Moving Out of Poverty

The words of US President John F. Kennedy, "the rising tide lifts all boats," can be applied to inclusive growth in contemporary Asia, where the poor are able to participate in and benefit from economic growth. *Moving Out of Poverty* explores three channels through which economic growth confers gains to the poor and improves the status of women. The first is creation of productive employment, as labor is typically the most abundant asset of the poor, and economic growth has created jobs in labor-intensive sectors. The second is investment in schooling which, coupled with increased opportunities to earn income, has elevated womens' status in society. The third is increased availability of improved infrastructure, which directly impacts increasing household income from wage work and self-employment activities.

This book will be of great value to development economists, students and researchers interested in rural economies in Asia, and policymakers engaged in poverty reduction.

Jonna P. Estudillo is Professor at the National Graduate Institute for Policy Studies (GRIPS) in Tokyo, Japan.

Keijiro Otsuka is Senior Professor at the National Graduate Institute for Policy Studies (GRIPS) in Tokyo, Japan.

T0389282

Routledge Studies in the Modern World Economy

Moving Out of Poverty

An inquiry into the inclusive
growth in Asia

Jonna P. Estudillo and Keijiro Otsuka

Routledge
Taylor & Francis Group

LONDON AND NEW YORK

First published 2016 by Routledge

2 Park Square, Milton Park, Abingdon, Oxfordshire OX14 4RN
711 Third Avenue, New York, NY 10017

Routledge is an imprint of the Taylor & Francis Group, an informa business

First issued in paperback 2018

British Library Cataloguing-in-Publication Data
A catalogue record for this book is available from the British
Library

Library of Congress Cataloging-in-Publication Data
Estudillo, Jonna P.
  Moving out of poverty : an inquiry into the inclusive growth in
Asia / Jonna P. Estudillo and Keijiro Otsuka. — 1 Edition.
    pages cm. — (Routledge studies in the modern world economy)
  1. Poverty—Asia.   2. Asia—Economic conditions—21st century.
3. Economic development—Asia.   I. Otsuka, Keijiro.   II. Title.
  HC415.P6E88 2015
  339.4′6095—dc23
  2015014344

ISBN: 978-0-415-71443-3 (hbk)
ISBN: 978-1-138-31692-8 (pbk)

Typeset in Galliard
by Apex CoVantage, LLC

Contents

PART III
Summary and conclusions   185

Figures

Tables

Preface

This book is a sequel to our earlier work, *Rural Poverty and Income Dynamics in Asia and Africa* published by Routledge in 2009, which was inspired by our own detailed study for about 30 years of socioeconomic and institutional changes that took place in our two study villages in Central Luzon and another two on Panay Island in the Philippines. In these villages, we have observed that an initial rise in household income brought about by the Green Revolution has been used to send children to school, importantly girls, in secondary and tertiary levels. The more educated ones have left the villages to engage in nonfarm and overseas employment. The result is a remarkable increase in household income and a reduction in poverty. This book is wholeheartedly dedicated to the women and men in our study villages.

This new book has significantly expanded the scope and perspectives of our analysis on poverty dynamics in Asia, thanks to our close collaboration with our former students at the National Graduate Institute for Policy Studies in Tokyo, Japan. They were among those who benefited from inclusive growth in Asia, which is the main subject of this volume. Rapid economic growth in Asia has been accompanied by the improvement of schooling and by greater opportunities for productive employment that made it possible for our students to pursue graduate studies in Tokyo. Interestingly, a greater number of our collaborators are women from East Asia, where economic growth has been much faster and where gender inequality in terms of schooling and economic opportunities is much less pronounced.

In Laos, we are particularly grateful for the participation of our former master's students Saygnasak Seng-Arloun and Kinnalone Phimmavong of the National Economic Research Institute (NERI) of the Ministry of Planning and Investment and the research support from the NERI staff and from its leaders – namely, Leeber Leebouapao, Syviengxay Oraboune, Souphith Darachanthara, and Sthabandith Insisengmay. Saygnasak Seng-Arloun is one of the authors (along with the first author of this volume and Yukichi Mano of Hitotsubashi University) of the paper "Job Choice of Three Generations in Laos," which was published in the *Journal of Development Studies* in 2013. This paper forms part of Chapter 2 of this volume.

In Myanmar, we benefited from the help with data collection from Kyi Kyi Win and the staff of the Ministry of National Planning and Economic Development. Marlar Oo, Khin Maung Thet, Than Aye, Ohmar Tun, and Arelene Julia Malabayabas of the International Rice Research Institute (IRRI) and Yolanda T. Garcia and Arnulfo G. Garcia of the University of the Philippines Los Banos gave us useful information on the conduct of the surveys.

Yasuyuki Sawada of the University of Tokyo and Yukichi Mano are our co-authors on the paper "Poor Parents, Rich Children: The Role of Schooling, Nonfarm Work, and Migration in Rural Philippines" published in the *Philippine Review of Economics* (PRE) in December 2014. Emmanuel de Dios of the School of Economics of the University of the Philippines on the Diliman campus and an anonymous referee of the PRE gave insightful comments on this piece. Parts of this paper are included in Chapter 4.

Charity Gay Ramos of the National Economic Development Authority in the Philippines did her PhD dissertation at GRIPS under our supervision and is the main author of the paper "Transformation of the Rural Economy in the Philippines, 1988–2006" (jointly co-authored with us and Yasuyuki Sawada) published in the *Journal of Development Economics* in 2012. Portions of Chapter 6 are drawn from this paper.

Our former master's student, Le Thanh Hue from the Ministry of Finance, and our colleague Nguyen Thi Gam from Thai Nguyen University conducted the surveys in Vietnam. Former colleagues at IRRI Tran Thi Ut and KL Heong helped us with the groundwork for the Vietnam surveys.

Nandika Sanath Kumanayake of the Sri Lanka Customs, who was our PhD student at GRIPS, is the main author of our joint paper "Changing Sources of Household Income, Poverty, and Sectoral Inequality in Sri Lanka, 1990–2006" published in *Developing Economies* in March 2014. Chapter 7 draws some parts from this paper.

Maria Lourdes Lopez, our master's student who wrote her policy paper at GRIPS under the supervision of the first author, helped us with the analysis of children's schooling in Bangladesh (Chapter 8). Mahabub Hossain and Mahfuz Rahman of BRAC shared with us the data set that was collected partly by IRRI and partly by BRAC.

Teresita V. Rola did an excellent editing job, Francis Mark Quimba helped with the graphics, and Yasuko Maeshima formatted the manuscript based on the Routledge style. Finally, the Global Center of Excellence Program of the Japan Society for the Promotion of Science (JSPS), GRIPS Grants-in-Aid for Scientific Research (JSPS KAKENHI Grant Number 22402023), GRIPS Emerging State Project (JSPS KAKENHI Grant Number 25101002), and the Tokyo Center for Economic Research (TCER) provided funding on the surveys and post-survey activities. The authors would like to express their deepest gratitude to these people, JSPS, TCER, and others whose contributions we have failed to mention in this preface.

1 Introduction

An overview and conceptual framework

Introduction

The World Bank Group has recently announced the twin goal for sustainable development, "ending poverty and sharing prosperity" (World Bank 2014). This is inspired by the world's success in reaching the Millennium Development Goal (MDG) target of halving the proportion of people living in extreme poverty 5 years ahead of the 2015 deadline. The World Bank (2014, p. 160) reported that, in developing regions as a whole, the proportion of the population living on less than $1.25 a day fell by more than one half from 43 percent in 1990 to 17 percent in 2011. The major contributing factor to global poverty reduction is the rapid economic growth in East Asia, most notably in China. Worldwide in 2011, just over 1 billion people live on $1.25 a day, which is 14.5 percent of the world's population (World Bank, 2014, p.2). The new goal is to virtually eliminate extreme poverty by 2030 by reducing the current proportion of poor people from 14.5 percent to 3 percent.

Economic growth for an extended period of time is the main driver of poverty reduction in the developing world (Dollar and Kraay 2002). Countries experiencing higher rates of economic growth are oftentimes observed to reduce poverty much faster than those that grow more slowly. In a cross-country study, Kraay (2004) shows that growth in average income explains 70 percent of the reduction in head count ratio in the short term and as much as 97 percent in the long term. Lopez and Servén (2004) suggest that, for a given level of income inequality, the poorer the country, the more important economic growth is in reducing poverty. The World Bank (1989, 2000, 2014) predicts that in order to eliminate extreme poverty by 2030 (get into the 3 percent target), per capita consumption of every country around the world must grow by 4 percent annually without any change in the distribution of income in each country. This new target needs the strong commitment of each country to reduce poverty. Simultaneously, we must have a clearer understanding of how poverty reduction can be achieved.

High growth rates could be effectively transmitted into poverty reduction if many of the poor receive gains in the expansion process. What is needed is inclusive growth, which is defined as "growth coupled with equality of opportunity" (Zhuang and Ali 2010, p. 9): growth is inclusive if a large segment of the population is able to participate in and benefit from it. Inclusive growth is about enlarging the "economic pie" – raising the pace of growth, creating a level playing field for investment, and increasing productive employment opportunities (Ianchovichina and Lundstrom 2009).

Asia, which is the most economically dynamic region of the world, is believed to be undergoing the process of inclusive growth. Sustained high growth rates in East Asia have been transmitted to a remarkable decline in poverty, enabling this region to attain the MDG target of halving extreme poverty ahead of the deadline and earlier than other regions (United Nations 2014). The main characteristic feature of the Asian growth pattern is that the growth is broad based, inclusive of the large part of the country's labor force. Creating jobs for the poor is important for poverty reduction inasmuch as labor is typically the most abundant asset of the poor (Fields 2012; World Bank 2012). Jobs in the more labor-intensive sectors (such as agriculture and informal service sectors and, to a varying extent, in construction, transport, and low-skilled manufacturing) tend to have stronger effects on poverty reduction.

The nature of inclusive growth, however, is not well understood. The major purpose of the present volume is to investigate the three channels – productive employment, higher schooling, and improved infrastructure – through which economic growth in Asia serves as a springboard of poverty reduction in its rural areas, where poverty is most prevalent and persistent. Since jobs are the key elements in making growth inclusive of the poor, we focus on the role of generating productive job opportunities. The novel approach here is to explore dynamic changes in the labor market through the lens of the job choices of women and men and to track changes in household income structure. The poor seldom take a unilateral strategy in fighting poverty, as they dynamically allocate their labor to various economic activities, where labor could be profitably employed (Baulch 2011). We also focus on the improvement of infrastructure, which has a direct impact on household income growth by increasing income from wage work and self-employment activities. It also has an indirect impact, as it stimulates the development of nonfarm sectors that create jobs in rural and urban areas.

While economic growth has been documented as a powerful force in reducing poverty (United Nations 2013; World Bank 1989, 2000, 2014; Zhuang and Ali 2010), the literature remains elusive on how and to what extent women have benefited from the process of inclusive growth. A level playing field would mean that women vis-à-vis men are able to have equal access to economic resources (importantly, land and schooling), opportunities in nonfarm wage employment, and political participation, which is consistent with MDG3, "promote gender equality and empower women." Among the three dimensions of equality, gender parity in schooling is the closest to being achieved (United Nations 2013). In fact, in more recent years, a clear gender bias that favors girls in tertiary school enrollment has emerged in developing countries (World Bank 2011d).

Globally, there is an increase in the number of wage-earning jobs held by women in the nonfarm sector, although women in developing regions remain more likely than men to work as unpaid family workers or to engage in low-paying jobs in the informal sector (World Bank 2011d). Worldwide, women held a mere one fifth of the proportion of seats in single or lower houses of national parliaments in 2013 (United Nations 2013). Overall, while a clear gender bias that favors men continues to persist in terms of wage employment and parliamentary representation, there have been major developments in this arena, which could be attributed to economic growth and affirmative actions that tend to promote women's welfare.

The present study fills the two missing gaps in the literature by (1) exploring how the three channels – productive employment, better education, and good infrastructure – are able to transmit the benefits of economic growth to the poor and (2) tracking the pathways by which growth has narrowed gender disparity in schooling and employment opportunities between women and men in Asia. Economic growth has stimulated the growth of nonfarm labor income from the informal and labor-intensive sectors and remittance income coming from migrants in local towns, cities, and other countries. Importantly, economic growth in Asia has created jobs for a large part of the labor force, even for the marginalized groups, including youth, women, and the unskilled, who are more likely to be poor. Initial sparks of income growth stimulated by modern agricultural technology and early development of the nonfarm sector have enabled rural households to invest equally in the schooling of girls and boys (Otsuka *et al.* 2009). Investments in the human capital of women consequently served as an important pillar in fostering gender equality in employment opportunities. Detailed case studies of rural households have been conducted in six countries in Asia: Laos, Myanmar, the Philippines, Vietnam, Sri Lanka, and Bangladesh. We have chosen these countries as we know relatively little about the process of inclusive growth in these regions.

Essence of inclusive growth in Asia

Moving out of poverty

Around 70 percent of the world's poor live and work in rural areas (United Nations 2010a). They live in remote areas, cultivate dry and marginal land, have few earning opportunities off the farm, and cannot read or write (International Fund for Agricultural Development [IFAD] 2000). Others live in favorable agricultural areas, but they do not possess farmland and work as agricultural laborers (David and Otsuka 1994; Otsuka *et al.* 2009; IFAD 2010; World Bank 2001, 2007b).

There are fears that rural poverty may increase further in Asia because of the high growth rates of the rural labor force on fixed land resources, leading to a decrease in farm size and creating a large group of landless workers (Hayami and Kikuchi 2000). Alongside this is the decline in agricultural employment opportunities because of the acceleration in the use of labor-saving technologies (Estudillo *et al*. 1999; Jayasuriya and Shand 1986). Thus, it is likely that the children of the rural poor will be unable to escape poverty. This scenario has not happened in Asia, however, because households strategically combined various strategies in raising income in response to changing resource scarcities.

There are three complementary pathways out of poverty: (1) farming, (2) off-farm and rural nonfarm work, and (3) migration to cities and overseas (World Bank 2007b). In China and India, rural poverty has declined drastically because of increased agricultural productivity, development of infrastructure, and expansion of the nonfarm sector (Ravallion and Chen 2007; Chaudhuri and Ravallion 2006). Women in northern Vietnam, where farm sizes are relatively small, have ventured into production of nontraditional high-value crops (vegetables, fruits, cut flowers, and tea) and livestock (Chapter 5). In Tanzania and Uganda, those most successful in moving out of poverty are farmers who have diversified their farming activities by growing food crops, fruits, and vegetables and raising livestock (World Bank 2007b). There has been increasing participation of women as wage workers in export-oriented agribusiness firms in labor-intensive processes such as the packing and processing of fresh vegetables, fruits, and flowers (Lastarria-Cornhiel 2006). In brief, the "high-value revolution" (a term coined by the World Bank [2007b]) in horticulture, livestock, and other high-value products could offer a new wave of employment opportunities in rural areas, particularly for women.

In some parts of Asia, farming has become a side enterprise, and groups of landless workers who traditionally eke out their living from casual daily wage work on farms have become nonfarm workers in village communities where farmland has become scarce (Hayami and Kikuchi 2000). This is a sensible change, as agricultural labor markets alone will not reduce poverty to a significant extent because agricultural wage income is low and agricultural work is declining in importance as a source of household income (Otsuka *et al*. 2007).

Overseas migration has been playing a more important role in poverty reduction (World Bank 2007b, 2012b). Females and males are equally likely to migrate overseas: the current share of females in the world's international migrant population is close to one half (United Nations 2010b). If male outmigration leaves females on the farm and if females have less access to inputs, extension services, and credit (World Bank 2011d), farm productivity may fall. In the Philippines, the increase in farm income due to the Green Revolution, implementation of land reform, and infrastructure development was used as funds to invest in children's schooling, particularly for girls, who then migrated out of the villages to urban areas and overseas and sent remittances (Quisumbing *et al*. 2004; Estudillo *et al*. 2008; Chapters 4 and 6). Young uneducated women in Laos cross the border to join the informal sector in Thailand in the midst of increasing scarcity of farmland and slow development of the nonfarm sector in their country (Chapter 2).

Occupational choice and the resultant household income structure embody sources of livelihood and combinations of strategies for raising income. This study looks closely at different sources of household income to examine the depth and breadth of poverty and to identify strategies in moving out of poverty while paying special attention to the specificity of such strategies in each study area. Our foremost hypothesis is that income growth and poverty reduction take place when the rural poor find jobs in lucrative, labor-intensive activities in agriculture and in the informal nonfarm sector where unskilled labor is productively utilized. Migration that does not entail large fixed costs such as migration to local towns and cities and neighboring countries (as in the case of Laos) is an integral part of this process. Many of these poor are uneducated landless or near-landless workers who are pushed out of agriculture amidst the increasing scarcity of farmland and who could not find jobs in the formal nonfarm wage sector requiring decent education as a major qualification.

Improving women's status

Schooling investments, ownership of physical assets, and improved access to job opportunities could improve women's status. In rural communities, physical assets mean farmland, and job opportunities mean opportunities to earn income in the emerging nonfarm sectors and in the production of high-value agricultural products. Gender differences in the inheritance of farmland and schooling attainment critically affect the decisions of women and men to venture into different types of employment (Estudillo *et al.* 2013). Inheritance of farmland by males is particularly common in areas where farming is intensive in male labor; hence, farmland stands as a far more valuable asset to sons than to daughters (Quisumbing *et al.* 2004). In developing countries, women-operated farms are smaller than farms run by men, and these farms produce lower output per unit of land because women have limited access to inputs and resources such as fertilizer, tools, extension services, and credit (Quisumbing *et al.* 2014).

Worldwide, in more recent years, parents have been investing relatively equally in the schooling of girls and boys at the primary and secondary schooling levels, and a clear bias that favors girls at the tertiary level has appeared (World Bank 2011d; United Nations 2014).[1] Progress in women's schooling is explained by the (1) rise in nonfarm employment opportunities for women, (2) lower cost of schooling, and (3) higher and more stable household income (World Bank 2011d). Schooling gives women better access to lucrative nonfarm jobs and enables them to migrate and send remittances that mitigate income shocks and protect households from depleting their asset base (World Bank 1989, 2000, 2013b).

This volume attempts to inquire into the routes out of poverty by exploring the job choices of women and men over generations. Our second major hypothesis is that women's status is enhanced primarily when women obtain higher levels of schooling, are able to migrate, and become employed in productive jobs, not only in agriculture but also, more importantly, in the nonfarm sector. The growth of the nonfarm sector can effectively elevate women's status because there are, generally, no innate differences in work ability in nonfarm jobs between women and men. Also, the development of the nonfarm sector stimulates the integration of women and men in the workplace and creates a greater degree of gender specialization.

This study has shown that parents tend to substitute schooling for farmland as a form of inheritance to their daughters. Data from three generations of women show that the younger women obtain more schooling and have a greater tendency to redefine their roles away from traditional housekeeping and helping their husbands on their farms to become independent workers in the expanding nonfarm sector. The less educated women venture into informal service jobs and low-skilled manufacturing jobs within the villages or in nearby towns and cities, while the more educated ones become employed in the formal wage sector or migrate overseas. Gender specialization takes place when the nonfarm economy is expanding, as in our case study in northern Vietnam, where men abandon farming to migrate to cities, while women are left behind on the farms to cultivate high-value crops and raise livestock (Chapter 5). To our knowledge, this is the first systematic comparative study on how economic growth in Asia has stimulated schooling investments and occupational and geographic mobility of women and men in rural areas of Asia over three generations of household members, which is reported in Part 1 of this volume.

Developing nonfarm sectors

Considering the utmost importance of the development of the rural nonfarm sector, it is vitally important to investigate its evolutionary processes and locational dynamics. To date, there are three strands of thought that trace the development of the rural nonfarm sector: (1) "geography of economic development" – there is a proliferation of rural nonfarm activities in areas near urban centers and in areas where infrastructure is well developed; (2) "the role of human capital" – the development of the nonfarm sector could be stimulated by investments in schooling, which leads to the increased supply of an educated labor force; and (3) "agricultural growth linkages" – agricultural development could spur the development of the nonfarm sector through several forward and backward linkages.

A major purpose of Part 2 of this volume is to identify the factors affecting the development of rural nonfarm sectors by exploring changes in household income sources with a particular focus on the role of improved infrastructure. The results of case studies in the Philippines, Sri Lanka, and Bangladesh are presented.

An overview of inclusive growth in Asia

Structural transformation and economic growth

One distinctive feature of rural Asia is the remarkable movement out of poverty in the midst of the unfavorable scenario of the increasing scarcity of farmland

Table 1.1 Arable land per capita in selected countries in Asia, 1990–2012

Country	1990	2012
	Arable land per capita[a]	
Laos	0.41	0.43
Myanmar	0.48	0.35
Philippines	0.23	0.13
Vietnam	0.16	0.13
Sri Lanka	0.14	0.14
Bangladesh	0.20	0.10

a   Total arable land divided by population between 15 and 60 years old.

Source: Authors' calculations from the World Development Indicators database.

and the declining availability of employment opportunities in agriculture (Otsuka *et al.* 2009). In the six study countries, with the exception of Laos and Sri Lanka, arable land per capita declined precipitously from 1990 to 2012 (Table 1.1). The Philippines, Vietnam, Sri Lanka, and Bangladesh could be characterized as land scarce, as arable land per capita was relatively small (compared with Laos and Myanmar) as early as 1990.

To avoid poverty, what has to take place is structural transformation, which is defined by Hayami and Godo (2005, p. 36) as the shift of the locus of economic activity away from agriculture to the industry and service sectors. A measure of structural transformation is the declining share of agriculture in the gross domestic product (GDP). Figure 1.1 shows that the share of agriculture in GDP declined between 1990 and 2012 in all six countries. A greater percentage point decline can be observed in Laos and Myanmar, when in 1990, agriculture had the highest share (about 60 percent) of GDP. With the exception of Vietnam, the service sector has become the more dominant component of GDP in 2012. Since this sector is made up of largely heterogeneous segments, including the labor-intensive ones that employ the unskilled or uneducated, it appears that the service sector could act as a depository of excess labor from agriculture.

While agriculture's share in GDP is less than 20 percent in 2012 in the Philippines, Vietnam, Sri Lanka, and Bangladesh, the share of the labor force in the sector is more than one third and is particularly high in Vietnam and Bangladesh (about 50 percent) and Sri Lanka (40 percent) (Figure 1.2). In Laos, 78 percent of the labor force remains in agriculture, and this is more than 60 percent in Myanmar. This difference between shares of agricultural GDP and employment is explained partly by the high proportion of part-time farmers and agricultural workers. Yet, this would also indicate that labor productivity in agriculture is low, and there is thus a push to allocate labor to more productive endeavors in the nonfarm sectors and also within agriculture to the

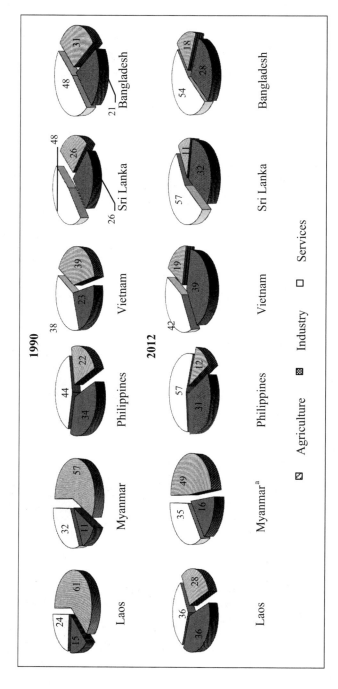

Figure 1.1 Composition of the gross domestic product in selected countries in Asia, 1990–2012

a Refers to 2004.

Source: World Development Indicators database.

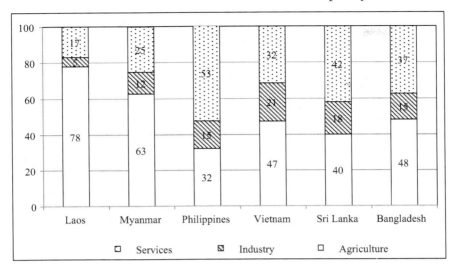

Figure 1.2 Composition of labor force in selected countries in Asia

Note: Data on Laos and Bangladesh refer to 2005; Myanmar data refer to 1998; and data on the Philippines, Vietnam, and Sri Lanka refer to 2012.

Source: World Development Indicators database.

high-value sector, which has the potential to create new jobs and spark growth in labor productivity within agriculture.

GDP per capita in absolute terms and its growth rate are higher in economies that are more diversified (Sri Lanka and Vietnam) and where industry and services are the most important sectors (Table 1.2 and Figure 1.1). The high growth rate of GDP per capita in Laos can be traced to the expanding mining and quarrying sector, whose share in GDP rose from less than 1 percent in 2002 to more than 6 percent in 2008, a span of only 6 years. This has contributed to an increase in GDP per capita by 2.7 times and a growth rate of 4.6 percent per annum. Yet, this sector is hardly the driver of poverty reduction because mining and quarrying, in combination with water and electricity, while contributing about 10 percent to total GDP in 2008, employ only 14,500 workers (Estudillo *et al.* 2013).

Women in the labor force, schooling, and infrastructure

Female share in the labor force is about 50 percent in Laos, Myanmar, and Vietnam, countries located in the Greater Mekong Subregion, which is by far the most dynamic region in Southeast Asia (Figure 1.3). Female labor force participation (FLFP) – defined as the percentage of women who are currently employed, are expecting to begin new work, or are looking for work – is also highest (close to 80 percent) in these countries (Figure 1.4). In Sri Lanka and

Table 1.2 Gross domestic product per capita and its growth rate in selected countries in Asia, 1990–2012

Country	1990	2012
	Gross domestic product (GDP) per capita (international dollars in 2011)	
Laos	1,622	4,388
Philippines	4,010	6,004
Vietnam	1,501	4,912
Sri Lanka	3,339	8,855
Bangladesh	1,067	2,363
	Annual growth rate of GDP per capita, 1990–2012[a]	
Laos	4.6	
Philippines	2.0	
Vietnam	5.4	
Sri Lanka	4.2	
Bangladesh	3.6	

a   Growth rates were calculated using regression.

Note: Data on Myanmar are not available.

Source: Authors' calculations from the World Development Indicators database.

Bangladesh, female share in the labor force and FLFP are lower because women in these countries are traditionally bound to stay home. In the Philippines, FLFP is low because of the higher number of small children and the low level of physical infrastructure (particularly electricity and tube water) that create a heavy burden on home production activities (Estudillo and Ducanes 2014).

Enrollment rates in primary school are well over 80 percent, except in Myanmar, and there is almost equal enrollment of girls and boys (Figure 1.5). Enrollment in secondary school varies widely from a low of about 40 percent in Laos to a high of more than 80 percent in Sri Lanka. There is a clear gender bias in favor of girls (the points are above the 45-degree line), particularly evident in the Philippines and Bangladesh. School enrollment at the tertiary level remains low, partly because tertiary schools are commonly not publicly provided and partly because the opportunity cost of sending students to high school is considerably high.

There was a remarkable increase in the proportion of the population with access to electricity, except in the case of Myanmar, where more than 50 percent of the population had no access to electricity even as late as 2012 (Table 1.3). This is in contrast to Vietnam, where 96 percent of its population had access (Table 1.3). In accordance with MDG7 – "halving the proportion of people

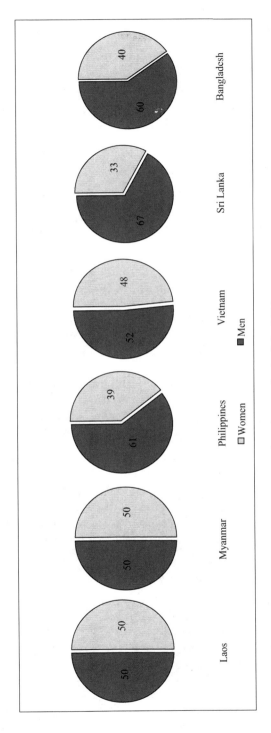

Figure 1.3 Share of women in the labor force in selected countries in Asia, 2012

Source: World Development Indicators database.

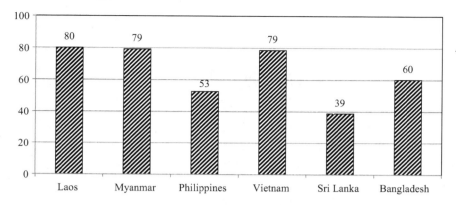

Figure 1.4 Female labor force participation (%) in selected countries in Asia, 2012
Source: World Development Indicators database.

without sustainable access to safe drinking water and basic sanitation" – three countries (the Philippines, Vietnam, and Sri Lanka) were able to increase the proportion of their population with an improved water source to well over 90 percent and two countries (Myanmar and Bangladesh) to well over 80 percent in 2012. Laos lags behind these five countries, reaching only about 70 percent in the same year.

Road density (in terms of kilometers of road per 100 km² of land area) had remained low and did not increase much in Laos, Myanmar, and the Philippines, and was comparatively higher in Sri Lanka and Bangladesh as early as the 2000s with modest increases (Table 1.3). There was also an increase in access to telephone lines and, more importantly, in mobile cellular subscriptions per 100 people. The Philippines and Vietnam had the most extensive mobile telephony access (105 cellular phone subscriptions per 100 people in the Philippines and 147 in Vietnam), perhaps due to the more liberalized telecommunications industry in these countries. Myanmar and Bangladesh had the lowest (7 and 62 per 100 people, respectively). Overall, access to clean water and telephones improved substantially in the six countries, while road density remained low.

Changes in income, poverty, and inequality

In general, there was a greater reduction in poverty in countries where the economic growth rate was higher. The most spectacular decline is evident in Vietnam (61 percentage points between 1990 and 2012), Bangladesh (27 percentage points), and Laos (25 percentage points) (Table 1.4). These are also the countries that started with higher poverty rates. The reduction in the Philippines was modest, given its modest economic growth performance. Sri Lanka had rapid economic growth, but because it started with the lowest level of poverty (15 percent), the proportion of extremely poor people declined by

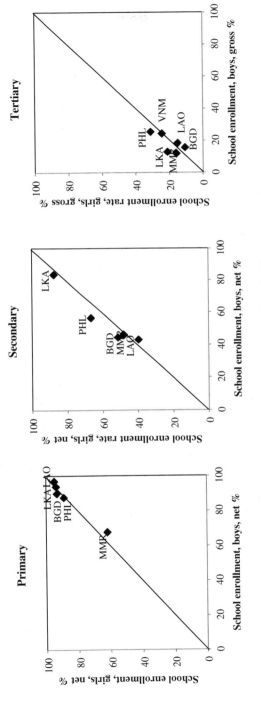

Figure 1.5 Enrollment rate in school, by gender, in selected countries in Asia, 2012

Note: LAO = Laos, MMR = Myanmar, PHL = Philippines, VNM = Vietnam, LKA = Sri Lanka, and BGD = Bangladesh.

Source: World Development Indicators database.

Table 1.3 Infrastructure in selected countries in Asia, 1990–2012

Country	1990	2012
	Access to electricity (% of population)	
Laos	51	78
Myanmar	43	48
Philippines	65	70
Vietnam	87	96
Sri Lanka	78	85
Bangladesh	21	59
	Improved water source (% of population)	
Laos	39[a]	71
Myanmar	55	85
Philippines	83	91
Vietnam	61	95
Sri Lanka	67	93
Bangladesh	68	84
	Road density (km of road per 100 km^2 of land area)	
Laos	9.1[b]	17.3[d]
Myanmar	3.9[b]	5.5[d]
Philippines	67.1[b]	67.3[e]
Vietnam	N/A[h]	48.3[f]
Sri Lanka	139.9[c]	173.9[g]
Bangladesh	144.0[b]	166.1[e]
	Telephone lines per 100 people (mobile cellular subscriptions per 100 people)	
Laos	0.16	67.7 (64)
Myanmar	0.17	0.99 (7)
Philippines	0.98	3.61 (105)
Vietnam	0.14	11.22 (147)
Sri Lanka	0.70	16.35 (91)
Bangladesh	0.20	0.62 (62)

a   Refers to 1994.
b   Refers to 2000.
c   Refers to 2002.
d   Refers to 2011.
e   Refers to 2003.
f   Refers to 2007.
g   Refers to 2010.
h   Not available.

Source: World Development Indicators database.

Table 1.4 Poverty and inequality in selected countries in Asia, 1990–2012

Country	1990	2012
	Poverty incidence at $1.25-a-day line (%)	
Laos	55[a]	30
Philippines	33[b]	18
Vietnam	63[a]	2
Sri Lanka	15	4[c]
Bangladesh	70[b]	43[d]
	Poverty gap ratio at $1.25-a-day line	
Laos	16.2[a]	7.6
Philippines	9.6[b]	4.0
Vietnam	23.5[a]	0.5
Sri Lanka	2.7	0.6[c]
Bangladesh	23.8[b]	11.1[d]
	Gini coefficient	
Laos	0.30[a]	0.36
Myanmar	N/A[e]	N/A
Philippines	0.44[b]	0.43
Vietnam	0.36[a]	0.37
Sri Lanka	0.33[b]	0.36[c]
Bangladesh	0.28	0.32[d]

a Refers to 1992.
b Refers to 1991.
c Refers to 2009.
d Refers to 2010.
e Not available.

Note: Data on Myanmar are not available.

Source: Authors' calculations from PovcalNet. This is the online tool for poverty measurement developed by the Development Research Group of the World Bank. Visit http://iresearch. worldbank.org/PovcalNet/index.htm?5,0.

only about 11 percentage points. Using a nationally representative data set and domestic poverty line, the Ministry of National Planning and Economic Development of Myanmar (MNPED) announced that the country's poverty incidence declined from 32.1 percent in 2005 to 25.6 percent in 2010 (MNPED 2011, Table 4, p. 16) – i.e., one in every three Myanmar citizens was poor in 2005, but only one in four citizens remained poor 5 years later. The poverty gap ratio (which measures the depth of poverty) was highest in Bangladesh and Laos in 2012.

The power of economic growth to reduce poverty cannot be fully realized if it is accompanied by rising inequality. In all five countries, where relevant data are available, the income share of the lowest 10 percent of the population had remained between 3 and 4 percent from the early 1990s to the late 2000s, while the income share of the highest 10 percent rose from about 25 to 30 percent in Laos, Sri Lanka, and Bangladesh. Consequently, the Gini coefficient of income inequality had remained fairly the same in the Philippines and Vietnam but increased slightly in Laos, Sri Lanka, and Bangladesh (Table 1.4). Nonetheless, the annual growth in mean consumption (or income) per capita of the bottom 40 percent was much higher than that of the total population in the Philippines, Sri Lanka, and Bangladesh (Table 1.5). Vietnam had the highest growth rate of per capita income, even though the growth rate of the income of the bottom 40 percent was lower than that of the total population. Thus, it is clear that economic growth did not harm the poor – in fact, the evidence shows that it benefits both the poor and those who are not. Indeed, as the late US President John F. Kennedy said, "the rising tide raises all boats."

A conceptual framework and hypotheses

Farm and nonfarm incomes of rural households are affected by a number of factors in a variety of ways. For example, improvements in infrastructures – e.g., irrigation, roads, electricity, and communication facilities – will increase farm income by enhancing the efficiency of farming, increasing farm gate prices of agricultural products, and reducing input prices. Such improvements also affect nonfarm income by improving access to outside markets, including urban and overseas labor markets. While farm income is governed by access to land, nonfarm income is critically affected by human capital. Nonfarm income is also directly affected by the development of the rural nonfarm, urban, and overseas labor markets. Gender matters in job choice and farm and nonfarm income, partly because access to land and education is often differentiated by gender and partly because the comparative advantages of male and female workers are different (Quisumbing *et al.* 2004). It is also important to note that investment in schooling of children is affected by income of parents, which in turn is affected by their access to land and their education level. Such relationships are illustrated in Figure 1.6. To substantiate these relationships, we provide a series of hypotheses to be tested in subsequent chapters.

In the early stage of economic development, when farming is a dominant source of income, access to land is a major determinant of rural household income (David and Otsuka 1994). Human capital, represented particularly by schooling, is in general not a major determinant of farm income (Otsuka *et al.* 2009), presumably because farm tasks carried out by farmers tend to be routinized, as in the case of "traditional agriculture" discussed by Schultz (1964). In other words, the return to education is relatively low in farming, as the farm sector grows less dynamically than do the nonfarm sectors; hence, the "ability to deal with disequilibria" (to use Schultz's [1975] term) is less needed in

Table 1.5 Growth of mean income (or consumption) of the bottom 40 percent in selected countries in Asia, 2005–2012

| Country | Period | Type^a | Annual growth in mean consumption or income per capita (%) | | Mean consumption or income per capita at $ a day (2005 purchasing power parity [PPP]) | | | |
| | | | | | Baseline | | Most recent year | |
			Bottom 40%	Total population	Bottom 40%	Total population	Bottom 40%	Total population
Laos	2007–12	C	1.40	1.98	0.97	1.98	1.04	2.18
Philippines	2006–12	C	1.37	0.68	1.20	3.26	1.30	3.39
Vietnam	2004–10	I	6.22	7.81	1.38	3.27	1.99	5.13
Sri Lanka	2007–10	C	2.99	-0.39	1.69	3.91	1.85	3.87
Bangladesh	2005–10	C	1.75	1.37	0.83	1.59	0.90	1.70

a C = consumption; I = income.

Note: Data on Myanmar are not available.

Source: Global Database of Shared Prosperity of the World Bank.

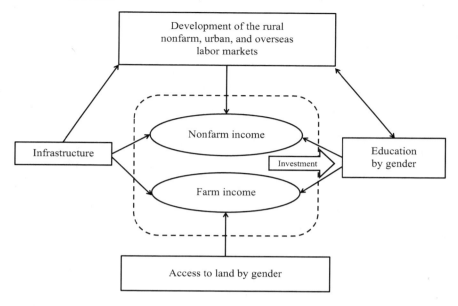

Figure 1.6 An illustration of determinants of rural household income

farming.[2] As the economy develops, the availability of nonfarm jobs increases, which increases the share of the nonfarm income of rural households and also the return to schooling. Based on such arguments, it seems reasonable to postulate the following hypothesis:

> *Hypothesis 1: Since access to farmland is a major determinant of farm income, whereas education is a major determinant of nonfarm income, as the nonfarm sector develops, the importance of farmland declines and that of human capital rises as a determinant of the total income of rural households.*

Since farmland is a major input in farm production and schooling is a major component of human capital useful in nonfarm activities, parents' decisions to bequeath farmland and invest in schooling of children critically affect the job choices of their children. As a corollary to Hypothesis 1, we would like to postulate the following:

> *Hypothesis 2: Inheritance of farmland positively affects the probability that children choose farming as a major occupation, whereas schooling investment increases the probability that children choose nonfarm jobs.*

The poorest of the poor in rural areas in Asia are landless agricultural workers (David and Otsuka 1994). They are poor as they are engaged in simple, manual, and seasonal tasks such as weeding and harvesting (Hayami and Otsuka 1993). Moreover, they do not possess useful knowledge specific to farming, such as knowledge on soil quality. This implies that their opportunity cost of leaving farm jobs tends to be lower than that of farmers who own land, possess farm-specific knowledge, and are engaged in farm tasks requiring care and judgment, such as water management and fertilizer application. As a result, landless workers are more mobile occupationally and geographically than members of farm households. To the extent that the nonfarm sector develops faster and that earnings in nonfarm jobs grow faster than expected, the disadvantage of the landless labor class in income earnings compared with the landed class may decline over time. It is therefore of interest to test the following hypothesis:

> *Hypothesis 3: Because of the increasing importance of nonfarm income and higher geographical and occupational mobility of landless households, the income gap between landed and landless households declines over time.*

Among nonfarm jobs, formal jobs tend to be more skill- and knowledge-intensive than informal jobs. Thus, we expect to observe that educated and uneducated workers self-select into formal and informal jobs, respectively. Insofar as the poor are less educated, we expect the informal sector to provide employment opportunities that are particularly conducive to poverty reduction. Thus, we postulate the following hypothesis:

> *Hypothesis 4: The formal nonfarm sector provides lucrative employment opportunities for the educated labor force, whereas the informal nonfarm sector provides employment opportunities for the uneducated labor force, thereby assisting them to move out of poverty.*

Although empirical testing is hard to implement, we presume that women do not have a comparative advantage in farming vis-à-vis men, particularly crop farming, which requires muscle work. However, women may have a comparative advantage in the production of labor-intensive high-value crops, such as flowers and vegetables, which requires careful management. Labor markets in nonfarm sectors are generally competitive and, as Becker (1957) argued, discrimination by gender and race tends to be suppressed under such a condition. Thus, women generally have strong incentives to work in the nonfarm sector, unless they are engaged in the production of high-value crops. To the extent that return to education in the nonfarm sector is high, there is a strong incentive for parents to invest in the schooling of their daughters. Such arguments may be summarized by the following hypothesis:

> *Hypothesis 5: The development of the nonfarm sector contributes to the improvement of women's educational and income status by providing equal employment opportunities for women and men.*

Infrastructure affects household income, not only directly by affecting input–output price ratios and the profitability of adopting new technologies, but also indirectly by affecting the development of nonfarm sectors. For instance, infrastructure, such as irrigation, affects agricultural income by improving the efficiency of farming and facilitating the adoption of new agricultural technologies, whereas transportation and communication infrastructure affects both farm and nonfarm incomes by reducing transport as well as transaction costs. In the longer run, infrastructure development may affect the development of nonfarm sectors and access to nonfarm labor markets, including overseas markets. The development of nonfarm sectors is also stimulated by the adoption of new agricultural technology and by the supply of the labor force from the farm sector in general and the educated labor force in particular. In this study, we assess the factors affecting the development of the farm and nonfarm sectors by analyzing the determinants of household income generated from farm and rural nonfarm activities. More specifically, we would like to postulate the following hypothesis:

> *Hypothesis 6: Development of the rural nonfarm sector is promoted by (1) investment in infrastructure, (2) the availability of an educated labor force, and (3) the adoption of modern agricultural technology.*

While Hypothesis 4 argues that landless workers actively participate in informal nonfarm jobs through labor markets, such an argument may not hold, however, in economies where labor markets are underdeveloped or in areas where finding nonfarm jobs requires considerably advanced investments. Since ownership of farmland generates income and farmland can be used as collateral, access to farmland may be an important factor affecting access to nonfarm jobs. Thus, we may test the validity of the following hypothesis:

> *Hypothesis 7: Larger endowment of farmland relative to labor promotes nonfarm self-employment activities and overseas migration because land represents wealth that can be used to finance start-up costs in these activities.*

A road map to the book

There are nine chapters in total – an introduction, seven chapters divided into two thematic parts, and a concluding chapter. The first theme – *Land, Schooling, and Occupational Choice* – examines how parental transfers of wealth in terms of farmland and schooling investments have affected their children's choice of occupations and incomes. We also examine differences in the income of the rural households of two generations and the changing pattern of income disparity between the landed and landless households. The second theme – *Infrastructure and Changing Landscape of Rural Economies* – examines the impacts of infrastructure on the changing sources of household livelihood. Poverty is measured by income, as we focus on the importance of the changing sources of income on poverty reduction. We also pay special attention to other indicators of poverty such as schooling and access to land, tube water, and electricity.

Throughout the entire study, we focus on the extent to which economic growth in Asia is inclusive of the poor, particularly through their participation in the nonfarm labor markets. Since the inclusiveness of growth varies from country to country, this study covers developing countries in Asia with distinctly different socioeconomic environments. We also attempt to distinguish between general and common features of inclusive growth among Asian countries and describe the specific features in each country.

We are particularly interested in the impacts of physical assets (inherited farmland), human capital (schooling, gender, and age), and infrastructure (road and electricity) on the labor earnings of the poor. We expect that their impacts are affected by land policies, educational policies, industrial policies, and policies on infrastructure development. For example, the success of industrial policies in promoting the development of industries intensive in the use of the young, female, and unskilled members of the labor force will be reflected in the effect of age, gender, and education on occupational choice and individual nonfarm incomes. The importance of infrastructure in moving the poor out of poverty will be revealed, not only by the significant effects of road density, the quality of the roads, and the availability of electricity, but also by enhanced effects of endowed resources in the labor earnings function. We hope that, by identifying the impacts of these variables and comparing their magnitudes across countries in Asia, we will be able to draw a rich set of policy implications to promote the inclusive growth conducive to income growth and poverty reduction. The major findings of each chapter are discussed in the following.

Chapter 2 explores the role of education and farmland on the job choices of three generations of household members in rural Laos. While the first (G1) and second (G2) generations are mainly engaged in farming, as in the other countries under study, the youngest generation (G3) is engaged primarily in nonfarm wage and overseas work. Education matters in nonfarm wage work but not necessarily in overseas work of Lao migrants in Thailand. The female members of G3, who are less educated than their male siblings, are found to be more likely to migrate. Our findings strongly indicate a shortage of available jobs for unskilled workers in Laos, pushing youth, women, and the less educated to cross the border to Thailand.

Chapter 3 aims to identify the changing sources of livelihood and poverty reduction in Myanmar in 1996 and 2012. There was a marked shift in the household income structure away from farm to nonfarm sources, accompanied by income growth and poverty reduction. The major sources of income growth are rice production and formal wage work for farmer households and informal wage work and self-employment for the landless. Income growth has come from the progress in secondary and tertiary schooling in conjunction with enhanced market returns to these human assets. For the landless poor, the major driver of poverty reduction is improved market returns to unskilled labor in informal wage work.

Chapter 4 explores how migration to local towns, big cities, and overseas has halted the transmission of poverty from parents to children in the rural Philippines. While parents' main source of livelihood was farming, their children had diversified into nonfarm work. Initially, poverty incidence is much higher among the landless households than farmer households. However, children from poor landless households are able to map their way out of poverty by acquiring more education; participating in the rural nonfarm labor market; and migrating more actively to local towns, big cities, and overseas. Migrant children have significantly higher total income coming almost exclusively from nonfarm sources, which is significantly affected by education. In brief, this chapter has clearly demonstrated that intergenerational economic mobility can be dictated by acquiring education and by migration.

Chapter 5 examines how schooling and inherited farmland have affected the job choices of three generations of rural households in rural Vietnam. Females in the older generations have been disfavored with respect to both schooling and farmland inheritance, whereas the inheritance of both females and males in the younger generation has been relatively equal. The first (G1) and second generations (G2) are largely engaged in farming, while the third generation (G3) has moved away from farming to nonfarm wage work. In the northern villages, gender specialization appears to exist among G3 – more men choose nonfarm work; more women choose farming. In southern villages, gender specialization on job choice is largely absent, in which husband and wife work together on the farm to exploit scale economies of mechanized rice farming.

Chapter 6 inquires into the process of the changing structure of the rural economy in the Philippines from 1988 to 2006. The expansion and upgrade of infrastructure such as electricity and roads and investment in secondary and tertiary education are important factors that induce the economic transformation of the rural economy. The importance of higher education as a requirement for entry into the nonfarm labor market has declined over time, indicating that the rural nonfarm sector has been increasingly providing employment opportunities to the unskilled and the uneducated, who form the bulk of the rural poor.

Chapter 7 compares changes in household income structure and poverty reduction among urban, rural, and estate sectors in Sri Lanka from 1990 to 2006. A shift of the household income structure away from agriculture to nonfarm sources is accompanied by income growth and reduction in poverty, particularly in the rural sector. Major contributing factors are the rise in returns to labor in general and educated labor in particular due to the development of the nonfarm labor market. Estate households continue to have persistently low income because of inadequate access to improved infrastructure, the limited availability of nonfarm employment opportunities, and the low education levels of working members.

Chapter 8 explores changes in girls' and boys' schooling in Bangladesh and the underlying factors. In more recent years, girls have tended to outnumber boys in enrollment in secondary and tertiary schools because of the increase in household income, rising employment opportunities for young girls, and affirmative actions that tend to support girls' schooling.

Clearly, the summary of findings indicates that the seven hypotheses postulated in this chapter are empirically supported. Chapter 9 concludes this volume by synthesizing major findings in such a way as to draw clear policy implications for the role of inclusive growth in poverty reduction and improvement of women's status.

Acknowledgment

The authors wish to thank Francis Mark Quimba for research assistance.

Notes

1 Gender parity in education means a gender parity index (GPI) between 0.97 and 1.03 (United Nations 2014, p. 20). The GPI is defined as the girls' gross school enrollment ratio divided by the corresponding ratio for boys.
2 See also Rosenzweig (1995). To our knowledge, a major study reporting significant impacts of schooling on the efficiency of farming was conducted by Foster and Rosenzweig (1996), who analyzed the adoption of new Green Revolution technology in the early 1970s in India, where schooling levels are generally low. We believe that their finding is the exception rather than the rule.

Part I

Land, schooling, and occupational choice

2 Off to cities and to Thailand

Job choice in Laos

Introduction

The labor market could serve as a key transmission mechanism to enable the rural poor to overcome poverty, as unskilled labor is regarded as the main asset of the poor (Fields 2012). Labor markets consist of (1) farm, (2) nonfarm, and (3) overseas markets, each one with different skill requirements and wage schemes (Estudillo *et al.* 2010). Using a rare individual-level data set, this chapter explores the dynamic changes occurring in the rural labor market structure through the lens of the employment sector that involves members belonging to three generations of households. We chose the Lao People's Democratic Republic (Laos), a country that has undergone the transition from a command- to a market-based economy. One important finding is the shift of the rural labor away from the farm sector to the non-farm sector in Laos and overseas. The underlying forces appear to be the decrease in size of farmland in this largely traditional agricultural setting, the lack of nonfarm employment opportunities in the country, and the rising demand for overseas workers in neighboring Thailand. This shift appears to be pro-poor, as it opens up job opportunities to the youth, the less educated, and the women who have limited options in agriculture and who are susceptible to spells of poverty. Reducing poverty in Laos means investing in people – portable investments (primary education and basic health) – which stimulates mobility (World Bank 2008b, Chapter 8). Another critical point to emphasize is that creating lucrative nonfarm jobs within the country remains a major challenge.

This chapter has five remaining sections. The second section describes the structure of and changes in the Lao economy; the third explains the characteristics of the study villages and sample individuals; the fourth identifies the determinants of inherited farmland, schooling, and job choice in three generations; and the fifth examines the results of estimated income functions. Finally, the sixth section presents the summary and conclusions of the study.

Changing economic structure in Laos

Laos in brief

Laos is a small country in Southeast Asia with a population of about 6 million people in 2009 (Asian Development Bank 2010b). It is classified by the United Nations (UN) as one of the least developed countries in the world (United Nations 2011). The country, with a transition economy, has transformed gradually from a command- to a market-based economy since the implementation of a new economic mechanism in 1986. Its gross domestic product (GDP) has grown at a reasonably high rate of 6–7 percent annually from 1990 to 2008 (World Bank 2011c), with industry (particularly garments, mining, and hydroelectricity) leading the way. The share of agriculture in GDP declined from 61 percent in 1992 to 31 percent in 2010 (World Bank 2011c). Ironically, 78 percent of the workforce continued to be engaged in agriculture even as late as 2005 (United Nations Development Programme [UNDP] 2009). Meanwhile, the incidence of poverty declined from 55 percent in 1992 to 34 percent in 2008, accompanied by a rise in inequality – the Gini coefficient of income inequality rose from 0.304 in 1992 to 0.367 in 2008 (World Bank 2011c).

Composition of GDP and labor force

Laos has experienced a shift of its aggregate output away from agriculture to the other sectors. In 1992, agriculture was the dominant sector, but its share of GDP declined by about 30 percentage points from 1992 to 2010; its GDP share became almost equal that of industry and services in 2010 (Table 2.1). The industry sector employs less than 5 percent of the labor force, while its share in total GDP is about one third. Mining, quarrying, and hydroelectricity are the major industries which, when combined, contributed about 10 percent to total GDP in 2008 (Ministry of Planning and Investments 2009a) while employing only 14,500 workers (UNDP 2009, pp. 82–3). Labor productivity in industry was about 10 times more compared with agriculture and 3.8 times more compared with the service sector in 1992.

Agriculture remains lowly productive, as only 16 percent of the cropland is irrigated. Nonetheless, the yield of rice, which is the major crop, rose from 2.6 to 3.6 tons per ha from 1992 to 2009, presumably because of the increasing rate of adoption of modern varieties (MVs) from 30 percent in the 1990s to 50 percent in the 2000s (Asian Development Bank 2006). Farm size is declining and landlessness is increasing because of the high population growth rate, which exceeded 2 percent annually in the 1980s and 1990s, pressing hard on a land frontier that is beginning to close. In the service sector, major employers are the government, education, and wholesale and retail trade sectors. While the more educated labor force tends to enter the government and education quarters, the service sector,

Table 2.1 Distribution of gross domestic product and workers among various sectors, Laos, 1992–2010

Sector	1992	1997	2002	2008	2010
Gross domestic product (GDP) per capita (international dollars in 2005, constant)	765	1,040	1,323	2,140	2,449
	Percentage distribution of GDP				
Agriculture	61.8	52.8	50.3	34.4	31.3
Industry	17.8	21.0	24.7	28.0	31.8
Mining and quarrying	N/A[a]	(0.19)	(0.05)	(6.42)	N/A
Electricity and water	N/A	(3.03)	(4.71)	(2.78)	N/A
Service	20.4	26.2	25.0	37.6	36.9
	Percentage distribution of workers				
Agriculture	N/A	85.4[b]	N/A	78.5[c]	N/A
Industry	N/A	3.5	N/A	4.8	N/A
Service	N/A	11.1	N/A	16.7	N/A

a N/A = not available.
b Refers to 1995.
c Refers to 2005.

Note: Numbers in parentheses are percentage of GDP.

Sources: World Bank (2011c), United Nations Development Programme (UNDP) (2009), and Ministry of Planning and Investment (MPI) (2009a).

as a whole, has low productivity inasmuch as an adult Lao employee has an average schooling of only about 4 years.

Income growth and poverty reduction

The high growth rate in GDP was accompanied by a reduction in the poverty head count ratio by 22 percentage points from 1992 to 2008 (Table 2.2). Growth and poverty reduction appear to move in tandem. GDP grew at an annual rate of 6.84 percent during 1992–7, along with a reduction in the head count ratio by 4.9 percentage points. When GDP slumped to a lower growth rate of 5.71 percent in 1997–2002, the reduction in the head count ratio was only 3.0 percentage points. And when GDP grew rapidly at 7.01 percent from 2002 to 2008, the reduction in poverty was more pronounced at 10.9 percentage points during the same period. Yet, the Gini coefficient (based on consumption) has continued to rise over time, attaining the highest level in 2008, when the income share of the richest decile reached more than 30 percent. It thus appears that growth is accompanied by a rise in inequality, which may mean that, in the case of Laos, the benefits of economic growth do not trickle down to the ultra-poor.

Table 2.2 Growth rate of gross domestic product, poverty, and inequality, Laos, 1992–2008

Description	1992	1997	2002	2008	2010
	Percentage of population living below the poverty line ($1.25 purchasing power parity [PPP] a day)				
Head count ratio	55.7	49.3	43.9	33.9	N/A[a]
Poverty gap ratio	16.2	14.9	12.1	8.9	N/A
	Percentage of population living below the poverty line ($2 PPP a day)				
Head count ratio	84.8	79.9	76.9	66.0	N/A
Poverty gap ratio	37.6	34.4	31.0	24.8	N/A
	Inequality				
Gini coefficient	30.43	34.91	32.63	36.74	N/A
Income share held by highest 10 percent	25.8	28.9	27.1	30.3	N/A
	Percentage annual growth rate				
		1992–97	1997–2002	2002–08	2008–10
Growth rate of GDP[b]		6.84	5.71	7.01	7.61

a   N/A = not available.
b   Authors' calculations based on regression runs.

Source: World Bank (2011c).

International migration

International Lao migrants commonly go to neighboring Thailand, with which Laos shares a similar culture and language and a long border. These migrants comprise about 8 percent of the total labor force, and their savings and remittances constitute about 7 percent of the Lao GDP (UNDP 2009). A large majority of outbound migrants to Thailand are undocumented because crossing the border illegally is easy. Lao migrants continue to flock to Thailand, motivated primarily by prospects of getting higher wages, having better jobs, and gaining access to modern urban amenities.

Study villages and sample individuals

Location

Our study villages are located in three provinces: Xayaboury, Champasak, and Savanakhet (Figure 2.1). A benchmark survey was conducted among 610 households in six villages (two villages in each province) in 2007 by the National Economic Research Institute (NERI) of the Lao Ministry of Planning and

Figure 2.1 Location of the study sites in Laos

Investment (MPI). Since the benchmark survey aimed to explore migration to Thailand, these three provinces were purposely selected because they posted the highest rate of circulatory and permanent outmigration. Two villages (one near the Thai border, one farther away) were thus selected for each province.

The two study villages in Champasak have a higher population density (96 and 56 people per square kilometer, respectively, compared with 25 for Laos as a whole in 2007), as they are respectively located 19 km and 20 km away from the city of Pakse. In Savanakhet, one study village has 60 people per square kilometer and the other village, 10; their distances from the city of Kaysone-phomvihane are 71 km and 52 km, respectively. In Xayaboury, the two study villages are thinly populated, with only 16 and 19 people per square kilometer, as these villages are far from the city of Xayaboury (250 km and 214 km, respectively). In brief, our study villages fall within the spectrum of typical Lao villages in terms of distance and population density.

The survey

In 2010, in collaboration with the NERI, the National Graduate Institute for Policy Studies (GRIPS) in Tokyo (with generous funding from the Japan Society for the Promotion of Science) conducted a retrospective schooling and inheritance survey among three generations of household members. Our respondents were the heads of households. We were able to reach 528 out of the original 610 households (i.e., attrition was as small as 13 percent); these 528 households

Table 2.3 Number of respondents in sample provinces in Laos, 2010

Province	Number	Percentage
Xayaboury	166	31
Savanakhet	194	37
Champasak	168	32
Total	528	100

were almost equally distributed across the three provinces (Table 2.3). The major reasons for attrition were outmigration, refusal of interview, and absence during the survey. We ran a probit function on the probability of being present in the 2010 survey using baseline information in 2007 such as age, education, and inherited farmland of the head of household. All the coefficients of these variables were not statistically significant, indicating that attrition is largely random.

Characteristics of households

All households in our study villages belonged to the dominant Lao–Thai ethnic group, which comprised about 60 percent of the entire population in 2005.[1] Ninety-eight percent of the 528 households have electricity, and 80 percent have access to tubewell water. About 50 percent have houses built with concrete and semi-concrete materials, yet only 1 percent have water-flushed latrines, indicating that housing standards in rural Laos are far from modern. Seventy-six percent of households have at least one mobile phone. The average household size in our study villages was 5.9, comparable with rural Laos' average of 5.8 in 2007–08 (MPI 2009b).

Average farm size was 2.92 ha, bigger than the 2-ha country average. Ninety-two percent of the households reported income earnings from rice production. The average yield of rice in the wet season crop was only 1.84 tons per hectare, which is lower than the Lao average of 3.8 tons per ha. The low yield was attributed to low adoption of MVs (only 66 percent of farmers in the study villages have adopted MVs), inadequate irrigation (only 17 percent have access to irrigation water), and low fertilizer use (only 40 percent apply inorganic fertilizer).

Sources of household income

The households in our study villages derived their income from agricultural and nonfarm activities (Table 2.4). Agricultural income comprised 55 percent of total household income: 37 percent from rice, 8 percent from nonrice crops, and 10 percent from livestock. Agricultural wages from planting, weeding, and harvesting of rice consisted of less than 1 percent of total income. Nonfarm income contributed 45 percent to total income: 8 percent from rural

Table 2.4 Sources of household income of respondents in sample villages in Laos, 2010

Description	Average
Total household income (current US$)[a]	4,381
Total household income (international dollars in 2005)	8,795
Household size	5.97
Household per capita income (current US$)	734
Household per capita income (international dollars in 2005)	1,473
	Share of total income (%)
Agricultural income	55
Rice production	37
Nonrice production	8
Livestock production	10
Agricultural wage work	0[b]
Nonfarm income	45
Nonfarm self-employment income	8
Nonfarm wage income	26
Earned in Laos	11
Earned in Thailand	15
Remittances and others	11
Total	100

a   Exchange rate is the average of the market rate in 2009 and 2010.
b   Less than 1 percent.

Note: This table refers to the period from September 2009 to August 2010.

self-employment activities (e.g., retail and trade, transport, restaurants, equipment rental, rural manufacturing, services, etc.)[2]; 26 percent from nonfarm wages earned mainly in urban Laos and Thailand (e.g., construction, domestic, factory, government, military, teaching, etc.); and 11 percent from remittances and other sources.[3] Nonfarm wage income could be earned within Laos (comprising 11 percent of total income) and through seasonal migration in Thailand (comprising 15 percent). Close to 30 percent of our sample households reported that at least one of their members goes to nearby Thailand to look for seasonal jobs. These seasonal migrants were mainly engaged in domestic, factory, and construction work.

The average per capita income was US$734 at the current market exchange rate, which is comparable with the US$800 national average in 2007 and is much higher than the US$299 average reflected in the results of a nationally representative household survey conducted by the UNDP in 2007–08.

Interestingly, the structure of household income in our study villages was fairly similar to that found by the UNDP survey (UNDP 2009, p. 124). In this particular survey, agricultural sources contributed 60 percent to total household income (in our study villages, 55 percent), and nonfarm sources contributed 40 percent (in our study villages, 45 percent). The 60 percent was further divided into 44 percent from crop production, 9 percent from livestock, and 7 percent from common property resource, whereas the 40 percent was broken down into 30 percent from wage work and self-employment activities combined, 8 percent from remittances, and 2 percent from other sources. Overall, in terms of household and farm characteristics, as well as sources of household income, our sample household could very well represent a typical rural Lao household.

Jobs

We classified jobs into five distinct categories: (1) farming, (2) nonfarm self-employment, (3) nonfarm wage work, (4) overseas work, and (5) others. Farming includes self-cultivation of crops and livestock, fishing, forestry, and negligible cases of casual agricultural wage work. Nonfarm self-employment includes retail trade and commerce, operation of rural transport, and the traditional manufacturing industry. Nonfarm wage work includes jobs in the government (e.g., teachers, military personnel, office workers, and rural health workers); in manufacturing, mining, and construction; and in services such as hotels, restaurants, and domestic work. Overseas jobs are largely concentrated in urban Thailand. "Others" largely refers to retired workers and housekeepers.

Of the 528 households, 458 were headed by males born in 1958, on average (Table 2.5). Male heads of households completed 4.6 years of schooling, whereas

Table 2.5 Characteristics of heads of households in sample villages in Laos, 2010

Characteristic	Male head of household	Female head of household	Total or average
Number of observations	458	70	528
Year of birth	1958	1954	1958
Completed years in school	4.6	2.3	4.3
Primary occupation			
Farming (%)	84	74	83
Nonfarm self-employment (%)	3	3	3
Nonfarm wage (%)	7	3	7
Others (%)[a]	6	20	7
Total (%)	100	100	100

a   Includes housekeepers and those who are retired, unemployed, disabled, or unreported.

female heads of households completed only half of that; the difference of 2.3 years was statistically significant. Farming was the predominant occupation among heads of households, while a small number were engaged in nonfarm wage employment (more than 80 percent were government employees), indicating that the private formal wage sector remains thin. Nonfarm self-employment (or home-based enterprises) was also not common. Surprisingly, the proportion of female heads of households in other job categories (consisting of housekeepers and those who are retired, unemployed, have a disability, or unreported) was considerably higher (20 percent) than that of male heads of households (6 percent) because there are more retired female heads of households: the retirement age is 55 for females and 60 for males, a practice mandated by the civil service law.

Members of the first generation (G1), consisting of the father (male G1) and the mother (female G1) of the respondents, were born around 1930 (Table 2.6). The male G1 inherited significantly more farmland than did the female G1 (4.0 ha compared with 2.3 ha) and obtained significantly more education (1.1 years compared with 0.4 years). This means that parents disfavored females in both schooling investments and farmland bequests. A large majority of G1 were engaged in farming, indicating that the nonfarm labor market is largely undeveloped.[4]

The second generation (G2) consists of the male respondents and brothers of respondents (male G2) and the female respondents and sisters of respondents (female G2). We have a total of 1,052 male G2 and 830 female G2, who were born in 1965, on average (Table 2.6).[5] G2 received significantly more education than their parents in G1 – a difference of about 3–4 years. Similar to their mothers, female G2 remained at a significant disadvantage with respect to schooling, but they received significantly more farmland. This pattern shows the emergence of gender specificity in parental bequest decisions: sons received more education, while daughters received more farmland, which largely

Table 2.6 Characteristics of three generations of household members in sample villages in Laos, 2010

Characteristic	First generation (G1)	
	Fathers of respondents	Mothers of respondents
Number of observations	528	528
Year of birth	1928	1934
Completed years in school	1.1	0.4
Inherited landholdings (ha)	4.0	2.3
Primary occupation		
Farming (%)	93	99
Nonfarm (%)	7	1
Total (%)	100	100

(*Continued*)

Table 2.6 (Continued)

Characteristic	First generation (G1)	
	Fathers of respondents	*Mothers of respondents*
	Second generation (G2)	
	Male respondents and brothers	Female respondents and sisters
Number of observations[a]	1,052	830
Year of birth	1965	1965
Completed years in school	5.4	3.9
Inherited landholdings (ha)[b]	0.63	0.86
Primary occupation		
Farming (%)[c]	88	91
Nonfarm self-employment (%)	2	3
Nonfarm wage (%)	10	5
Others (%)[d]	0	1
Total (%)	100	100
Characteristic	Third generation (G3)	
	Sons of respondents	Daughters of respondents
Number of observations[a]	732	772
Year of birth	1981	1981
Completed years in school	6.5	5.5
Primary occupation		
Farming (%)[c]	63	65
Nonfarm self-employment (%)	2	4
Nonfarm wage work in rural villages (%)	10	6
Nonfarm wage work in local towns and cities (%)	10	3
Overseas (%)	14	20
Others (%)[d]	1	2
Total	100	100

a   Consists of those who were 17 to 60 years old at the time of the survey.
b   Refers to those whose bequests have been completed.
c   Includes a negligible number of casual agricultural workers.
d   Includes housekeepers and those who are retired, unemployed, disabled, or unreported.

characterizes the matrilineal system of farmland inheritance in Southeast Asia (Quisumbing *et al.* 2004). Having received a piece of farmland, female G2 chose to become farmers (not housewives) – 91 percent classified themselves as farmers.

Like their parents, a large number of G2 continued to engage in farming (90 percent). Nonfarm self-employment was rather limited (2 percent), and nonfarm wage employment was confined mainly to government service (8 percent) (Table 2.6). It appears that the rural labor market in rural Laos in the 1970s and 1980s consisted of two large groups – farming and formal employment in the government sector. Rather unique in Laos is the small size of the nonfarm self-employment sector which, in many developing countries, is largely dominated by retail trade, services, and operation of rural transport.

The third generation (G3) consists of sons of respondents (male G3) and daughters of respondents (female G3) who were born in 1981, on average. We have 732 male G3 and 772 female G3.[6] G3 received significantly more schooling than G2, higher by about 1–2 years. Yet, female G3 continued to be at a significant disadvantage in schooling, although the schooling gap between males and females has declined from 1.5 years in G2 to only 1 year in G3. This implies that rural Laotian parents have become more egalitarian with respect to schooling investments.

At the time of our survey in 2010, 79 percent of the children mentioned that their parents were still undecided on farmland bequests. For the remaining 21 percent, we found that bequests to male G3 were almost the same as those to female G3 (1.28 ha for the male G3 compared with 1.21 ha for the female G3), a discontinuation of the traditional practice in the previous generation of giving more farmland to females.

In contrast to the older generations – G1 and G2, who were primarily engaged in farming – the job choice of G3 shifted away from farming in rural villages to nonfarm jobs in local towns and cities within Laos (including the main city of Vientiane) and to overseas jobs in Thailand. This change of preference tends to be more pronounced among female G3, who are traditionally the caretakers of farmland.

Around the mid-1990s (10 years after liberalization), a larger nonfarm sector emerged, along with a higher incidence of overseas work. While 65 percent of male G3 were farmers, about one third of male G3 have diversified into nonfarm wage work and overseas work, and the tiny minority who remained in the rural villages engaged in nonfarm self-employment (Table 2.6). This pattern was true for female G3 as well, although there was a much smaller proportion of female G3 in nonfarm wage work and a larger proportion working in Thailand.[7] Females made up 61 percent of overseas workers in G3. Overseas work was mainly confined to low-productivity, "last-resort" jobs undertaken by the unskilled and less educated workers who were "pushed out" of the domestic labor market because of the lack of alternative options domestically. The nonfarm wage sector and the self-employment sector in retail and rural transport remained thin: nonfarm wage income earned within Laos comprised a mere 11 percent of total household income, and nonfarm self-employment a mere 8 percent (Table 2.4).

For female G3, the most common jobs in Thailand were domestic, factory, and farm wage work; informal trade and commerce; and casual work in hotels, restaurants, and beauty shops. For male G3, the most common jobs were construction, transport, factory, and farm wage work. While the 2010 data do not give the exact place of workers' destinations in Thailand, the 2007 benchmark survey shows that a large majority of outbound Lao overseas workers went to Bangkok (62 percent) and other cities (21 percent), while the rest went to bordering provinces (10 percent) and other rural areas (7 percent).

Statistical tests revealed significant differences in education level across types of workers (Table 2.7). Farmers among male G3 have an average schooling of 5.5 years; nonfarm workers, including self-employed and wage workers, 9.0 years; and overseas workers, 5.5 years. Farmers among female G3 have an average of 4.5 years of schooling, nonfarm workers have 8.1, and overseas workers have 5.6. Inasmuch as overseas workers have comparable levels of education with farmers and much lower education than those in the nonfarm sector for both sons and daughters, there appears to be a push to migrate. This supports Hypothesis 2 on the choice of children's occupation based on education. Overseas workers were disproportionately young (28 years old, on average) and obtained jobs offering wages that were even lower than those prevailing in Laos. Most likely, many such jobs are informal. Yet, urban Thailand remains attractive because it has a huge job market and offers modern amenities.

In brief, our evidence shows that, while the rural labor market in Laos consists largely of farming in G1 and G2, it has subsequently evolved in G3 to become highly diversified (including jobs in the nonfarm and overseas sectors) and highly segmented in terms of schooling and gender. This development tends to reduce gender inequality, giving support to Hypothesis 5 on the improvement of women's status; it induced G2 to make equal investments in the schooling of both female G3 and male G3. The availability of nonfarm jobs and overseas work reduced poverty, as wages paid for this kind of work were higher.

Table 2.7 Year of birth and schooling of children, by type of employment, in selected villages in Laos, 2010

Characteristics of household members	Type of employment of the third generation (G3)			
	Farming	Nonfarm self-employment	Nonfarm wage employment	Overseas work
Sons of respondents				
Year of birth	1981	1976	1980	1980
Completed years in school	5.5	8.5	9.5	5.5
Daughters of respondents				
Year of birth	1980	1979	1981	1982
Completed years in school	4.5	7.3	9.0	5.6

Farmland, schooling, and job choice

Econometric model

Farmland and schooling are the most important forms of wealth transfer in rural communities in developing countries. Here, we explore the factors affecting farmland bequests and schooling investments from the older to the younger generations: i.e., (1) from G1 to G2 and (2) from G2 to G3. We specify the linear latent functions of inherited farmland L^* and completed years in school E^* of individual i of household h as follows:

$$L_{ih}^* = \sum_j a_j (\text{own characteristics})_{jih} + \sum_k b_k (\text{parent characteristics})_{kh}$$

$$+ \sum_k c_k (\text{female dummy}) \times (\text{parent characteristics})_{kh}$$

$$+ \text{intercept} + e_{1h} + e_{2ih} \qquad (1)$$

where we observe that $L = L^*$ if $L^* > 0$ and $L = 0$ if otherwise; a, b, and c are regression parameters; e_1 denotes the household-specific effect; and the error term e_2 is assumed to be independent and identically distributed (i.i.d.) across individuals according to $N(0, \sigma_2^2)$.

$$E_{ih}^* = \sum_j \alpha_j (\text{own characteristics})_{jih} + \sum_k \beta_k (\text{parent characteristics})_{kh}$$

$$+ \sum_k \gamma_k (\text{female dummy}) \times (\text{parent characteristics})_{kh}$$

$$+ \text{intercept} + e_{3h} + e_{4ih} \qquad (2)$$

where we observe that $E = E^*$ if $E^* > 0$ and $E = 0$ if otherwise; α, β, and γ are regression parameters; e_3 denotes the household-specific effect; and the error term e_4 is assumed to be i.i.d. across individuals according to $N(0, \sigma_4^2)$. Household-specific effects e_1 and e_3 are included in Equations (1) and (2) to account for the unobserved heterogeneity at the household level. Specifically, the presence of children belonging to the same household enables us to address potential bias emanating from unobservable household-specific factors that may be correlated with the explanatory variables.

We use the following as explanatory variables: (1) characteristics of the child, (2) parents' characteristics, and (3) interaction term between parental characteristics and female child dummy. Characteristics of the child include year of birth, birth order (shown as a dummy for the youngest child and eldest child), female child dummy, and number of siblings. From the estimated coefficients of these three dummies, we can test whether there is autonomous discrimination against daughters and younger children within a household: that is, if a_i and α_i have opposite signs, we can infer that schooling and farmland are alternative forms of transferring wealth.

Parental characteristics include father's and mother's completed years in school and father's and mother's inherited farmland in hectares: b_k and β_j are expected to measure the effects of parental characteristics on a son's farmland inheritance and schooling, while c_k and γ_k capture the gender bias associated with parental characteristics. Thus, for example, if an educated mother particularly favors a daughter in schooling investments, then the coefficient of the term *mother's education × female child dummy* is positive in schooling regression.

Equations (1) and (2) are estimated separately for the wealth transfers from G1 to G2 and only Equation (2) for transfers from G2 to G3. This is because, at the time of the 2010 survey, G2 was largely undecided on farmland bequests to G3; we thus skipped the analysis of farmland bequests from G2 to G3. Since not all children received transfers from the older generation, either schooling or farmland or both, we estimated Equations (1) and (2) as a tobit using household fixed effect (FE) (Honore 1992) and random effect (RE) models.

We explored the roles of education and inherited farmland, as these are the major forms of parental bequests that profoundly affect the job choices of children. Since education and farmland inheritance could be correlated with unobserved determinants of job choice (e.g., ability), we considered the two as endogenous variables. In the analysis of job choice of G2, we used both education and farmland inheritance. In G3, however, we used a parent's inherited farmland in place of children's inherited farmland because a large number of G3 have not yet received farmland bequests.

In G2, we were able to identify two alternative job choices: (1) farm job and (2) nonfarm job; in G3, there were three alternatives: (1) farm job, (2) nonfarm job, and (3) overseas job.

Let us define Υ_i^* as a latent variable corresponding to alternative k, which follows

$$\Upsilon_{kih}^{\cdot} = \sum_j \phi_{kj} \left(\text{own characteristics}\right)_{jih} + \theta_k L_{ih} + \psi_k E_{ih} + e_{5kh} + e_{6kih} \tag{3}$$

where we observe that $\Upsilon_{kih} = 1$ if and only if $\Upsilon_{kih}^{\cdot} > \Upsilon_{mih}^{\cdot}$ for $m \neq k$; i.e., alternative k is chosen over other types of jobs, and $\Upsilon_k = 0$ if otherwise. L denotes inherited farmland of G2, whereas in G3, it denotes inherited farmland of their parents; E denotes the completed years of schooling; φ, θ, and ψ are regression parameters; $e_5 k$ is the household-level random effect; and error term $e_6 k$ is assumed to be i.i.d. In the analysis of the job choice of G2, we used Rivers and Vuong's (1988) method in estimating the probit model with endogenous regressors and household random effects. We hereafter call this model the instrumental variable random effect (IV RE) probit model. To control for the endogeneity of land and education in the job choice function, we incorporate in Equation (3) the residuals obtained from the first-stage regressions of education and farmland bequest in Equations (1) and (2). We applied the same methodology to the analysis of job choice of G3, but incorporated only the residuals of education obtained in the first-stage regression, since we treated inherited farmland of parents as exogenous.

Determinants of farmland bequests and schooling

Table 2.8 shows the household FE and RE tobit regressions with respect to parental bequest decisions on schooling and farmland: columns A and B for

Table 2.8 Determinants of schooling and farmland inheritance in sample villages in Laos (tobit with household fixed and random effects)

Variable	Respondents and siblings (G2)				Respondents' children (G3)	
	A	B	C	D	E	F
	Education		Inherited farmland		Education	
	FE tobit[a]	RE tobit[a]	FE tobit	RE tobit	FE tobit	RE tobit
Year of birth	0.0356*	0.0446***	0.0034	-0.0032	0.0777***	0.0560***
	(1.610)	(3.295)	(0.219)	(-0.301)	(3.021)	(2.790)
Youngest dummy	0.4580*	0.3565*	0.4639	0.4808***	0.2635	0.3866
	(1.952)	(1.651)	(1.454)	(2.977)	(0.897)	(1.442)
Eldest dummy	-0.5474**	-0.6293***	0.6187***	0.6418***	0.8312***	0.7155***
	(-2.020)	(-2.853)	(2.726)	(4.107)	(2.698)	(2.806)
Female child dummy	-2.6128***	-2.9688***	1.2142	0.8511***	-0.4406	-0.1842
	(-5.852)	(-7.447)	(1.429)	(3.066)	(-0.536)	(-0.353)
Number of siblings		0.0265		-0.0610		0.1587
		(0.348)		(-1.096)		(1.552)
Education of father		0.1866**		0.1010*		0.3147***
		(2.385)		(1.899)		(3.517)
Education of mother		0.0296		-0.1171		-0.0885
		(0.198)		(-0.960)		(-0.808)
Size of farmland inherited by parents						0.3269***
						(2.633)
Number of siblings × female child dummy	0.1781**	0.1981***	-0.0948	-0.0203	-0.1027	-0.1447**
	(2.312)	(2.817)	(-0.782)	(-0.375)	(-1.142)	(-2.281)
Education of father × female child dummy	0.0549	0.1137	0.0278	-0.0162	-0.1974	-0.1615**
	(0.638)	(1.356)	(0.304)	(-0.269)	(-1.378)	(-2.007)

(Continued)

Table 2.8 (Continued)

Variable	Respondents and siblings (G2)				Respondents' children (G3)	
	Education		Inherited farmland		Education	
	A	B	C	D	E	F
	FE tobit[a]	RE tobit[a]	FE tobit	RE tobit	FE tobit	RE tobit
Education of mother × female child dummy	0.1021 (0.952)	0.1707 (1.153)	-0.0990 (-0.926)	-0.0408 (-0.290)	0.2765* (1.799)	0.2469** (2.515)
Size of farmland inherited by parents × female child dummy					-0.2763 (-1.375)	-0.2451** (-2.498)
Champasak I dummy						3.3216*** (4.269)
Champasak II dummy						4.7700*** (5.781)
Savanakhet I dummy						5.3627*** (7.582)
Savanakhet II dummy						3.8860*** (5.111)
Xayaboury I dummy						6.0834*** (6.966)
Constant		82.81*** (3.210)		5.792 (0.280)		103.4851*** (2.602)
Observations	1,795	1,795	1,243	1,243	1,009	1,009
Number of groups		423		328		288

a   FE = fixed effects; RE = random effects.
*Significant at 10% level. **Significant at 5% level. ***Significant at 1% level.

Note: Numbers in parentheses are z-statistics.

schooling, columns C and D for farmland inheritance of G2, and columns E and F for schooling of G3. We show results from the FE tobit (Honore 1992) and RE tobit models. Nonetheless, we have also estimated the linear FE and RE models and calculated the Hausman statistics accordingly. The estimation results, by using the four methods (i.e., the FE and RE tobit models and the linear FE and RE models), were remarkably similar to each other, and the Hausman tests did not reject the consistency of the linear RE. We decided to report the estimation results of the FE and RE tobit models below as these results were, by far, the best.

Year of birth had a positive and significant coefficient in the schooling function of G2, suggesting that later-born children have received more schooling. The youngest children were significantly favored, whereas the eldest children were significantly disfavored compared with the middle children (control group). The female G2 were significantly disfavored in schooling (receiving about 3 years less than what the male G2 got), while they were favored in terms of farmland inheritance (receiving about 1 ha more than what was given to the male G2) (after controlling for other child characteristics and parental wealth). There seemed to be no significant sibling rivalry in terms of schooling and farmland inheritance. Schooling and farmland are substitute forms of wealth transfers to children in G2 (Table 2.8, columns A to D).

Fathers' education assumed a positive and significant coefficient in schooling and farmland inheritance. Mothers' education did not matter much, primarily because female G1 had very low schooling: 87 percent of them finished only 1 year of schooling; the rest never went to formal school. Parental gender preferences with respect to resources under their control were largely absent, indicating the egalitarian characteristics of G1.

Later-born children in G3 continued to receive significantly higher levels of schooling (Table 2.8, columns E and F). The eldest child received the highest schooling in G3, while he or she received the lowest schooling in G2. Female G3 were no longer at a significant disadvantage with respect to schooling investments. Sibling rivalry was also absent in G3. The education of fathers has continued to exert a positive and significant impact on the schooling of G3. The size of parental farmland had a positive effect on child schooling (after controlling for parental education). The same gender principle was applied in G3: the more educated mothers preferred daughters for schooling investments, the more educated fathers preferred sons. Village dummies were all significant, reflecting differences in the supply of educational services and complementary infrastructure.

To summarize, our results show that parental wealth transfer decisions on farmland and schooling have changed dynamically over time. G1 invested significantly much less on schooling of female G2, but nonetheless compensated for it with farmland inheritance. G2 invested relatively equally on schooling of G3, when farmland has become scarce and the labor market has evolved to give relatively equal job opportunities to both female and male workers alike.

Determinants of job choice

Table 2.9 identifies the determinants of job choice of G2 and G3 with a focus on the role of education and inherited farmland. For G3, we used the multinomial probit model because the coefficients of the residual terms were not statistically significant, which indicates the absence of the endogeneity problem.

In G2, the choice was between farming and nonfarm jobs (Table 2.9, columns A and B). The impact of education on the choice of nonfarm jobs was not statistically clear: the coefficient of education was positive and significant only in the IV RE probit model II (column B). The impact of inherited farmland on the choice of nonfarm jobs of G2 was consistently positive and significant (columns A and B). This may be attributed to the fact that nonfarm jobs in rural areas primarily involved self-employment, which requires initial investment, so that large and wealthy farmers had the advantage. Females and males are equally likely to get a nonfarm job after controlling for both education and inherited farmland, indicating the absence of discrimination against females in nonfarm labor markets. Village dummies were largely insignificant. In short, inherited farmland in G2 is an important linkage between parental decisions and children's job choices.

In G3, there were three choices: (1) farming (control), (2) nonfarm, and (3) overseas jobs. Turning to nonfarm jobs in G3 (Table 2.9, column C), education exerted a positive and significant impact on the choice of nonfarm jobs. This is consistent with Hypothesis 2, which states that education is a major determinant in choosing nonfarm jobs. Female G3 had a higher probability of getting a nonfarm job, in contrast to G2, when both females and males have equal probability. As is argued in Hypothesis 5, the development of nonfarm sectors seems to contribute to the improvement of women's income status. Turning to overseas jobs in G3 (Table 2.9, column D), education had no significant coefficient with respect to the probability of having an overseas job, which means that both the highly and lowly educated have an equal probability of moving overseas to engage in informal wage jobs. Female G3 were more likely to cross the border (after controlling for education and parental farmland). G3 whose parents have larger inherited farmland were more likely to engage in nonfarm jobs and migrate to Thailand, which is consistent with Hypothesis 7, which posits the positive relationship between farm size and participation in nonfarm work. The wealth effect conferred by farmland on job choice, however, declined from G2 to G3, as shown by the decline in magnitude of the coefficient of farmland. These results show that the labor market in Laos has evolved dynamically to become pro-poor, offering a new and broader set of job choices to the more marginalized segment of the community – youth, women, and the less educated – who are more likely to fall into the poverty trap.

It is reasonable to speculate that the dynamic changes in the rural labor market in Laos have been brought about by the declining supply of farmland under a scenario of stagnant agriculture (low irrigation, MV adoption ratio, and fertilizer use), as well as the rising demand for overseas workers in Thailand.

Table 2.9 Determinants of job choice in sample villages in Laos

Variable	Respondents and siblings (G2)		Children of respondents (G3)	
	A	B	C	D
	Nonfarm	Nonfarm	Nonfarm	Overseas
	IV RE probit I[a]	IV RE probit II[a]	Multinomial probit	
Year of birth	-0.0107	-0.0102	0.0036	0.0219**
	(-0.756)	(-0.830)	(0.281)	(2.495)
Female child dummy	-0.5139	-0.3994	0.6867***	0.4001***
	(-1.431)	(-1.437)	(3.134)	(3.095)
Education of the child	0.1959	0.2387**	0.0980***	0.0025
	(0.984)	(2.088)	(2.976)	(0.125)
Size of farmland inherited from parents	0.3838*	0.3771**	0.1287*	0.0663*
	(1.771)	(2.251)	(1.930)	(1.912)
Residual of education function from FE tobit[a]	0.0501			
	(0.250)			
Residual of farmland inheritance function from FE tobit[a]	-0.3674*			
	(-1.688)			
Residual of education function from RE tobit[a]		0.0042		
		(0.036)		
Residual of farmland function from RE tobit[a]		-0.3613**		
		(-2.166)		

(Continued)

Table 2.9 (Continued)

Variable	Respondents and siblings (G2)		Children of respondents (G3)	
	A	B	C	D
	Nonfarm	Nonfarm	Nonfarm	Overseas
	IV RE probit I[a]	IV RE probit II[a]	Multinomial probit	
Champasak I dummy			0.3006 (0.759)	0.2191 (0.783)
Champasak II dummy			-0.3886 (-0.906)	-0.8400** (-2.272)
Savanakhet II dummy			-1.4605** (-2.488)	0.0662 (0.236)
Savanakhet I dummy			-0.5954 (-1.152)	0.4362 (1.634)
Xayaboury I dummy			-1.2803** (-2.074)	-1.4560*** (-4.074)
Constant	19.0138 (1.020)	17.2003 (0.726)	-10.2966 (-0.409)	-44.9819*** (-2.582)
Number of observations	1,183	1,183	1,127	1,127

a IV RE = instrumental variable random effects; FE = fixed effects; and RE = random effects. Education and farmland are corrected for endogeneity using the residuals of farmland and education function from the first-stage FE tobit model.
*Significant at 1% level. **Significant at 5% level. ***Significant at 1% level.

Note: Numbers in parentheses are z-statistics.

Lao migrants to Thailand consist largely of unskilled wage workers who are employed in informal jobs that a wealthy Thai would rather opt to decline – jobs that the youth, the less educated, and the women in Laos would accept.

Determinants of household income

Since G3 are geographically mobile, it was extremely difficult to apply random sampling and inquire about their incomes by activity. As a result, we failed to collect unbiased data. Thus, we report the estimation results of household income functions by source and by total income of only G2, which are shown in Table 2.10. There are several interesting findings. First, farm size had significantly positive effects on agricultural income, remittances, and total income. In an agriculture-dominated economy such as Laos, access to farmland is still a decisive factor that affects total income as well as income from remittances, which is consistent with the results of Table 2.9. Second, schooling was the most important factor affecting nonfarm income and total income. This is consistent with Hypothesis 1, which argues for the increasing importance of human capital as a determinant of rural household income. Third, as may be expected, schooling was unimportant in informal wage jobs in Thailand. These three findings are also consistent with Hypothesis 4, which states that the formal domestic sector provides lucrative jobs for the educated labor force, whereas the informal (overseas) sector provides employment opportunities for less educated workers. Fourth, the proportion of female working members had a significant effect on remittances. Combined with earlier findings that female children tend to choose nonfarm jobs and informal overseas jobs (Table 2.9) and that female G3 receive as much schooling as males do (Table 2.8), it is clear that the availability of nonfarm and overseas jobs contributes to the improvement of women's educational and income status (cf. Hypothesis 5).

In short, changes in schooling and job choices and determinants of rural household income in Laos are remarkably consistent with the hypotheses we put forth in Chapter 1.

Summary and conclusions

The key to enabling the poor to move out of poverty is to give them the opportunity to put their abundant asset – unskilled labor – into profitable use. Using a rare individual-level data set, this chapter explored how the rural labor market has changed in structure over time by analyzing the job choices of three generations of household members. We chose Laos because its labor market is gradually evolving, accompanying its transition toward a market-based economy that began in 1986. We found evolutionary changes in its rural labor market that may serve as an important catalyst for income growth and poverty reduction.

Three major conclusions have emerged from this chapter. First, there is a gradual transformation of the rural labor market away from farming to nonfarm

Table 2.10 Determinants of household income of respondents in the study villages in Laos, 2010

Variable	Log agricultural income	Log nonfarm income earned in Laos	Log nonfarm income earned in Thailand	Log remittances	Log total income
Log farm size	0.299***	−0.082	0.097	0.412***	0.226***
	(5.508)	(−0.625)	(0.719)	(3.370)	(3.908)
Log number of working-age members	0.197*	0.814***	0.760**	−0.004	0.495***
	(1.758)	(3.018)	(2.582)	(−0.017)	(4.296)
Proportion of working-age members					
Female	−0.387	−0.515		1.032*	
	(−1.460)	(−0.798)		(1.920)	
Between 25 and 34 years old	0.018	1.056**	−0.031	−0.280	−0.019
	(0.081)	(2.016)	(−0.058)	(−0.573)	(−0.083)
Between 35 and 44 years old	0.148	1.002	0.681	−0.738	0.055
	(0.528)	(1.588)	(0.857)	(−1.237)	(0.191)
Between 45 and 60 years old	0.330	1.960***	0.678	−0.399	0.562*
	(1.082)	(2.705)	(0.871)	(−0.610)	(1.784)
With primary schooling (1–5 years in school)	0.201	1.654***	0.138	0.501	0.467**
	(0.903)	(3.148)	(0.242)	(1.030)	(1.981)
With secondary schooling (6–9 years in school)	0.431*	3.025***	0.766	0.909*	0.784***
	(1.861)	(5.519)	(1.266)	(1.835)	(3.202)
With tertiary schooling (more than 10 years in school)	−0.096	3.374***	1.515	1.847**	1.859***
	(−0.242)	(4.546)	(1.553)	(2.380)	(4.439)

Dummy for Savannakhet (1 = yes)	-0.714*** (-5.655)	-0.723** (-2.303)	0.566** (2.119)	-0.669** (-2.384)	-0.703*** (-5.216)
Dummy for Champasak (1 = yes)	-0.616*** (-4.852)	-0.164 (-0.599)	0.041 (0.133)	-0.619** (-2.130)	-0.594*** (-4.422)
Constant	7.262*** (19.644)	3.950*** (4.689)	6.153*** (7.045)	5.955*** (7.906)	7.298*** (20.317)
Observations	415	181	118	194	426
R^2	0.174	0.321	0.203	0.149	0.234

*Significant at 10% level. **Significant at 5% level. ***Significant at 1% level.

Note: Numbers in parentheses are *t*-statistics.

wage work and overseas work, indicating the evolution of a labor market that offers a broader set of jobs with vastly different skill requirements. This development appears to have been induced by the decline in farmland size in largely traditional agriculture and the rise in Thailand's demand for overseas workers, particularly in the informal sector. Second, while there has been a decline in the size of inherited farmland, there has been an improvement in the schooling attainment of three generations of household members. Parental preferences with respect to bequest decisions on schooling and farmland have moved away from pro-male bias to gender equality: female G1 were not favored; female G2 were disfavored in schooling but nevertheless were compensated for this lack with more farmland; and female G3 and male G3 received relatively equal schooling. This has enabled younger females to have far greater access to economic resources than ever before. Third, and finally, education significantly matters in the choice of nonfarm jobs in G3 but does not significantly matter in selecting overseas jobs, indicating that the poorly educated have an equal opportunity to work in Thailand; female G3 are more likely to cross the border. This last finding indicates that youth, the poorly educated, and women appear to have been "pushed out" of the domestic labor market because of the scarcity of jobs.

This study is able to identify two strategic policies to enhance the workings of the labor market to effectively address poverty problems in Laos. First, investments in human capital, in primary education and basic health, are fundamental, as these two factors are clearly linked to employment by bringing jobs to people and encouraging migration. This strategy strongly corroborates with the policy priorities set forth by the Sixth National Socio-Economic Development Plan of promoting development in human capital by putting the top priority on education and health. To date, the Lao government has spent less than 3 percent of its GDP on education and less than 1 percent on health, which falls far short (6 percent on education and 2.5 on health) of the spending of countries that achieve rapid progress on this front (UNDP 2009).

Second, public investments in entrepreneurship training, infrastructure, and expansion of credit facilities cannot be ignored in order to stimulate industrial development. A fundamental reason for the outmigration of many Lao people to Thailand is the lack of development of labor-intensive industries in this country. Sonobe and Otsuka (2014) strongly argue that management as well as technological training provided by the public sector and international organizations holds the key to boosting the development of industrial sectors in developing countries. In the Philippines, electricity and road quality have exerted positive impacts on the development of the trade, transport, and communications sector, which employs a large number of the rural poor (Chapter 6). In Bangladesh, the development of rural roads has boosted the rural transport sector, while micro-credit has created a large number of small businesses opening up jobs for the poor (Hossain and Bayes 2009). While returns to investments in infrastructure are expected to be higher in areas closer to ports, natural resources, or large cities, the World Bank (2008b, Map 8.5, p. 243), on the other hand, argues that for poverty reduction, public investments in infrastructure should be spatially neutral since the poor in Laos are spread out quite uniformly across the country. To sum up, with the strong commitment of the government to remove the country from the UN roster of least developed countries, it seems that stimulating the growth of the rural nonfarm sector is a step in the right direction, as it is through the rural nonfarm labor market that the poor can participate in and benefit from economic growth.

Acknowledgment

The contribution of NERI staff to the data collection is highly appreciated. Some parts of this chapter are drawn from Estudillo *et al.* (2013) with permission from Taylor & Francis under license number 3550590099509.

Notes

1 There are 50 ethnic groups in Laos (Steering Committee for Census of Population and Housing 2006, Table 1.6, p. 15).
2 Retail and trade comprise small village stores and the buying and selling of fruits, vegetables, livestock, and meat. Transport means operation of public and cargo transport, vehicle repair, car rental, and services. Renting of equipment is confined to tractors and threshers only. Rural manufacturing refers to furniture shops, while services refer largely to beauty parlors and barbershops.
3 In Laos, urbanization is the main motor of rural nonfarm growth (Haggblade *et al.* 2007), driven by growing urban markets, high urban wages, commuting, and migration. Much of it emanates from nearby Thailand, as only 27 percent of the Lao population lives in urban areas (about one third of the 27 percent lives in the main city of Vientiane).
4 The Lao War from the mid-1950s to the mid-1970s appears to have had an impact on occupational structure: 18 male G1, consisting of about 4 percent of our sample, were identified as soldiers.
5 We have a total of 2,044 male G2 and female G2. A total of 162 individuals were dropped because they were dead, are on disability, are retired, or have missing or unreported occupation data.
6 We have a total of 1,597 male G3 and female G3. A total of 93 individuals were dropped because they were dead, are on disability, or are currently in school.
7 While Thailand is documented to accommodate Lao sex workers, we found that only 10 out of 772 female G3 are working in hotels, restaurants, and salons (supposedly where female sex workers are concentrated), indicating that much of the demand for overseas female G3 falls on domestic and factory work.

3   Evolution of jobs in Myanmar

Introduction

Poor households seldom take a single unilateral strategy to escape poverty, as they accumulate assets and dynamically allocate their endowments to economic activities where returns to factors are rising (Baulch 2011). The aim of this chapter is to identify sources of income growth and poverty reduction in rural Myanmar in 1996 and 2012. In line with Hypothesis 4 postulated in Chapter 1, our major hypothesis is that poverty reduction takes place when the rural poor find jobs in the slowly growing informal wage sector. Many of them are uneducated landless workers who move out of agriculture amidst the increasing scarcity of farmland and cannot find jobs in the largely stagnant formal nonfarm wage sector.

We chose Myanmar because, unlike many Asian countries, it was much less integrated with the global economy from 1962 to 2011 and, like many, it has been facing unfavorable conditions that can cause further impoverishment: increasing scarcity of farmland and slow development of the nonfarm sector. We found, on the contrary, a modest increase in household income and a reduction in poverty. Major sources of income growth were rice farming and nonfarm formal work for the farmer households and self-employment and informal work for the landless. Poverty reduction took place because of the accumulation of secondary and tertiary schooling and enhanced market returns to these endowments. Particularly important was the rise in returns to unskilled labor in informal wage work, which has largely conferred benefits to the landless poor. Our findings highlight the important role of the informal sector in poverty reduction at the time Myanmar was less integrated with the global economy.

This chapter has six remaining sections. The second section gives an overview of Myanmar's economy. The third section describes the study villages and sample households, identifies the sources of household income, and presents poverty trends. The fourth section identifies the determinants of household income. Finally, the fifth section provides the summary and conclusions.

Myanmar economy in brief

From 1962 to 1988, Myanmar was under a centrally planned economic regime. In 1988, the government announced a transition to a market-oriented economy, while the features of a command system remained largely visible. Marketing of agricultural commodities was dominated by the state under its procurement and distribution system; the industry and service sectors, as well as foreign trade, were also monopolized by the state. The installation of a new government in March 2011 paved the way for political and economic reforms, raising hopes for further integration and economic growth.

Myanmar had a population of about 60 million in 2011 (Central Statistical Organization 2011). Mandalay, Yangon, and Ayeyawady are the most populous regions. There were 31 million people in the labor force in 2011 – the labor force participation rate for men stood at 82 percent and that for women was only 50 percent. Agriculture remained the dominant sector, and rice was the single most important crop grown in almost half of the country's arable land. The rural economy of Myanmar faces two unfavorable conditions: increasing scarcity of farmland and slow expansion of the nonfarm sector, particularly the formal nonfarm wage sector. These are expected to cause an increase in poverty but, on the contrary, our data have shown a decline. It is thus the purpose of this chapter to explore the underlying mechanisms.

Arable land declined from 0.45 ha per person in 1960 to only 0.21 ha in 2011 (Figure 3.1) because of population pressure on a land frontier that is beginning to close. The average population growth rate is about 2 percent annually, whereas arable land has increased by a mere 0.8 million ha for about five decades since the 1960s. Given the limits to arable land, rapid growth in the labor force will not be productively absorbed in agriculture; the industry and service sectors must pick up the slack. In the 1990s, a few years after partial liberalization in 1988, the economy experienced a structural shift of its economy away from agriculture to industry and services (Figure 3.2).

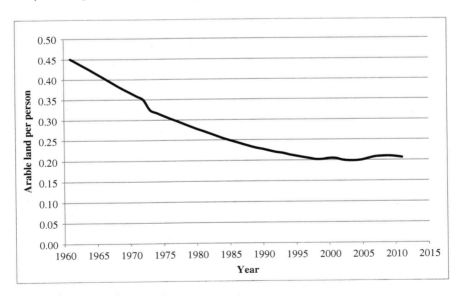

Figure 3.1 Arable land per person, Myanmar, 1960–2012
Data source: World Bank (2013a).

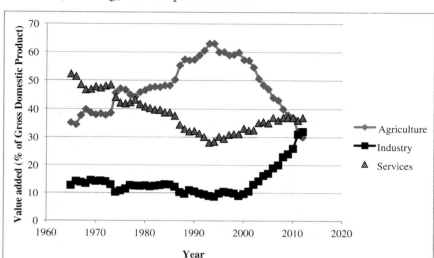

Figure 3.2 Share of sectors in value added of gross domestic product, Myanmar, 1960–2012

Data source: World Bank (2013a).

In 2012, the share of agricultural value added to gross domestic product (GDP) was 30 percent, the share of industry was 32 percent, and the share of services was 38 percent. The share of the labor force in agriculture was 60 percent in 1994 (the latest data available).

Myanmar has a GDP per capita (in US$ purchasing power parity [PPP] in 2005) of $1,801, which is the lowest in Southeast Asia (Asian Development Bank 2013). Real GDP per capita grew between 5 and 11 percent from 2000 to 2011 which, according to the Asian Development Bank (2013, p. 1), could be overstated, given the country's poor statistical capacity and use of outdated methodologies. Using its own poverty line, Myanmar's poverty incidence (in terms of consumption expenditure) declined slowly from 32.1 percent in 2005 to 25.6 percent in 2010 (Ministry of National Planning and Economic Development [MNPED] 2011, Table 4, p. 16) – i.e., one in every four Myanmar citizens remained poor in 2010.

Study sites and sample households

Study sites

Our study villages are located in one township in the Ayeyawady Division, south of the main city of Yangon (Figure 3.3). Historically, the Ayeyawady delta has been the largest rice-producing region in Myanmar, contributing about one third of the country's total rice production (Central Statistical Organization

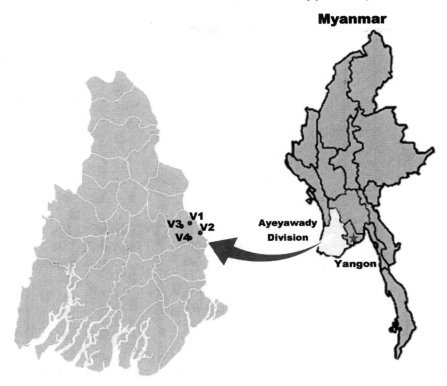

Figure 3.3 Location of the study villages in Myanmar

2011). Ayeyawady has a poverty incidence of 32 percent (based on the domestic poverty line), the highest contribution to the national poverty incidence (19 percent) in 2010, and the highest incidence of landless households, which are mainly engaged in agricultural wage work (MNPED 2011).

The four study villages were selected by the International Rice Research Institute (IRRI) as representatives of various ecosystems and topography in the delta (Garcia *et al.* 2000, p. 121). V1 represents the irrigated upper terrace; V2, the irrigated lower terrace; V3, the typical rainfed environment; and V4, the deepwater ecosystem (Figure 3.3). The main source of irrigation in V1 and V2 is the Pan Hlaing River Dam.

V1 is located about 50 km away from Yangon, V2 is 45 km, V3 is 58 km, and V4 is 60 km. V2 and V4 are accessible by boat from the main road. V4, which is quite remote, can be reached by a 45-minute boat ride from the main highway. The person–land ratio in 2012 in terms of paddy area per person was 0.62 ha in V1, 0.29 ha in V2, 0.23 ha in V3, and 0.38 in V4. Paddy production is the main source of livelihood in these four villages, whereas fish farming in V2 and open fishing in V4 are common.

Households and farms

Surveys were conducted in the study villages in 1996 and 2012.[1] The 1996 survey was conducted by IRRI with headquarters in the Philippines (Garcia *et al.* 2000). The current authors undertook the 2012 survey with funding from the National Graduate Institute for Policy Studies in Tokyo in collaboration with the MNPED of the government of Myanmar in Naypyidaw.

A total of 739 households were interviewed in 1996, and 900 were interviewed in 2012 (Table 3.1). Our sample villages are composite villages consisting of sub-villages: V1 has five sub-villages, V2 has 10, V3 has 12, and V4 has five. The 1996 survey entailed a complete enumeration of all households in a sub-village in each of the four composite villages. The current authors were unable to follow up the original household survey in 1996 because the names of the sub-villages and the names of the heads of households are not available in the IRRI data set. In 2012, sample households in each of the sub-villages were selected based on housing quality that may well represent various living standards in the sub-villages.[2]

Households in the villages consisted of farmer and landless households. Farmer households included those who are currently cultivating rice land, which are predominantly owner cultivators.[3] Landless households included those households not currently cultivating rice land, such as owners who are renting out their

Table 3.1 Number of households in sample villages in Myanmar, 1996 and 2012

Description	1996	2012
Number of sample households		
Irrigated upper terrace (V1)	179	200
Irrigated lower terrace (V2)	202	310
Rainfed lowland (V3)	158	180
Deep water (V4)	200	210
Total	739	900
Proportion of households		
Farmer (%)	60	21
Landless (%)	40	79
Total (%)	100	100
Households with electricity (%)	N/A[a]	2
Households with access to improved water source (%)	N/A	4

a N/A = not available.

Sources: Data in 1996 were downloaded from the International Rice Research Institute (IRRI) Farm Household Survey Database in Myanmar in 1996. Data in 2012 were collected by the current authors.

entire land, agricultural wage worker households, and nonagricultural worker households that are purely dependent on nonagricultural wage employment.

The proportion of landless households rose from 40 to 79 percent (Table 3.1). Some of these households were owner cultivators whose farms are currently under mortgage arrangement, whereby the farmer temporarily transfers his cultivation rights on the land in exchange for cash with an agreement to redeem it in the future. Landlessness is becoming prevalent because of the increasing scarcity of farmland due to strong population pressure and legal prohibition of share tenancy, as mandated in the Tenancy Law of 1963, which states that "the [land] renting fee shall be paid in cash." Yet, in poor village economies in Asia, share tenancy is often preferred over a land rental contract due to its risk-sharing features (Hayami and Otsuka 1993).

Our study villages were poorly endowed with infrastructure, as only a negligible number of households had access to electricity and improved water supply in 2012 (Table 3.1).[4] The MNPED (2011) reports that 34 percent of rural households in the whole country (30 percent in Ayeyawady) had access to electricity and 65 percent had access to safe drinking water in 2010.

The average household size declined from 5.3 members in 1996 to 4.7 members in 2012 (5.2 nationwide in 2010), and average schooling of the head of household was about 5 years (Table 3.2). Heads of households were involved in six job categories: (1) farming, (2) landless agricultural wage work, (3) nonfarm formal wage work, (4) nonfarm informal wage work, (5) nonfarm self-employment, and (6) others. There was a decline in the proportion of heads of households who are involved in farming and an increase of those who are engaged in nonfarm informal wage work.

The average number of working-age members between 15 and 60 years old declined from 3.1 to 2.7 (Table 3.2). There was an increase in the proportion of working-age members who completed secondary (7–10 years) and tertiary schooling (more than 10 years). For farmer households, the proportion of working-age members with secondary schooling rose from 26 to 32 percent and from 5 to 20 percent for tertiary schooling; for the landless, it rose from 14 to 24 percent for secondary and from 3 to 9 percent for tertiary schooling. Clearly, there has been an improvement in the quality characteristics of labor resources.

Village heads stated that open forests were no longer available in the villages in 2012. Indeed, the average farm size declined from 2.62 ha in 1996 to 1.63 ha in 2012 (Table 3.3); this is smaller than the national average of 2.71 ha in 2010. Owner cultivation is the major form of land tenure in rice cultivation. Landlessness is fairly common, while there are a negligible number of share and leasehold tenants. It appears that the village community has been largely divided into landowning and landless classes.[5]

Mortgage arrangement, which accounted for 29 percent of the rice area in 2012 (Table 3.3), is an arrangement whereby a creditor advances money to a farmer debtor in exchange for the right to cultivate his or her farm. The

Table 3.2 Characteristics of sample households in Myanmar, 1996 and 2012

Description	1996	2012
Average household size (no. of persons)	5.3	4.7
Average age of head of household (years)	46.8	46.5
Average schooling of head of household (years)	5.0	5.3
Households with female heads of households (%)	9	11
Primary occupation of head of household		
Farming (%)	55	30
Agricultural work (%)	24	20
Nonfarm formal wage work (%)	↑	2
Nonfarm informal wage work (%)	18	34
Nonfarm self-employment activities (%)	↓	12
Others (%)[a]	3	2
Total (%)	100	100
Average number of working-age members[b]	3.1	2.7
Working-age members		
With 0–6 years schooling (%)	74	63
With 7–10 years of schooling (%)	21	26
With more than 10 years of schooling (%)	5	11
Total (%)	100	100

a   Refers to housekeepers and those who are unemployed, retired, or have a disability.
b   Refers to members between 15 and 60 years old.

Sources: Data in 1996 were downloaded from the International Rice Research Institute (IRRI) Farm Household Survey Database in Myanmar in 1996. Data in 2012 were collected by the current authors.

creditor assumes the cultivation of the farm until such time that the debtor is able to pay the principal plus interest. The farmer debtor could become a hired agricultural laborer on the same piece of land. Fifteen percent of farmers in the study villages advanced money to a debtor and currently cultivate land under a mortgage arrangement.

The two most popular rice varieties in 2012 are Sinn Tuka and Ma Naw Thuka. Ma Naw Thuka, introduced by IRRI, is for export. Its yield in farmers' plots is only 3 tons per ha, far lower than the usual modern variety (MV) yield of 4–5 tons per ha, possibly because of low fertilizer application. Among our farmer respondents, 80 percent used fertilizer, 35 percent practiced double cropping, 50 percent used tractors, and 80 percent used threshers. These indicate that rice farming is modernizing, albeit slowly. Rice farming could be a major source of income and livelihood in this region.

Table 3.3 Characteristics of farms of sample households in Myanmar, 1996 and 2012

Characteristic	1996	2012
Average farm size (ha)	2.62	1.63
Distribution of rice area		
Ownership (%)	95	67
Leasehold (%)	↑	1
Share tenancy (%)	5	3
Mortgaged out (%)	↓	29
Total (%)	100	100
Modern rice (% users)	56[a]	100
Irrigation (% users)	25[b]	35
Average rice yield (tons per ha)	1.8[a]	2.8

a See Garcia *et al.* (2000, Table 3, p. 124).
b Proportion of plots.

Sources: Data in 1996 were downloaded from the International Rice Research Institute (IRRI) Farm Household Survey Database in Myanmar in 1996. Data in 2012 were collected by the current authors.

The average rice yield in 1996 was 1.8 tons per ha,[6] rising to 2.8 tons in 2012. This is lower than the average in Bogale Township and Mawlamyine-gyun Township in Ayeyawady, which is about 3.5 tons per ha (based on 2013 IRRI surveys) and lower than the national average of 4.0 tons per ha (Food and Agriculture Organization [FAO] 2014). Farmers buy fertilizer in retail stores downtown and sell their paddies to rice millers within the village or contiguous villages – 38 rice mills buy paddies from the farmers in the study villages, indicating the presence of fairly competitive fertilizer and paddy markets.

Sources of household income

We classified the sources of household incomes into (1) rice production; (2) non-rice crops, fish, and livestock production; (3) agricultural wage work and other agricultural income; (4) nonfarm formal wage work; (5) nonfarm informal wage work; (6) nonfarm self-employment activities; and (7) pensions, remittances, and others (Table 3.4). We compared changes in the household income structure of the farmer and landless households in 1996 and 2012.

Income from rice production comes predominantly from owner-cultivated rice farms. Nonrice crops include maize, pulses, oilseeds, jute, cowpea, black gram, mung bean, groundnut, vegetables, fruits, and fuel wood. Livestock and poultry income comes from the production of milk, pigs, cattle, chickens, goats, chicken eggs, fish, and cow dung. Fishing is an important source of

Table 3.4 Sources of household income in sample villages in Myanmar, 1996 and
2012

Income source	1996		2012[a]	
	Farmer	Landless	Farmer	Landless
Agriculture	2,207 (91)[b]	736 (68)	3,602 (82)	833 (38)
Rice production	624 (26)	0	1,539 (35)	0
Nonrice crops, livestock, and poultry	↑ 1,583 (65)	N/A[c]	1,328 (30)	573 (26)
Agricultural wage work	↓	N/A	735 (17)	260 (12)
Nonagriculture	209 (9)	340 (32)	785 (18)	1,330 (62)
Nonfarm formal wage work	N/A	N/A	300 (7)	103 (5)
Nonfarm informal wage work	N/A	N/A	127 (3)	653 (30)
Nonfarm self-employment activities	N/A[c]	N/A[c]	185 (4)	513 (24)
Pensions, remittances, and others[d]	N/A	N/A	173 (4)	61 (3)
Total annual household income (US$ purchasing power parity [PPP] in 2005)	2,416 (100)	1,076 (100)	4,387 (100)	2,163 (100)
Average household size (no. of persons)	5.5	4.9	4.8	4.6
Per capita annual income (US$ PPP in 2005)	439	219	914	470
Poverty incidence (%)	51	85	39	74
Poverty gap ratio (%)	18	44	19	42

a   Refers to December 2011–November 2012.
b   Numbers in parentheses are percentages.
c   N/A = not available.
d   Refers to gifts, rental income, interests, and others.

Sources: Data in 1996 were downloaded from the International Rice Research Institute (IRRI)
Farm Household Survey Database in Myanmar in 1996. Data in 2012 were collected by the
current authors.

income in V2 and V4. Income from agricultural wage work comes from the
planting, weeding, and harvesting of paddies. Other agricultural income
refers to imputed in-kind gifts (e.g., paddies, fruits, vegetables, livestock,
and fish), rentals of agricultural machinery, and land rent. Nonfarm formal
employment is dominated by jobs in the service sector in the government
and formal private sector, mainly in factories in Yangon and a few rural
enterprises within the villages. Nonfarm informal wage income comes from
employment in rural manufacturing (e.g., brickmaking, fish feed milling, fish

processing, rice milling, and battery charging), vegetable gardening, livestock raising, shopkeeping, transport operation, retail and trade, bicycle driving, tailoring, road construction, personal services, and domestic services. Non-farm self-employment activities include operation of rural manufacturing, operation of retail and trade, trading, rural transport, beauty parlors, and tailor shops. Pensions are received mainly by retired government employees. Remittances come largely from migrant workers in Yangon and overseas workers in Thailand, Malaysia, and Singapore. Other income refers to gifts, rental income, interest payments, etc.

Income in 1996 included incomes between January and December, while income in 2012 included those between December 2011 and November 2012. In 1996, agricultural income was the most important source, accounting for 91 percent of total income of farmer households and 68 percent of the landless (Table 3.4). Income from nonrice crops, livestock, and poultry production was almost as important as rice farming for the farmer households (35 percent versus 30 percent) and was the most important agricultural income source of the landless (26 percent) in 2012. There was a shift of the household income structure away from agriculture to nonfarm sources. The share of agricultural income of farmer households declined from 91 to 82 percent and that of the landless from 68 to 38 percent. Formal wage work was the most important nonfarm source for farmers in 2012. Landless households appear to have sub-stituted informal wage work and self-employment activities for agricultural wage work in 2012, presumably because of the declining labor employment oppor-tunities in rice farming due to decreasing farm sizes coupled with low rice yield and low cropping intensity.

Total household income in international dollars in 2005 increased about 1.8 times for the farmer and 2.0 times for the landless, which led to the decline in the income gap (from 2.2 to 2.0) between the two groups (Table 3.4). The major sources of income growth were rice farming and formal wage work for farmers inasmuch as income from formal work became the dominant source of nonfarm income in 2012. Nonfarm informal wage work and nonfarm self-employment activities were the main sources of income growth for the landless. Accordingly, per capita income rose (from $439 to $914 for farmers and from $219 to $470 for the landless) because of the rise in total household income and the decline in household size.

Farmer households experienced an increase in rice income because of increases in rice yield and rice price. Rice yield rose from 1.8 to 2.8 tons per ha because of increased adoption of MVs. Rice prices increased because the rice production quota, which was still in practice in 1996, was completely abolished in 2003. Under the quota system, farmers are mandated to sell 0.5 tons per ha of rice produce to the government at a predetermined price. In 1996, the private traders' rice price was about three times that of the government price ($22.70 versus $7.42 in US$ PPP in 2005 per 100 kg of paddy). Our sample farmers sold about 25 percent of their produce to the government and about 30 percent to private middlemen, and the rest went largely to home consumption. In 2012, all paddy produce went to private traders at a price of $33.90 in US$ PPP per 100 kg of paddy. This means that farmers received an increase in the rice price of about 50 percent.

Poverty

We used the international poverty line, which is pegged at $1.25 per capita per day, and calculated the poverty line (L_{1996}) in the local currency unit in the 1996 price as follows:

$$L_{1996} = PPP_{2005}\,(37.89)(12)\frac{CPI_{1996}}{CPI_{2005}}, \tag{1}$$

where PPP_{2005} is the consumption-based PPP exchange rate in 2005; CPI_{1996} is the consumer price index (CPI) in 1996; and CPI_{2005} is the CPI in 2005. PPP has been widely used in converting $1.25 into the local currency equivalent. The number 37.89 is the monthly equivalent of $1.25 per day, and 12 is the number of months per year. PPP_{2005} is 266, CPI_{1996} is 14.5, and CPI_{2005} is 100 drawn from the World Bank (2013a): the poverty line in 1996 was 17,537 kyats. If we substitute CPI_{2012} (which is 237) in Equation (1), the poverty line in 2012 is 289,058 kyats. We used the Foster–Greer–Thorbecke (FGT) index in calculating the incidence and depth of poverty.

Poverty incidence declined from 51 to 39 percent from 1996 to 2012 among farmer households and from 85 to 74 percent among the landless (Table 3.4) following an increase in income that largely came from rice production and formal wage work for farmers and nonfarm informal wage work and self-employment activities for the landless. Surprisingly, the poverty gap ratio did not change, which means that the depth of poverty remained the same. Poverty incidence (particularly among the landless) in our study villages was much higher than the national figure, which was 25 percent in 2010. Jobs are limited in Ayeyawady because of the slow development of the nonfarm sector and declining farm size. High poverty among the landless could also be related to the relatively high level of land inequality: the Gini coefficient of land distribution was 0.75 because landlessness is pervasive.

Choice of jobs

We did a retrospective survey of the job choices of two generations of household members. The first generation (G1) consists of the male respondents and their brothers (male G1) and the female respondents and their sisters (female G1). The second generation (G2) consists of the respondents' sons (male G2) and daughters (female G2). These individuals were between 17 and 60 years old at the time of the survey.[7]

We have 1,604 male G1 and 894 female G1 who, on average, were born in 1970 (Table 3.5).[8] The male G1 completed an average of 5.0 years of schooling

Table 3.5 Characteristics of two generations of household members in sample villages in Myanmar, 2012

Characteristics of household members	First generation (G1): respondents and siblings	
	Male respondents and brothers (male G1)	Female respondents and sisters (female G1)
Number of observations[a]	1,604	894
Year of birth	1970	1970
Completed years in school	5.0	4.3
Inherited landholdings (ha)[b]	1.6	1.5
Primary occupation		
Farming (%)	30	26
Agricultural work (%)	18	16
Nonfarm formal wage work (%)	2	3
Nonfarm informal wage work (%)	33	21
Nonfarm self-employment activities (%)	12	11
Others (%)[c]	5	23
Total (%)	100	100

	Second generation (G2): children of respondents			
	Farming households		Landless households	
	Sons (male G2)	Daughters (female G2)	Sons (male G2)	Daughters (female G2)
Number of observations[a]	199	196	278	214
Year of birth	1985	1983	1986	1986
Completed years in school	7.7	7.2	5.9	5.5
Primary occupation				
Farming (%)	49	44	3	3
Agricultural work (%)	10	14	3	5
Nonfarm formal wage work (%)	11	8	9	7
Nonfarm informal wage work (%)	13	7	61	37
Nonfarm self-employment activities (%)	6	9	13	16
Others (%)[c]	11	18	11	32
Total (%)	100	100	100	100

a   Consists of those who are 17–60 years old, excluding students at the time of the survey.
b   Refers to those whose bequests have been reported.
c   Refers to housewives, overseas workers, those with a disability, and unreported cases.

Source: Data were collected by the current authors.

and the female G1, 4.3; the difference of 0.7 was statistically significant, indicating that the female G1 are worse off with respect to schooling investments.[9] About half of the male G1 and about a third of the female G1 were engaged in nonfarm work in the informal sector and in self-employment activities. Common nonfarm jobs for the male G1 were construction, carpentry, and transport; for the female G1, these were domestic work, dressmaking, personal services, and shopkeeping. A high proportion of the female G1 declared that they are housewives, indicating that profitable job opportunities were largely absent for the female G1, who were less educated than their male counterparts.

We grouped G2 into sons (male G2) and daughters (female G2) of farmer and landless households (Table 3.5). Farmers' children have completed more years of schooling than the landless (7.4 versus 5.7; the difference of 1.7 was statistically significant). The difference in schooling between the male G2 and the female G2 was no longer significant, indicating that parents have been investing relatively equally in the schooling of boys and girls.

The largest proportion of farmers' children was engaged in farming (49 percent of male G2, 44 percent of female G2) (Table 3.5). A larger proportion of farmers' children were engaged in formal wage work because they were more educated than the landless children. The male G2 and the female G2 from landless households largely abandoned agricultural wage work (which was the main job of their parents) and ventured into informal wage work and self-employment. This job choice is consistent with the shift of the income structure of the landless households to nonfarm informal wage work and self-employment and away from agricultural wage work.

We estimated a multinomial probit function on the choice of jobs of G2 using the year of birth of the child, gender dummy (1 = female), completed years in school, and farmland of the parents as explanatory variables (Table 3.6). This function uses the job categories given in Table 3.5 using "others" as default. We obtained the following important findings: (1) later-born children were less likely to farm and less likely to engage in nonfarm self-employment; (2) female G2 were significantly less likely to engage in a job (more likely to be housekeepers); (3) the more educated G2 were significantly more likely to work in the nonfarm formal sector and to engage in nonfarm self-employment and less likely to become agricultural wage workers; and (4) children of those with large farms were more likely to farm, while children of those with small farms and landless workers were more likely to become employed in nonfarm informal work. The second finding is not consistent with Hypothesis 5, which suggests that the nonfarm sector provides equal employment opportunities for females and males, which may be attributed to the underdevelopment of the nonfarm sector in this country.

Overall, our results support Hypothesis 1 on the increasing importance of human capital and the declining importance of farmland as determinants of income and Hypothesis 4 on the association between the higher (lower) education and formal (informal) jobs. It is also worth emphasizing that the informal nonfarm sector was able to accommodate the youth and uneducated children whose parents have small landholdings, including the landless – groups of people who are more

Table 3.6 Determinants of job choices of children of respondents in sample villages in Myanmar, 2012 (multinomial probit)

Variable	Farming	Landless agricultural work	Nonfarm formal work	Nonfarm informal work	Nonfarm self-employment
Year of birth	-0.0401***	0.0183	0.0119	-0.0029	-0.0656***
	(-2.890)*	(1.125)	(0.704)	(-0.201)	(-4.490)
Female dummy (1 = yes)	-1.5409***	-1.2221***	-1.7454***	-2.0490***	-1.4300***
	(-5.384)	(-3.989)	(-5.824)	(-7.130)	(-4.824)
Education	0.0493	-0.1120***	0.1296***	-0.0452	0.0695**
	(1.637)	(-3.089)	(4.109)	(-1.473)	(2.172)
Parents' landholdings	0.1534**	0.0527	-0.0918	-1.1082***	-0.0504
	(2.479)	(0.715)	(-1.275)	(-8.452)	(-0.758)
Constant	80.9096***	-34.6652	-22.9155	8.9503	131.1295***
	(2.941)	(-1.075)	(-0.685)	(0.312)	(4.525)
Number of observations	792	792	792	792	792

Note: Numbers in parentheses are z-statistics.

*Significant at 10% level. **Significant at 5% level. ***Significant at 1% level.

susceptible to spells of unemployment and poverty. It may well be that the land-less are made better off by finding informal nonfarm jobs, thereby catching up with landed farmers in income earnings, as argued by Hypothesis 3.

Determinants of household income

To identify sources of household income growth, we estimated regression functions for different sources of income in 1996 and 2012. The dependent variables are (1) agricultural income and (2) nonfarm income (Table 3.7). Explanatory variables were (1) farm size; (2) technology, represented by the proportion of areas with irrigation; (3) the number of working-age members (between 15 and 60 years old); (4) proxies for the quality of labor of working members in terms of age, schooling, and gender; and (5) village dummies. We classified age into various age groups of household members using the youngest category (between 15 and 25 years old) as default. To represent schooling, we grouped household members by completed years in school – zero and primary schooling (0–5 years) combined (control), secondary (7–10 years), and tertiary (more than 10 years). To represent gender, we used male as control. Incomes were in US$ PPP in 2005, and the income determination functions were estimated using the ordinary least squares (OLS) separately for farmer and landless households. The difference in coefficients between 1996 and 2012 could well represent the change in market returns to endowments of land and quantity and quality characteristics of labor.

We obtained several important findings from Table 3.7. First, market returns to land increased; an additional 1 ha of land increased the agricultural income of farmer households by $402.61 in 1996 and by $1,410.19 in 2012 (Table 3.7, columns A and E). Second, availability of irrigation raised agricultural income significantly in 2012, presumably because irrigation expansion induced the adoption of MVs (column E). Third, an additional working-age member (which is a measure of household labor endowment) increased agricultural income significantly by about the same magnitude for farmer and landless households alike in 1996 ($312.24 versus $304.43, columns A and C). Importantly, for landless households, the value of endowment of pure labor in raising nonfarm income became much greater in 2012 ($78.29 versus $140.82, columns D and H). Fourth, while age does not seem to have a significant impact in raising income, secondary and tertiary schooling significantly raised nonfarm income, and such an impact has increased over time, particularly that of tertiary educa-tion (columns B, D, F, and H). Also, for landless households, secondary schooling significantly increased nonfarm income in both 1996 and 2012, and its impact grew in 2012 (columns D and H). The increasing importance of schooling in nonfarm income regression is consistent with Hypothesis 1. Fifth, the coefficient of gender was largely not significant, indicating the absence of significant gender discrimination in the labor market in Myanmar. Sixth, non-farm income of landless households in 2012 was significantly greater in the rainfed, irrigated lower, and irrigated upper terrace villages relative to the

Table 3.7 Determinants of household income in sample villages in Myanmar, 1996 and 2012 (ordinary least squares)

Variable	1996				2012			
	Farmer		Landless		Farmer		Landless	
	Agricultural income (A)	Nonfarm income (B)	Agricultural income (C)	Nonfarm income (D)	Agricultural income (E)	Nonfarm income (F)	Agricultural income (G)	Nonfarm income (H)
Farm size (ha)	402.61*** (8.113)[a]	93.25***[b] (3.691)			1,410.19*** (8.762)	-59.65 (-0.733)		
Irrigation (% area)	58.71 (0.251)	145.77 (1.227)			2,232.56*** (3.044)	-53.58 (-0.145)		
Number of working-age members[c]	312.24*** (4.643)	22.07 (0.645)	304.43*** (6.753)	78.29*** (2.632)	164.24 (0.694)	28.50 (0.238)	73.08 (0.244)	140.83* (1.776)
Characteristics of working–age members								
Between 26 and 35 years old (%)	-92.65 (-0.235)	55.36 (0.276)	144.33 (0.818)	72.10 (0.619)	1,034.33 (0.757)	37.99 (0.055)	-350.73 (-0.292)	-151.33 (-0.476)
Between 36 and 45 years old (%)	490.05 (1.110)	19.86 (0.088)	245.46 (1.191)	234.75* (1.727)	2,070.60 (1.365)	-192.68 (-0.251)	1,277.06 (0.929)	425.87 (1.170)
Between 46 and 60 years old (%)	-43.17 (-0.079)	-94.66 (-0.339)	-247.41 (-1.018)	135.60 (0.846)	2,152.22 (1.440)	88.90 (0.118)	-395.91 (-0.288)	-316.49 (-0.871)
With secondary schooling (%)[d]	525.14 (1.558)	251.37 (1.465)	-178.35 (-0.950)	245.43** (1.980)	568.75 (0.640)	127.71 (0.284)	-537.93 (-0.554)	567.79** (2.209)
With tertiary schooling (%)[c]	266.41 (0.401)	1,699.40*** (5.019)	450.76 (1.274)	568.91** (2.437)	2,444.44** (2.219)	1,801.42*** (3.236)	1,076.69 (0.732)	1,224.66*** (3.145)

(Continued)

Table 3.7 (Continued)

Variable	1996				2012			
	Farmer		Landless		Farmer		Landless	
	Agricultural income (A)	Nonfarm income (B)	Agricultural income (C)	Nonfarm income (D)	Agricultural income (E)	Nonfarm income (F)	Agricultural income (G)	Nonfarm income (H)
Female (%)	-696.02	-7.26	-104.81	-198.79	-472.39	272.96	20.86	91.45
	(-1.462)	(-0.030)	(-0.435)	(-1.251)	(-0.804)	(0.920)	(0.030)	(0.502)
Rainfed village (1 = yes)	605.01**	-286.99**	143.03	-83.62	-588.35	231.43	-806.86	1,099.88***
	(2.177)	(-2.028)	(0.894)	(-0.792)	(-0.731)	(0.569)	(-0.883)	(4.549)
Irrigated lower terrace (1 = yes)	79.97	-223.02*	191.21	-116.12	5,841.69***	218.59	-424.40	943.12***
	(0.324)	(-1.776)	(1.198)	(-1.102)	(2.805)	(0.208)	(-0.565)	(4.748)
Irrigated upper terrace (1 = yes)	370.96	-191.37	-122.42	-99.01	-414.53	291.22	-865.96	544.75**
	(1.378)	(-1.397)	(-0.782)	(-0.959)	(-0.545)	(0.757)	(-0.887)	(2.108)
Constant	156.88	-115.04	-114.13	169.40	-1,626.72	34.71	1,033.47	-23.91
	(0.317)	(-0.457)	(-0.429)	(0.966)	(-0.857)	(0.036)	(0.625)	(-0.055)
Number of observations	437	437	288	288	182	182	663	663
R²	0.278	0.151	0.186	0.087	0.479	0.086	0.008	0.083

a   Between 15 and 60 years old.
b   Refers to 6–10 years of schooling.
c   Refers to more than 10 years of schooling.
*Significant at 10% level. **Significant at 5% level. ***Significant at 1% level.

Note: Numbers in parentheses are t-values.

deepwater village (control), mainly because of easier access to Yangon. Seventh, and finally, the irrigated lower terrace had a significantly higher agricultural income of farmer households in 2012 than the other three villages because some villagers in the former village started commercial fish production with buyers from overseas.

Table 3.8 shows the results of ordinary least squares (OLS) regressions for components of nonfarm income such as (1) formal wage, (2) informal wage, and (3) self-employment in 2012 for farmer and landless households separately. Such data were available only for this year. We obtained a few important findings. First, returns to endowment of pure labor of landless households raised income significantly from informal wage work (the coefficient of working-age members was 126.33 [Table 3.8, column E]), indicating that landless labor was allocated more profitably to informal wage work and away from agricultural wage work. Second, the impact of secondary education in increasing income in 2012 was significant for landless households in formal wage work and self-employment (columns D and F). Third, and finally, the impact of tertiary education was significant in raising income in formal wage work and self-employment for both farmer and landless households alike. Interestingly, the impact of tertiary schooling was highest in formal wage work for the farmer households (column A) and in self-employment for the landless (column F). The associations between higher education and formal jobs and between lower education and informal jobs are consistent with Hypothesis 4.

Our regression results indicate that enhanced market returns to land and to quantity and quality characteristics of labor were the major underlying factors behind income growth and poverty reduction in Myanmar. The impact of one additional hectare of land on increasing agricultural income rose by about threefold from 1996 to 2012 (Table 3.7, columns A and E), while endowment of farmland declined; average farm size declined from 2.62 to 1.63 ha (Table 3.3). For the landless households, incremental nonfarm income associated with one additional working-age member (which represents unskilled labor) approximately doubled, and such additional income has come importantly from informal wage work. Inasmuch as unskilled labor is the most abundant asset of the landless poor, it is reasonable to conclude that enhanced market returns to unskilled landless labor in informal wage work explain much of the income growth of the landless (the average number of working-age members remained at 2.6). This result corroborates the occupational choice of landless children, who increasingly favor nonfarm informal jobs, presumably because they are more lucrative and are available year round. This result is consistent with Hypothesis 3, which argues for the declining income gap between landless workers and farmers due to the development of informal nonfarm sectors.

The rise in endowment of secondary and tertiary schooling and the rise in market returns to these endowments are also important forces for income growth. Yet secondary schooling was more important for the landless in raising nonfarm income. For farmer households, tertiary schooling significantly increased nonfarm income from formal wage work and in self-employment activities for

Table 3.8 Determinants of nonfarm income in sample villages in Myanmar, 2012 (ordinary least squares and tobit)

Variable	Farmer			Landless		
	Formal wage (tobit) (A)	Informal wage (tobit) (B)	Self-employment (OLS) (C)	Formal wage (tobit) (D)	Informal wage (tobit) (E)	Self-employment (OLS) (F)
2012						
Farm size (ha)	-40.93 (-0.903)		32.53 (0.873)			
Irrigation (% area)	-44.18 (-0.214)		-49.11 (-0.289)			
Number of working-age members[a]	10.99 (0.165)	18.59 (0.395)	40.66 (0.742)	-1.08 (-0.055)	126.33*** (3.858)	23.67 (0.321)
Characteristics of working-age members						
Between 26 and 35 years old (%)	-382.18 (-0.994)	-34.22 (-0.126)	246.03 (0.778)	-38.12 (-0.485)	-45.48 (-0.347)	-46.73 (-0.158)
Between 36 and 45 years old (%)	-503.38 (-1.179)	-219.90 (-0.731)	730.87** (2.081)	73.97 (0.823)	-11.16 (-0.074)	304.49 (0.899)
Between 46 and 60 years old (%)	-288.04 (-0.684)	-120.90 (-0.407)	546.63 (1.579)	64.51 (0.718)	-361.97** (-2.412)	-53.92 (-0.159)
With secondary schooling (%)[b]	-99.75 (-0.399)	249.07 (1.434)	127.66 (0.621)	180.31*** (2.838)	-201.65* (-1.899)	609.71** (2.548)
With tertiary schooling (%)[c]	1,216.19*** (3.922)	-148.03 (-0.704)	487.62* (1.912)	387.27*** (4.024)	-446.55*** (-2.776)	1,274.44*** (3.515)

Female (%)	182.04 (1.101)	-69.46 (-0.594)	320.70** (2.358)	-10.54 (-0.234)	-22.44 (-0.298)	145.47 (0.858)
Rainfed village (1 = yes)	181.77 (0.803)	13.13 (0.082)	57.44 (0.308)	99.59* (1.667)	111.18 (1.113)	876.32*** (3.894)
Irrigated lower terrace (1 = yes)	323.94 (0.553)	-25.50 (-0.064)	-60.65 (-0.126)	-5.06 (-0.103)	720.49*** (8.783)	217.75 (1.178)
Irrigated upper terrace (1 = yes)	-0.63 (-0.003)	272.17* (1.854)	-41.06 (-0.233)	182.48*** (2.857)	173.72 (1.628)	40.94 (0.170)
Constant	257.69 (0.483)	34.04 (0.090)	-759.92* (-1.730)	-21.32 (-0.197)	175.47 (0.970)	-232.78 (-0.571)
Number of observations	182	182	182	663	663	663
Sigma	1,026.50*** (18.976)	732.39*** (50.834)		487.87*** (36.360)	815.26*** (36.362)	
R^2			0.099			0.060

a   Between 15 and 60 years old.
b   Refers to 6–10 years of schooling.
c   Refers to more than 10 years of schooling.
*Significant at 10% level. **Significant at 5% level. ***Significant at 1% level.

Notes: Numbers in parentheses are *t*-values in ordinary least squares (OLS) and *z*-values in tobit.

the landless. Briefly, our regression results point to the rising importance of schooling as a determinant of income in nonfarm sectors and poverty in Myanmar, as in other countries in Asia, even though this country is less developed and less integrated with the global economy.

Summary and conclusions

There have been fears that the Myanmar people have been trapped in a long spell of poverty since 1962, when the country started to become much less integrated from the global economy. Myanmar has also been facing two unfavorable conditions: population pressure and the slow development of the nonfarm sector, which could even deepen poverty. Landlessness has become pervasive because of population pressure and the legal prohibition of share tenancy. This chapter explored the changing sources of livelihood and trends in poverty by examining the composition of household income in 1996 and 2012. This study found that the household income structure has shifted away from agriculture to nonfarm sources, accompanied by income growth and poverty reduction from 1996 to 2012. The major sources of income growth are rice production and formal wage work for farmer households and informal wage work and self-employment for the landless. Income growth has come from the accumulation of secondary and tertiary schooling in conjunction with enhanced returns to human assets.

Importantly, for the landless households, enhanced market returns to uneducated labor in the informal wage sector have served as an important propelling force to raise income and reduce poverty. Workers from landless households, particularly the younger generation, have shifted their preferences to informal wage work and away from agricultural wage work amidst the increasing scarcity of farmland and slowly modernizing agriculture. Many of them are uneducated and cannot find employment opportunities in a largely stagnant formal nonfarm wage sector. Overall, this study found that the development of the nonfarm sector (the informal sector in the case of Myanmar) is pro-poor.

This study suggests a fivefold strategy to enhance the development of the nonfarm sector. First, since rice income has become a major source of income growth for the farmer households, it seems important to raise the productivity of the rice sector. Myanmar was one of the world's largest exporters of rice from around the 1850s to the 1940s during the British colonial period, indicating the existence of a strong comparative advantage of this country in rice production, given its vast water resources and inexpensive labor. Second, investment in human capital in health and schooling is clearly necessary, as Myanmar has one of the highest maternal and infant mortality rates in Southeast Asia, and the gross enrollment rate in tertiary schooling was only 13 percent in 2011 (World Bank 2013a). With the rising demand for a high-quality labor force, it is important to improve the quality of schooling at all levels, particularly in public schools where poor children are educated. Third, investments in physical infrastructure such as roads, electricity, and improved water sources cannot be ignored; infrastructure is an important pathway by which the poor could fully participate in economic growth, as was the experience in the rural Philippines (Chapter 6). Fourth, since landlessness is becoming common in rural communities, it is necessary to induce the development of a competitive land market. The enactment of the Farmland Law in March 2012, which repealed the Land Nationalization Act in 1953 and the Tenancy Law in 1963, could spark the development of a more active land market. It could allow landless households to move up the agricultural ladder from landless workers to tenant farmers and owner farmers, eventually allowing them to have far greater access to the credit market. Fifth, and finally, economic liberalization programs, which started in 2011, could pave the way to a more prosperous economy following the successful experience of former command economies in Asia such as China and Vietnam. Overall, there is great optimism for Myanmar's future with the serious government commitment to fostering economic growth and improving the welfare of its citizens.

Acknowledgment

The authors would like to thank the Ministry of National Planning and Economic Development for their cooperation in the survey. Marlar Oo, Khin Maung Thet, Than Aye, Ohmar Tun, Yolanda T. Garcia, Arnulfo G. Garcia, and Ikuko Okamoto gave useful comments on the conduct of the survey. Data in 1996 were drawn from the International Rice Research Institute (IRRI) Farm Household Survey Database in Myanmar. Data in 2012 were collected by the current authors with generous funding from the Global Center of Excellence Program of the National Graduate Institute for Policy Studies in Tokyo, Japan.

Notes

1 Another survey conducted by IRRI in 2004 used the same set of households as respondents in 1996.
2 This sampling design was suggested by a government staff member who is fairly knowledgeable about living standards in the villages.
3 The Constitution states that the state is the legal owner of the land. Households nevertheless classify themselves as owner cultivators because they can dispose of the land at will even without consent from the state.
4 A few households use battery lamps, solar panels, and diesel generators as electricity sources. Ponds, wells, rivers, canals, and groundwater are common sources of drinking water.
5 In the Philippines, as well as in India, the landless population has been created by the prohibition and suppression of land tenancy contracts (Otsuka 2010).
6 See Garcia *et al.* (2000, Table 3, p. 124).
7 Compulsory schooling age ends at 16.
8 The number of the female G1, consisting of respondents and their sisters, is substantially lower because female-headed households comprise only 11 percent of our sample households.
9 Fathers of respondents have an average schooling of 3.9 years and mothers have 3.5 years; the difference of 0.4 is statistically significant.

4 Poor parents, rich children

Migration and landlessness in the Philippines

Introduction

About 70 percent of the world's poor live in rural areas, and a large proportion of them are children and young people (International Fund for Agricultural Development [IFAD] 2010). This fact raises the question of whether poverty and inequality are being transmitted across generations in the rural areas of the developing world. A grandmother's favorite bedtime story to young kids, "a poor man's child becomes rich," emphasizes the thrift, initiative, and enterprise of the poor man. Yet, success hinges not only on personal drive but also on other characteristics such as education, good health, and inherited wealth from parents. And far beyond all of these are markets, infrastructure, and availability of economic opportunities.

This chapter inquires into the routes out of poverty of poor women and men in three generations of household members in the rural Philippines. We focus on the landless population in the rural Philippines or the "poor man" in the grandmother's tale whose parents have no farmland and have low levels of education, representing the poorest segment of the rural community in Asia in general and the Philippines in particular (David and Otsuka 1994).[1] We found that the most important strategy to move out of poverty is to take advantage of new economic opportunities within the rural nonfarm economy of the villages or to move out to explore job markets beyond the villages in local towns and big cities and even overseas for the younger generation.

Studies on intergenerational economic mobility in developing countries are rare, mainly because of the absence of a long-term panel data set that gives socioeconomic information on a pair of a parent and a child spanning at least two generations. This is mainly because of the difficulty of tracing the whereabouts of children after they leave their parents' homes in search of wage employment elsewhere. And this is particularly true for the landless households, which are the poorer and the more mobile population. We used a unique data set from surveys that enabled us to trace a parent–child pair across generations. To explore the changes in the breadth and depth of poverty across generations, we have given interviews to the children of parents who were residents in our study villages 23 years ago, thanks to the mobile phone technology that has enabled us to trace these children and give them personal in-house interviews in their respective places of residence. To our knowledge, this is the first study on economic mobility in the rural Philippines on three generations of household members.

This chapter is divided into five parts. The second section gives an overview of land and labor resources and poverty trends in the Philippines, whereas the third section gives a description of the study villages and sample individuals from three generations. The fourth section explores the factors affecting the residential and occupational choices of two generations and the structure and determinants of household income of the youngest generation. Finally, the fifth section provides the summary and conclusions.

Land, labor, and poverty in the Philippines

The Philippines has been facing an unfavorable scenario in agriculture – declining farm sizes – that could lead to impoverishment. Table 4.1 shows arable land per capita declining from 0.29 ha in 1980 to 0.13 ha in 2012. In contrast, rice yield has risen from 2.2 to 3.8 tons per ha during the same period because of the continuous adoption of newer and better varieties of rice, along with increased fertilizer application and expansion of irrigation coverage (Estudillo and Otsuka 2006).

The share of the labor force in agriculture declined from 51 percent in 1980 to 33 percent in 2012 and, consequently, the share of value added as a proportion of gross domestic product (GDP) coming from agriculture declined from 25 to 12 percent in the same period. The labor force share of agriculture (33 percent in 2012), which is much higher than the value-added share of agriculture in GDP (12 percent in 2012), indicates that labor productivity in agriculture is lower than that of industry and services. The share of women in the labor force rose from 36 percent in 1990 to 39 percent in 2012, indicating an increasing integration of women and men in the labor market.

The annual growth rate of GDP per capita was –0.70 between 1980 and 1989 (Table 4.1) because of the financial crises in 1984 and 1985 when annual GDP per capita growth was –9.81 percent and –9.78 percent, respectively (World Bank 2013a). The annual growth rate of GDP per capita rose to 0.41 percent between 1990 and 1999 because of the robust growth between 1994 and 1997 (with an annual GDP per capita growth rate of more than 2 percent). Between 2000 and 2009, the annual growth rate of GDP per capita was 2.49 percent and that between 2010 and 2012 was 4.23 percent. The poverty head count ratio was reduced from 34.9 percent in 1985 to 18.4 percent in 2009 because of the transformation of economic activities away from agriculture to industry and services, which accompanies overall economic growth. While agriculture remains important for poverty reduction, particularly in the "high-value revolution," which is highly labor intensive (World Bank 2007a), the industrial and service sectors appear to have a bigger role to play in the Philippines.

Table 4.1 Land and labor resources and poverty in the Philippines, 1980–2012

Resources	1980	1990	2000	2012
Arable land per unit labor (ha)[a]	0.29	0.22	0.16	0.13
Rice yield (tons/ha)	2.2	2.9	3.0	3.8
Share of women in the labor force (%)	N/A[b]	36	37	39
Proportion of labor force				
Agriculture (%)	51[c]	45	37	33
Industry (%)	15[c]	15	16	15
Services (%)	34[c]	40	47	52
Gross domestic product (GDP) per capita purchasing power parity (PPP) (international dollars in 2005)	2,807	2,538	2,685	3,801
Value added (% of GDP)				
Agriculture	25	21	14	12
Industry	39	34	34	31
Services	36	44	52	57
GDP per capita growth (annual, %)	−0.70[d]	0.41[e]	2.49[f]	4.23[g]
Poverty head count ratio (%)[b]	34.9[h]	30.6[i]	22.4	18.4[j]
Poverty gap ratio (%)	10.2[h]	8.5[i]	5.4	3.7[j]

a   Refers to arable land divided by population between 15 and 60 years old.
b   N/A = not available.
c   Refers to 1981.
d   Refers to 1980–9.
e   Refers to 1990–9.
f   Refers to 2000–9.
g   Refers to 2010–2.
h   Refers to 1985.
i   Refers to 1991.
j   Refers to 2009.

Sources: World Bank (2013a); Food and Agriculture Organization (2012); and the National Statistical Coordination Board [NSCB] (1990, 2000, 2012).

Study villages and sample individuals

The study villages and survey design

We have four study villages – two villages are located in Central Luzon and two are on Panay Island (Figure 4.1). These four villages were purposely selected from 50 villages drawn from representative irrigated and rainfed lowland rice areas in northern, central, and southern Luzon plus Panay Island in the Visayas.[2] The International Rice Research Institute (IRRI), in line with its research project *Differential Impact of Modern Rice Technology in Favorable and Unfavorable Areas* (David and Otsuka 1994), conducted a complete census of households

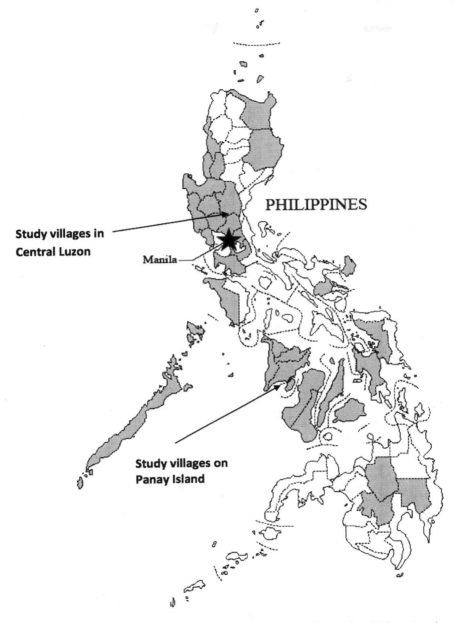

Study villages in Central Luzon

PHILIPPINES

Manila

Study villages on Panay Island

Figure 4.1 Location of study villages and residences of sample children in the Philippines

in the villages in 1985 to obtain basic information on farmland characteristics and tenure, as well as individual household member characteristics such as age, gender, education, and occupation. Based on access to farmland, households were grouped into two categories: (1) farmer households consisting of owner cultivators, leaseholders,[3] and share tenants and (2) landless households consisting of casual agricultural workers and nonagricultural households. We used the census in 1985 as the baseline data in our subsequent surveys in 2008.

Table 4.2 shows a total of 632 sample households in the four villages combined, consisting of 474 farmer households and 158 landless households in 1985; these data were drawn from the census of four villages. There were 2,490 children coming from farmer households and 728 coming from landless households. In the first phase of our research, we went back to the villages in 2008 in search of the 632 original households to administer a shortened version of the original 1985 census questionnaire in order to obtain information on the current contact addresses of the 3,218 children. We were able to successfully track 68 percent of the households (432 out of 632), which enabled us to update information on 48 percent of the children (1,522 out of 3,218).[4] The tracking rate on the landless households was lower because landless households are geographically more mobile – many of them were not available at the time of the resurvey or were no longer residing in the study villages in 2008, with hardly any information on their whereabouts.

In the second phase, we conducted a unique survey that directly reached out to children at their contact addresses. These children received a personal in-house interview at their current respective places of residence using questionnaires that contain questions on the demographic characteristics of their own households, migration and occupational history, and sources of income. The gray areas in Figure 4.1 show the locations of current residences of our sample children. Children tend to cluster in the northern and central parts of the country, where infrastructure is more developed and peace and order is not a problem. We divided children into four groups based on their residential addresses at the time of the 2008 resurvey: (1) study villages, (2) local towns, (3) big cities, and (4) overseas. Local towns refer to the *población* (town center) of the study villages, contiguous villages, towns located in the same province, small cities nearby, and cities and towns in other provinces. Big cities include metropolitan Manila, metropolitan Cebu, and Baguio. We were able to interview 27 overseas children, as it happened that they were visiting the study villages at the time of our survey.

We tried to track 100 percent of the children in big cities and 100 percent of the children in local towns but were able to give interviews to only about 80 percent of them. The main reasons for attrition were refusal of interview and absence during our survey visit. We selected 60 percent of the children residing in the villages using a lottery in order to make our sample selection truly random. Out of 1,522 children, we were able to give in-house interviews to 870 children (an interview rate of 57 percent) (Table 4.2).[5] We believe that this sample set is reasonable in size; it was randomly selected void of any sample selection bias that oftentimes occurs in panel surveys.

Table 4.2 Tracking and survey rates in the study villages in the Philippines, 2008

Category	Target population (A)	Population whose current residence was identified (B)	Tracking rate (%) (C = B/A)	Number of in-house interviews (D)	Interview rate (%) (E = D/B)
			Number of households in 1985 census		
Farmer households in 1985	474	340	71		
Landless households in 1985	158	92	58		
Total	632	432	68		
			Number of children in 1985 census		
Farmer households in 1985	2,490	1,202	49	695	58
Landless households in 1985	728	320	44	175	55
Total	3,218	1,522	48	870	57

Since we aim to explore whether poverty has been transmitted from parents to children, it is necessary to have data on the income of parents in 1985. We were able to obtain such data from a survey called an "intensive survey" of households conducted by IRRI (David and Otsuka 1994). This is an income survey on a sample set of farmer and landless households that were randomly selected from the census of households in the study villages in 1985, stratified by farm size for the farmer and by household size for the landless. The intensive survey has a sample size of 268, while the census has 632 households – that is, 42 percent of the population was included as sample households in the intensive survey.

We were able to obtain data on the characteristics of two generations of household members from a survey conducted by Quisumbing (1994) in 1989, which explores gender bias in traditional land inheritance customs. The first generation (G1) consists of parents of respondents, while the second generation (G2) consists of the respondents and their sisters and brothers. Quisumbing (1994) intended to conduct interviews on the full set of 268 households but successfully obtained only a smaller set of 192 households, which is 72 percent of the 268 households in the intensive survey in 1985. Attrition in the Quisumbing (1994) survey is explained by the low response rate of the landless households, as many of them have moved out of the study villages since 1989. Only a few outmovers were included in Quisumbing's (1994) survey because there was hardly any information on the contact addresses of the outmovers. Her data set contains a total of 1,485 individuals from G2. Quisumbing (1994) did not collect data on the household incomes of G2. Data on the respondents' children, the third generation (G3), were taken from our own survey in 2008. Overall, we have a total of 535 individuals from G1; 1,485 individuals from G2; and 1,516 individuals from G3 (1,197 from the farmer households and 319 from the landless households) (Table 4.3).[6]

The 1,516 members of G3 in the 2008 survey came from a complete enumeration of household members in the 1985 census. The sample consisting of the respondents and their siblings (G2) in the 1989 survey may not be purely random, as outmovers were excluded. Indeed, according to Rosenzweig (2003), long-term panel surveys that did not include members who separated from the

Table 4.3 Characteristics of sample individuals

Category	Number	%	Year of birth	Completed years in school	Inherited land (ha)
	Parents of respondents (G1)				
With job in agriculture	243	46	1907	3.4	1.14
With nonfarm job	38	7	1909	6.2	0.44
With overseas job	1	0	1910	N/A[a]	N/A
Unemployed and others[b]	253	47	1911	3.1	0.61
All	535	100	1909	3.4	0.83

			Respondents and siblings (G2)		
With job in agriculture	680	46	1940	6.0	0.57
With nonfarm job	259	17	1943	9.0	0.23
With job in the big cities	85	6	1944	9.3	0.08
With overseas job	48	3	1949	10.1	0.51
Unemployed and others	413	28	1940	6.0	0.24
All	1,485	100	1941	6.9	0.39
			Children of farmer households (G3)		
With job in agriculture in study villages	287	24	1971	8.8	0.17
With nonfarm job in study villages	202	17	1972	11.0	0.08
With job in agriculture in local towns[c]	45	4	1968	8.7	0.23
With nonfarm job in local towns[c]	76	6	1973	11.9	0.01
With job in the big cities	193	16	1973	11.1	0.03
With overseas job	78	6	1971	12.8	0.01
Unemployed and others	316	27	1972	10.2	0.02
All	1,197	100	1972	10.4	0.07
			Children of landless households (G3)		
With job in agriculture in study villages	46	14	1972	8.0	0
With nonfarm job in study villages	48	15	1974	10.9	0
With job in agriculture in local towns	11	4	1971	6.8	0
With nonfarm job in local towns	26	8	1974	10.8	0
With job in the big cities	56	18	1975	10.6	0
With overseas job	35	11	1973	12.9	0
Unemployed and others	97	30	1973	9.4	0
All	319	100	1974	10.0	0

a   N/A = not available.
b   Includes housekeepers, discouraged workers, retired workers, and people with a disability.
c   Includes small cities.

original households may create nonrandom subsamples of individuals. Yet, our panel data set, which gives data on three generations of household members, remains a rarity in developing countries. We believe that this data set could serve our purpose of exploring intergenerational economic mobility and poverty transition of household members.

Characteristics of sample individuals

We selected members of G2 and G3 who were 24 years old and above at the time of the 1989 and 2008 surveys, respectively. We chose 24 as the lower bound, as it is the age when tertiary schooling is expected to have been completed and farmland is bestowed to children commonly upon marriage, on average, at the age of 24 for G2. Schooling and farmland are the two most important forms of intergenerational wealth transfers in developing countries (Quisumbing *et al.* 2004).

We grouped G1, G2, and G3 based on the type of job. For G1, we have the following classifications: (1) with job in agriculture, (2) with nonfarm job, (3) with overseas job, and (4) unemployed and others (Table 4.3). Almost all male G1 were engaged in agriculture, and almost all female parents were unemployed, mainly housekeepers. The G1 were born around 1910; had very little schooling; and owned, on average, less than 1 ha of farmland per person. Fathers completed more years of schooling than did mothers (3.8 years versus 3.1 years) and inherited larger areas of farmland (1.1 ha versus 0.56 ha), indicating a gender bias in the transfer of wealth in favor of males. Interestingly, parents who were engaged in nonfarm work were men, who had the highest level of education – 6.2 years of completed years in school – indicating that the rural nonfarm labor market in the early 1990s was thin and dominated mainly by male jobs in the formal sector.

For G2, we have the following groupings: (1) with job in agriculture, (2) with nonfarm job, (3) with job in the big cities, (4) with overseas job, and (5) unemployed and others. The G2 were born around 1940, accomplished more than twice the length of education of their parents (6.9 versus 3.4 years), and inherited about half the size of their parents' farmland (0.39 versus 0.83 ha). The size of inherited farmland has declined over time, and males continue to receive farmland as bequests because rice farming is intensive in male labor (Estudillo *et al.* 2001). Brothers and sisters had about the same level of schooling, in contrast to their parents' generation, when females were disfavored. Females started to flock to school to take advantage of the American colonial policy of the free public primary school system that opened to both sexes, which was largely not available during the Spanish colonial period.[7] Interestingly, both male G2 and female G2 had become engaged in more diversified occupations, including overseas work.[8] There was also a rise in the incidence of nonfarm jobs and a decline in unemployment, indicating that the nonfarm labor market had started to develop.

We divided G3 based on parental endowment of farmland: (1) children originating from farmer households and (2) children from landless households (Table 4.3). These two groups were further subdivided into seven categories based on current residence and occupation: (1) with job in agriculture in the study villages, (2) with nonfarm job in the study villages, (3) with job in agriculture in local towns, (4) with nonfarm job in local towns, (5) with job in the big cities, (6) with overseas job, and (7) unemployed and others.

The G3 were born around 1973, had more than 10 years of schooling (3.3 years more than their parents), and had inherited farmland of less than one tenth of 1 ha. Children of farmers completed 0.4 more years of schooling than did landless children – a difference that was statistically significant at 5 percent. A larger proportion of children from farmer households opted to stay in the study villages. Landless children were geographically more mobile, residing in the big cities, local towns, and overseas. This was particularly true for female landless children, who are more educated than their brothers. Interestingly, female children of the landless had become more heavily engaged in nonfarm jobs and more actively sought overseas jobs than those of farmer households.

Overall, we have seen a secular increase in completed years in school and a decline in the size of inherited farmland. The major question is whether landless children, who came from poorly endowed households, have become worse off than farmers' children.

Sources of household income and poverty

Table 4.4 shows the sources of household income of G2 in 1985 and those of their children (G3) in 2008, classified as coming from farmer or landless households and as single or married. Sources of household income were the following: (1) rice income consisting of income from rice production and from off-farm wage activities; (2) nonrice farm income coming from the production of nonrice crops, livestock, and poultry; (3) nonfarm income consisting of wage income from nonfarm activities such as formal and informal salary work and from self-employed activities

Table 4.4 Composition of household income of respondents and their children from study villages in the Philippines (annual income in international dollars in 2005)

Source	Household income of respondents (G2) in 1985				
	Farmer households			Landless households	
	Income	%		Income	%
Rice income	1,104	58		329	36
Nonrice income	342	18		119	13
Nonfarm income	225	12		369	41
Remittances and others[a]	224	12		91	10
Total income	1,895	100		908	100
Poverty head count (%)[b]	42			65	
Poverty gap (%)[b]	20			26	
Number of observations	230			65	

(*Continued*)

Table 4.4 (Continued)

| | Household income of married children of respondents (G3) in 2008 | | | |
| | Married children of farmer households | | Married children of landless households | |
	Income	%	Income	%
Rice income	610	8	81	1
Nonrice income	757	9	484	7
Nonfarm income	5,452	67	5,372	81
Remittances and others	1,322	16	691	11
Total income	8,142	100	6,629	100
Poverty head count (%)	26		34	
Poverty gap (%)	12		16	
Number of observations	527		129	

| | Household income of single children of respondents (G3) in 2008 | | | |
| | Single children of farmer households | | Single children of landless households | |
	Income	%	Income	%
Rice income	772	12	116	2
Nonrice income	545	8	446	6
Nonfarm income	4,144	62	4,963	71
Remittances and others	1,194	18	1,443	21
Total income	6,656	100	6,970	100
Poverty head count (%)	25		16	
Poverty gap (%)	13		5	
Number of observations	167		43	

a   Refers to pensions, interest payments, gifts, etc.
b   Taken from Otsuka *et al.* (2009, Table 2.6, p. 33).

in trade, transport, and the communication sector; and (4) domestic and foreign remittances. Income data are in international dollars in 2005.

In 1985, a substantial portion of household income of G2 (76 percent for farmer households, 49 percent for landless households) came from agricultural sources such as the production of rice, nonrice crops, and livestock (Table 4.4). The income of farmer households was about twice that of landless house-holds – a difference that was statistically significant at the 1 percent level.

The major sources of disparity were incomes from rice and nonrice crop production, indicating that the size of farmland was the primary indicator of household economic well-being in earlier years, when nonfarm employment opportunities were still limited. Nonfarm income was higher for the landless, presumably coming from low-productivity livelihood activities and giving no significant income advantage to the landless poor. And because the landless are land poor, poverty was higher among the landless households (65 percent) than among the farmer households (42 percent). Poverty measures were estimated using the Foster–Greer–Thorbecke (FGT) index (Foster *et al.* 1984), with the US$1.25 per capita per day in PPP based on private consumption as the poverty line.

Interestingly, nonfarm income has become the major income source of farmer children in 2008 – 67 percent of their income – while it was only 12 percent for their parents. Income disparity between the farmer and landless households appears to have disappeared in the children's generation with nonfarm income as the major driver of income growth – the total income gap between the farmer and landless children was only $1,072 in PPP, which was not significantly different. Meanwhile, income from rice and nonrice farming remained significantly higher for the farmer children.

In the landless household category, the children's income is 7.4 times more than that of their parents', whereas in the farmer household category, the children's income is 4.1 times more than that of their parents', indicating a substantial growth of income of the landless children.

While incomes of children have largely equalized, poverty incidence among the landless children remained higher, but at a mere 8 percentage points compared with their parents, for whom poverty stood at 23 percentage points higher among the landless class. Landless children who migrated to local towns and big cities were the ones able to increase their income vis-à-vis that of farmer children. The poor in the village are mainly farm workers eking out their living doing casual daily wage work in rice farming. In brief, it is clear that participation in the nonfarm labor market and migration to local towns and big cities are the main pathways out of poverty for the landless poor. These observations are clearly consistent with Hypothesis 3, which points to the declining income gap between landed and landless households due to the greater geographical and occupational mobility of the landless class.

Children's income by place of residence

Table 4.5 shows the sources of household income of G3 by place of residence. Children working overseas had the highest income, followed by those in the big cities; children who reside in the study villages had the lowest. Accordingly, poverty incidence and depth of poverty were highest among children living in the villages, and that poverty did not exist among overseas children, while less than 10 percent of migrants in the big cities were poor. Migrant children were deeply engaged in nonfarm work; the largest proportion of their incomes had

Table 4.5 Household income composition of children of respondents in study villages in the Philippines by place of residence (annual income in purchasing power parity, international dollars in 2005)

Income source	Mean	%
	Local towns[a]	
Rice income	329	4
Nonrice income	410	5
Nonfarm income	6,886	78
Remittances and others[b]	1,252	14
Total income	8,877	100
Poverty head count ratio (%)	22	
Poverty gap ratio (%)	10	
Number of observations	255	
	Big cities	
Rice income	14	0
Nonrice income	15	0
Nonfarm income	8,545	82
Remittances and others	1,896	18
Total income	10,469	100
Poverty head count ratio (%)	9	
Poverty gap ratio (%)	3	
Number of observations	116	
	Overseas	
Rice income	499	2
Nonrice income	86	0
Nonfarm income	24,561	96
Remittances and others	423	2
Total income	25,570	100
Poverty head count ratio (%)	0	
Poverty gap ratio (%)	0	
Number of observations	27	
	Study villages	
Rice income	785	15
Nonrice income	990	19
Nonfarm income	2,269	44
Remittances and others	1,062	21
Total income	5,106	100
Poverty head count ratio (%)	36	
Poverty gap ratio (%)	17	
Number of observations	468	

a   Includes small cities.
b   Refers to pensions, interest payments, gifts, etc.

come from nonfarm income, which reinforces the validity of Hypothesis 3. Surprisingly, even those children who remain in the study villages derived 65 percent of their income from nonfarm sources, including nonfarm wage income (44 percent) and remittances and other sources (21 percent). Rice income has become a much less important source of income for G3, whereas it was the most important source, particularly for farmer households, for G2.

The importance of rice income has declined due to stagnant rice yield and declining labor use in the rice sector because of the accelerated adoption of labor-saving technologies. Also, it appears that production of high-value crops and livestock, the "high-value revolution" (World Bank 2007b), has become more common; the share of nonrice income among children living in the study villages was 19 percent, which is higher than the 15 percent share of rice income. Also, a relatively larger share of income of children in the study villages has come from remittances and other sources, attesting to the economic importance of transfer income from outside the villages. Clearly, nonfarm work, migration, and the production of high-value crops and livestock have served as an important pathway out of poverty for G3.

Correlation of parents' and children's characteristics

Correlation coefficients of parents' and children's schooling declined from 0.30 between G1 and G2 to 0.20 between G2 and G3. Children from less educated parents tended to catch up with children from highly educated parents in terms of schooling, with male children benefiting more. This could be partly attributed to the expansion of free public secondary schools in the villages since 1988 and the construction of bridges in two remote villages (in Central Luzon in 1992 and on Panay Island in 1995) connecting the two to the town centers, where secondary schools are located. The correlation coefficient between parental income and children's income was close to zero, and the coefficient of parental income in a regression function of children's income was statistically not significant, with a value of –0.1187. Clearly, the initial economic position of parents has weakened in explaining their children's economic destiny.

To identify pathways out of poverty and inequality more rigorously, we first explored parental bequest decisions on farmland and schooling and then assessed the extent to which bequeathed farmland and completed schooling affected the decisions of children on migration and occupational choices and their incomes.

Occupational choice and income determinants

Choice of occupation

Here, we explore the factors affecting children's residential and occupational choices. We focus on the role of education and inherited farmland, as these are the major forms of inter-generational wealth transfer that could potentially affect children's residential and occupational preferences.

For G2, we considered the following five alternatives: (1) agricultural work, (2) nonfarm job in rural areas, (3) job in the big cities, (4) overseas job, and (5) unemployed. Housewives, discouraged workers, retired workers, and people with a disability (except those residing overseas) were classified as unemployed. For G3, we have the following seven alternatives: (1) agricultural work in study villages, (2) nonfarm work in study villages, (3) agricultural work in local towns, (4) nonfarm work in local towns, (5) job in big cities, (6) job overseas, and (7) unemployed.

Let us define Υ^{*}_{i} as a latent variable corresponding to alternative k as follows:

$$\Upsilon^{*}_{i} = \delta E_{i} + \zeta L_{i} + \gamma X_{i} + e_{3}, \tag{1}$$

where Υ^{*}_{i} denotes the job choice of individual i, which is affected by schooling (E_{i}), inherited farmland (L_{i}), and his or her own characteristics (X_{i}) such as year of birth, birth order, and gender, while e_{3} is the error term. We observe that $\Upsilon^{*}_{i} = 1$ if and only if alternative k is chosen over other types of jobs; $\Upsilon^{*}_{i} = 0$ otherwise. We used the multinomial probit model in our estimation.

We initially treated inherited farmland L and schooling E as endogenous variables and inserted the predicted values obtained from estimates of farmland bequests and completed years in school from the earlier ordinary least squares (OLS) regressions into the multinomial probit function following the methodology of Rivers and Vuong (1988). We found that a large number of residuals were not significant, indicating that schooling and inherited farmland are largely devoid of endogeneity.

Table 4.6 shows the multinomial probit function of the choice of occupation of respondents and their siblings (G2). There were five choices, and we used unemployed as the default category. We obtained the following important findings: (1) education positively and significantly affected the choice of nonfarm work and migration to the cities, (2) children with larger inherited farmland were significantly more likely to work in agriculture and significantly less likely to engage in nonfarm work and to migrate to the cities, (3) later-born children were more likely to work overseas, (4) females were more likely to be housewives, (5) the youngest child was less likely to be an agricultural worker and a nonfarm worker, and (6) the eldest child was significantly less likely to stay on the farm. Findings (1) and (2) clearly support Hypothesis 2, which says that inheritance of farmland affects the choice of farming jobs, whereas schooling affects the choice of nonfarm jobs.

Table 4.7 shows the multinomial probit function of the choice of occupation of respondents' children (G3). We have seven job alternatives; unemployed was the default category. We obtained the following findings: (1) the more educated children were more likely to engage in nonfarm work in the village and local towns and migrate to the big cities and overseas; they were less likely to engage in agricultural work in the village and local towns; (2) similar to G2, children

Table 4.6 Determinants of choice of occupation of respondents and siblings in study villages in the Philippines (multinomial probit)

Variable	Agricultural work	Nonfarm work	Job in big cities	Job overseas
Education	−0.012	0.204***	0.206***	0.172***
	(0.022)	(0.022)	(0.027)	(0.031)
Inherited land	0.149*	−0.323***	−0.714***	0.039
	(0.084)	(0.101)	(0.199)	(0.125)
Year of birth	0.005	−0.005	−0.002	0.030***
	(0.006)	(0.006)	(0.007)	(0.010)
Female dummy	−3.327***	−2.046***	−1.845***	−1.723***
(1 = yes)	(0.150)	(0.159)	(0.190)	(0.225)
Married dummy	0.338	−0.175	−0.377	−0.426
(1 = yes)	(0.220)	(0.218)	(0.251)	(0.280)
Youngest dummy	−0.381*	−0.574***	0.223	0.287
(1 = yes)	(0.200)	(0.216)	(0.227)	(0.258)
Eldest dummy	−0.345*	−0.146	−0.055	−0.228
(1 = yes)	(0.200)	(0.211)	(0.270)	(0.372)
Constant	−7.543	9.481	2.770	−59.207***
	(11.065)	(11.576)	(14.499)	(19.429)
Number of observations	1,352	1,352	1,352	1,352

*Significant at 10% level. **Significant at 5% level. ***Significant at 1% level.

Note: Numbers in parentheses are standard errors.

with more inherited farmland were more likely to choose farming in the village and local towns; (3) later-born children in G3 were more likely to migrate to big cities to engage in the rapidly expanding nonfarm sector; (4) females were more likely to become housekeepers; (5) married children, regardless of gender, were more likely to migrate to local towns to engage in both agricultural and nonfarm work; (6) the youngest child in G3 was more likely to be a migrant in the big cities or to stay overseas; and (7) the eldest child in G3 was less likely to stay in the village and overseas. Particularly noteworthy are Findings (1) and (2), which confirm the validity of Hypothesis 2.

Summing up, schooling has enabled members of G2 and G3 to explore job opportunities in the nonfarm sector in the village and local towns and make them prepared to migrate to big cities and overseas. Inherited farmland remains a decisive factor in choosing farming vis-à-vis other occupations in the village and local towns. Since landless children in G3 obtained schooling levels that were less than but comparable with those of farmer children, it is reasonable to expect that they are equally likely to explore job opportunities in the nonfarm labor market in the village, local towns, and big cities. In fact, landless children have a higher propensity to migrate in search of economic opportunities elsewhere outside the village (Table 4.3).

Table 4.7 Determinants of choice of occupation of respondents' children from study villages in the Philippines (multinomial probit)

Variable	Agricultural work in the village	Nonfarm work in the village	Agricultural work in local towns	Nonfarm work in local towns	Job in big cities	Job overseas
Education	-0.069***	0.132***	-0.067**	0.180***	0.139***	0.326***
	(0.022)	(0.023)	(0.032)	(0.028)	(0.023)	(0.033)
Inherited land	1.085***	0.485	1.051***	-1.165	-0.293	-1.046
	(0.317)	(0.328)	(0.354)	(0.756)	(0.400)	(0.693)
Year of birth	-0.011	0.008	-0.027*	0.019	0.023**	-0.003
	(0.011)	(0.011)	(0.016)	(0.013)	(0.011)	(0.013)
Female dummy (1 = yes)	-2.683***	-1.753***	-2.248***	-1.538***	-1.806***	-1.579***
	(0.147)	(0.133)	(0.216)	(0.155)	(0.132)	(0.158)
Married dummy (1 = yes)	0.070	-0.253	1.066***	0.557***	0.098	-0.099
	(0.166)	(0.154)	(0.391)	(0.209)	(0.158)	(0.183)
Youngest dummy (1 = yes)	-0.349**	-0.441***	-0.277	-0.385**	-0.452***	-0.589***
	(0.159)	(0.151)	(0.235)	(0.181)	(0.150)	(0.186)
Eldest dummy (1 = yes)	-0.306**	-0.289**	-0.181	-0.034	-0.228	-0.442**
	(0.147)	(0.142)	(0.203)	(0.164)	(0.141)	(0.175)
Constant	23.770	-16.769	53.133*	-39.764	-46.220**	3.612
	(22.000)	(21.103)	(32.194)	(25.131)	(20.958)	(25.916)
Number of observations	1,479	1,479	1,479	1,479	1,479	1,479

*Significant at 10% level. **Significant at 5% level. ***Significant at 1% level.

Note: Numbers in parentheses are standard errors.

Determinants of children's income

Here, we estimate the household income function of the 880 members of G3 who we interviewed in their respective places of residence. We explore determinants of household income by place of residence: (1) big cities and overseas, (2) local towns, and (3) study villages.

Let Υ_i denote the income of a household living in place i = {big cities, local towns, overseas, study villages}. We considered the following model of income received by living in place i:

$$\Upsilon_i = \Sigma\mu_i \text{ (husband characteristics)} + \Sigma\nu_i \text{ (wife characteristics)} + c_i. \quad (2)$$

Own child and spouse characteristics include years of schooling and size of inherited farmland, respectively; μ and ν are regression parameters; and c is the error term. We used OLS in our estimation. We combined big cities and overseas because we were able to give in-house interviews to only 27 overseas workers. We estimated the function separately for married and single children.

We represented Υ_i in three components – (1) total income, (2) farm income, and (3) nonfarm income – because the impact of child characteristics and spouse characteristics may be different for each of the income components. Table 4.8 shows income functions for married children in four places of residence, while Table 4.9 shows those for single children.

We obtained several findings for the married children (Table 4.8). First, for G3 living in the big cities and overseas, the age and education of wives significantly increased the household's nonfarm income, while the age of husbands affected farm income. A few of the G3 living in big cities and overseas have farm income, if the husband or wife has inherited farmland. Importantly, the size of inherited farmland did not affect the total income of G3. Second, for G3 in local towns and for G3 who choose to remain in the villages, the education of both the husband and wife significantly increased nonfarm income, whereas farmland inherited by the husband significantly increased farm income. In brief, education significantly increased nonfarm income, while inherited farmland significantly increased farm income. This is consistent with Hypothesis 1, which points out the declining importance of farmland and the increasing importance of human capital as a determinant of household income. Furthermore, the size of inherited farmland did not affect the nonfarm income of G3, regardless of the fact that they are migrants in Manila, overseas, and in local towns or continue to stay behind in the villages. This indicates that G3 coming from landless parents have an equal chance of participating in nonfarm employment as those coming from farmer parents. For single children (Table 4.9), education was the only factor that significantly mattered, with a negative impact on farm income and a positive impact on nonfarm income. To the extent that higher education leads to a shift from informal to formal jobs, the decisive importance of education in nonfarm income is consistent with Hypothesis 4. Furthermore, it is important to note that the female dummy is insignificant,

Table 4.8 Determinants of household income of married children of respondents in study villages in the Philippines by place of residence, 2008 (ordinary least squares)

Variable	Manila and overseas		
	Total income	Farm income	Nonfarm income
Age of husband	−385.20 (254.450)	12.28*** (4.579)	−397.48 (254.224)
Education of husband	574.15 (611.243)	−1.39 (10.999)	575.54 (610.698)
Inherited land of husband	−3,211.74 (8,380.371)	236.01 (150.797)	−3,447.75 (8,372.903)
Age of wife	1,250.54*** (264.011)	−4.95 (4.751)	1,255.48*** (263.775)
Education of wife	3,156.50*** (618.535)	−14.72 (11.130)	3,171.21*** (617.984)
Inherited land of wife	1,597.50 (17,550.908)	−7.89 (315.812)	1,605.39 (17,535.268)
Constant	−56,350.82*** (10,093.465)	−33.20 (181.622)	−56,317.62*** (10,084.470)
Number of observations	97	97	97
R^2	0.448	0.137	0.449
	Local towns		
Age of husband	134.64 (317.567)	−21.47 (43.090)	156.12 (317.002)
Education of husband	1,794.83*** (609.803)	26.21 (82.743)	1,768.62*** (608.719)
Inherited land of husband	2,537.36 (4,198.091)	1,027.17* (569.635)	1,510.19 (4,190.631)
Age of wife	177.93 (319.862)	51.25 (43.402)	126.67 (319.294)
Education of wife	1,189.11** (579.587)	20.36 (78.644)	1,168.75** (578.557)
Inherited land of wife	−14,456.20 (15,434.737)	−782.60 (2,094.324)	−13,673.60 (15,407.307)
Constant	−32,008.42*** (9,828.811)	−781.26 (1,333.661)	−31,227.17*** (9,811.344)
Number of observations	180	180	180
R^2	0.167	0.034	0.161
	Study villages		
Age of husband in 2008	21.43 (55.071)	−3.00 (28.564)	24.43 (45.799)
Education of husband	379.66*** (103.313)	98.26* (53.586)	281.41*** (85.918)

Inherited land of husband	1,697.74***	1,899.60***	−201.87
	(449.135)	(232.958)	(373.513)
Age of wife in 2008	71.56	50.67*	20.89
	(54.344)	(28.187)	(45.194)
Education of wife	510.72***	41.64	469.08***
	(114.598)	(59.440)	(95.303)
Inherited land of wife	−934.53	1,054.11	−1,988.64
	(1,478.399)	(766.817)	(1,229.478)
Constant	−7,487.88***	−1,624.89	−5,862.98***
	(1,908.329)	(989.813)	(1,587.020)
Number of observations	359	359	359
R^2	0.186	0.201	0.148

*Significant at 10% level. **Significant at 5% level. ***Significant at 1% level.

Note: Numbers in parentheses are standard errors.

Table 4.9 Determinants of household income of single children of respondents in study villages in the Philippines, 2008 (ordinary least squares)

Variable	Total income	Farm income	Nonfarm income
Age in 2008	17.29	−0.90	18.19
	(71.508)	(30.454)	(64.106)
Education	494.04***	−217.95***	711.99***
	(168.498)	(71.760)	(151.056)
Female dummy (1 = yes)	1,012.88	701.30	311.57
	(1,057.013)	(450.165)	(947.599)
Inherited land	3,091.17	2,076.68	1,014.49
	(3,951.678)	(1,682.954)	(3,542.627)
Constant	−254.50	3,398.47***	−3,652.97
	(3,010.776)	(1,282.240)	(2,699.121)
Number of observations	130	130	130
R^2	0.095	0.084	0.174

*Significant at 10% level. **Significant at 5% level. ***Significant at 1% level.

Note: Numbers in parentheses are standard errors.

indicating that females are not handicapped in income-earning activities compared with males. Combined with findings from Tables 4.7 and 4.8 that females chose rural nonfarm and urban jobs and from Table 4.5 that incomes from nonfarm jobs were much higher than farming, it is clear that the development of nonfarm sectors contributes to the improvement of women's income status, as argued in Hypothesis 5.

To sum up, our results point to the importance of education and occupational mobility in avoiding poverty in a state of landlessness. Lack of access to land as well as education has induced the participation of landless children in nonfarm employment and the migration to big cities and local towns, strategies that have led to an increase in income and, importantly, income earned from nonfarm labor activities.

Summary and conclusions

This study is an inquiry on intergenerational economic mobility. Do rich parents produce rich children, and do poor parents produce poor children? Economic mobility means parental endowment during childhood not being reflected in a child's circumstance later in life – i.e., the grandmother's bedtime story of "a poor man's child becoming rich." Our aim is to explore whether poverty has been transmitted over generations of household members in selected villages in the northern and central Philippines.

This study uses a long-term panel data set that enables us to trace changes in the socioeconomic conditions of three generations of members belonging to the same households for a period of 23 years beginning in 1985. We examine dynamic changes in household members' decisions with respect to transfer of wealth, residential and occupational choices, and income-earning activities in response to changes in household resource endowments and factor prices. Our focus is on the landless children whose parents are poorly endowed with farmland and schooling.

To explore economic mobility, we identify the factors that affect the choice of the younger generation of their place of residence (big cities, local towns, overseas, and study villages), occupation (farm and nonfarm jobs), and income sources. Migration and labor employment decisions could be particularly important strategies for avoiding poverty for landless children whose parents have no access to farmland. We then examine to what extent inherited farmland and schooling have affected children's income in various residential places.

Our major finding is that landless children reach an educational level comparable with that of farmer children, thus enabling them to move up the ladder of economic mobility by participating in the rural nonfarm labor market and by migrating to big cities and local towns. Poverty has declined among landless children, and the income gap between farmer and landless households has narrowed. The findings in this study point to the expansion of labor demand in the nonfarm sector and the high geographical and occupational mobility of poor households as the major driving forces that improve the lot of the landless poor, leading to a decline in poverty and an improvement in income distribution.

Going back to the grandmother's story of "a poor man's child becoming rich," the question is how the poor children from our study villages are able to escape from poverty. It is obviously more than just their virtues of frugality, initiative, and enterprise. The poor man needs education, farmland, infrastructure, and economic opportunities outside the village in order to move up the economic ladder. With these elements, the grandmother's story will never be a fairy tale after all.

Acknowledgment

Parts of this chapter were drawn from Estudillo *et al.* (2014) with permission from the *Philippine Review of Economics*. Map in Figure 4.1 was drawn by Masatoshi Higuchi.

Notes

1 Otsuka (1991) suggests that the proportion of landless agricultural wage worker households is higher in the Philippines because of the suppression of tenancy markets by the land reform law.
2 Originally, there were five villages, but we dropped one village because of a failure to establish sufficient panel data.
3 Leaseholders include recipients of certificates of land transfer who are amortizing owners of farmland obtained through the land reform program.
4 There were 1,529 children, but seven did not have information on their current addresses.
5 We interviewed 881 children, but 11 did not have information on parental land-holdings in the 1985 census.
6 We have a total of 1,522 members of G3, but six of them did not have information on parental landholdings in 1985.
7 The Philippines was under the Spanish colonial regime for about 350 years from around the mid-1500s to the late 1800s and then under the American colonial regime from 1900 until its independence in 1946.
8 According to Capistrano and Sta. Maria (2007), the first wave of Filipino overseas migration started around the 1930s; they went to work as plantation laborers in Hawaii and fruit pickers in California. The second wave was in the mid-1940s after World War II; they worked as construction workers repairing the American military bases around the world. The third wave occurred in the 1970s in the Gulf states, where Filipinos were hired as skilled workers in the construction boom triggered by the oil price boom. The fourth wave was in the 1980s in the so-called newly industrializing countries in East Asia, where Filipinos were hired to satisfy the labor shortage in these countries.

5 Are younger women left on the farms in Vietnam?

Introduction

Using a rare individual-level data set, this chapter examines dynamic changes in the choice of occupation of three generations of members belonging to the same household in rural Vietnam. We focus on the role of schooling and inherited farmland, which exerts a profound impact on the gender patterns of employment and income. The main finding is that, although Vietnamese females in the older generations have been disfavored with respect to both schooling investments and farmland inheritance, both genders have been treated relatively equally in the younger generations. Furthermore, we found a gender-specific choice of occupation in the youngest generation in our study villages in the north – more men choose nonfarm work; more women choose farming – while such gender specialization is largely absent in our study villages in the south. This means that economic development in Vietnam has promoted women's schooling and their participation in the labor market either as wage workers in the evolving nonfarm sector or as workers on their own farms producing rice and high-value products.

This chapter has five remaining sections. The second section provides a brief description of Vietnam. The third section describes the study villages and sample households. The fourth section traces schooling investment, land inheritance, and job choice. The fifth section explains the regression model, while the sixth section shows the results of the determinants of schooling and farmland inheritance, as well as the job choices of individual members. Finally, the seventh section presents the summary and conclusions.

Vietnam in brief

Economic growth and poverty

Vietnam had a population of about 89 million in 2012 (World Bank 2013a) and is considered one of the fastest-growing economies in the Greater Mekong Sub-region (GMS). After the French colonial period, Vietnam experienced a political separation into North Vietnam (under a command economy) and South Vietnam (under a market economy). Conflict intensified between the two regions, which evolved into the Vietnam War in 1955. The war ended with the fall of Saigon in 1975. The victory of the north unified the country under communist rule. Yet, even under the same legal and political system, it is generally recognized that the business environment has been more favorable to the private sector in the south. Government regulations pertaining to the economy are more strictly implemented in the north, whereas the south continues to have a relatively decentralized atmosphere, with its markets functioning more smoothly. Although the Communist Party directly appoints the highest positions in city government in the north, such custom is observed to be much less strictly practiced in the south.

During the first 10 years of unification from 1975 to 1985, the state tried to control all farmland and natural resources and tried to organize agriculture under a collective system ("commune") with an emphasis on farming and crop specialization and the use of science and technology. In spite of the emphasis on agricultural development, the industrial sector continued to receive a larger chunk of the state investment because of heavy subsidies on state-owned enterprises that tended to favor heavy industry. During 1975–85, there were chronic food shortages, high unemployment rates, and poor overall economic performance, which created a strong social sentiment to introduce previous market elements such as the decentralization of the administration, profit-oriented production incentives, and private initiatives.

Economic liberalization ("Doi Moi"), which was launched in 1986 in the Sixth Party Congress, moved rapidly after 1994 with the removal of the US trade embargo. Table 5.1 shows a remarkable increase in the gross domestic

Table 5.1 Distribution of gross domestic product and number of workers in Vietnam, 1986–2011

Sector	1986	1991	1996	2001	2006	2011
Gross domestic product per capita (US$ purchasing power parity [PPP], 2005 constant)	806.8	941.3	1,324.3	1,685.8	2,313.3	3,012.6
Percentage distribution of gross domestic product						
Agriculture	38.0	40.4	27.7	23.2	20.4	19.6
Industry	28.8	23.7	29.7	38.1	41.5	40.6
Service	33.0	35.7	42.5	38.6	38.0	39.7
Percentage distribution of workers						
Agriculture			70.0	64.0	51.7	
Industry			10.6	13.8	20.2	
Service			19.4	22.1	28.2	

Sources: World Bank (2013a) and General Statistics Office of Vietnam (2011).

Table 5.2 Growth rate of gross domestic product, poverty, and inequality in Vietnam, 1986–2011

Description	1986	1991	1996	2001	2006	2011
		Percentage of population living below the poverty line at $1.25 a day				
Head count ratio		63.74[a]	49.65[b]	40.05[c]	21.42	16.85[d]
Poverty gap ratio		23.57[a]	15.05[b]	11.20[c]	5.30	3.75[d]
		Income share (%)				
Income share held by highest 10%		28.96[a]	29.34[b]	30.31[c]	27.79	28.21[d]
Income share held by lowest 10%		3.46	3.57	3.32	3.02	3.18[d]
		Annual growth rate (%)				
Annual growth rate of gross domestic product	2.78	5.96[a]	9.34	6.89	8.22	5.88

a   Refers to 1993.
b   Refers to 1998.
c   Refers to 2002.
d   Refers to 2008.

Source: World Bank (2013a).

product (GDP) per capita from 1991 to 1996 and a dramatic shift of GDP toward industry and services and away from agriculture beginning in 1996. The annual percentage growth of GDP was very low before the removal of the embargo, at only 2.78 percent in 1986 and 5.96 percent in 1991. GDP growth spiked at 9.34 percent in 1996 and then hovered between 6 and 7 percent from 2001 to 2011 (Table 5.2).

Concomitant with this swift transformation is the marked decline in the incidence of poverty by as much as 46 percentage points from 1991 to 2008 (Table 5.2). Also, when GDP growth rate was higher, the decline in poverty was greater. For example, when the growth rate of GDP rose from 5.96 percent in 1991 to 9.34 percent in 1996, the result was a greater decline in poverty of about 14 percentage points for a period of only 5 years. This is a clear indication that economic growth is inclusive of the poor in Vietnam. The income share held by the highest 10 percent remained at around 28 percent, and the income share held by the lowest 10 percent did not decrease below 3 percent. Incidentally, the proportion of vulnerable workers (defined as own-account and contributing family workers) to total employment declined from 82 to 62 percent between 1996 and 2012, indicating that vulnerable workers had joined the emerging formal sector.

In a span of merely 10 years from 1996 to 2006, the proportion of the labor force engaged in agriculture declined from 70.0 to 51.7 percent and, concomitantly, rose in the industry and service sectors (Table 5.1). In industry, the major depository of labor is manufacturing and construction; in services, wholesale and retail trade, repair of motor vehicles, public administration and defense, and education are important activities. New service jobs were also created in banking, hotels and restaurants, the computer and insurance sectors, new pharmaceuticals, and advertising.

Women in the labor force

The share of females in the total labor force has been close to 50 percent since 1989, which is higher than the average in East Asia (44 percent). A slightly lower female share was observed in the Mekong River Delta (MRD) and the Southeast (about 46 percent), where women are traditionally bound to perform housework. As Vietnam embarks into a more open economy, the female labor force participation rate (among those between 15 and 64 years old) declined from 81 percent in 1990 to 61 percent in 2011 and, similarly, the male labor force participation rate declined from 89 to 78 percent during the same period. This can be traced to the decline in labor force participation rates of those who are between 15 and 24 years old, as enrollment rates in the secondary and tertiary schools rose among females from 57 percent in 1999 to 80 percent in 2010 and among males from 63 to 73 percent during the same period. The gender gap in primary schooling in Vietnam has been eliminated, and females have caught up with and even surpassed males in acquiring college degrees, although there remains a significant degree of gender segregation in their respective fields of study, as is commonly observed in many developing countries.

Vietnamese females are increasing their roles in agricultural production. From 1993 to 1998, 92 percent of new participants in agriculture were women, while the number of male farmers was slowly decreasing by 0.3 percent annually (Asian Development Bank 2005). Vietnamese males were observed to migrate out of farming, leaving behind the farms to the female members (Paris *et al.* 2009). As a result, the shift out of agriculture is slower for females than for males (World Bank 2011b). In rural areas, male labor in the nonfarm sector is largely found in transport and communications, retail sales, and business and financial services, while female labor in the nonfarm sector is largely found in manufacturing (textiles, garments, wood, paper, food, and beverages), retail and wholesale trade, and education and cultural services (General Statistics Office of Vietnam 2011). Overall, we have seen dynamic changes in the labor market in Vietnam that appear to have strengthened job specialization between genders since the economic liberalization in 1986.

Land and economic reforms

During the French colonial period, most farmland in Vietnam was owned by French plantation owners or by elite Vietnamese landlords. Land became the property of the state in the late 1950s, and collective farming was implemented in the north.[1] In the early stage of collective farming, individual ownership of crop land, draft animals, and farm implements was preserved, and the members got a share of collective output in proportion to the amount of inputs they contributed. In the later stage, the payment system degenerated based solely on individual labor contribution, as all inputs were deemed the common property of the collective members. This payment system is similar to a fixed wage system and has led to weak work incentives and clamor to reclaim family farming.

Nonetheless, even under collective farming, the Communist Party has permitted households to privately own 5 percent of the cooperative's cultivated land (the "5 percent plots"), which is mainly intended for vegetable and fruit farming. Output from the 5 percent plots was much higher than that from the cooperative's land (Ravallion and van de Walle 2008; Kerkvliet 2005), and income from these plots comprised 60 to 75 percent of total household income. In the south, collectivization did not take place because of strong farmer resistance. Pingali and Xuan (1992) reported that, even as late as 1986, less than 6 percent of farmers in the south belonged to a cooperative.

In 1981, the household-specific production quota was implemented to replace the work contract in collective farming. Under the new scheme, any output in excess of the quota could be sold to the free market or to state trading agencies at a higher price. In 1986, the Doi Moi was launched, which many believe is the most important economic reform that propelled Vietnam into an era of a rapid growth rate. In 1988, the Communist Party granted households long-term user rights over the land while it remained the property of the state (15 years for annual crops and 40 years for perennial crops). In 1993, official land titles in the form of land-use certificates (LUCs) were issued, and land tenure was extended for 20 years for annual crops and 50 years for perennial crops. Importantly, the 1993 Land Law allowed LUCs to be transacted for transfer, exchange, inheritance, rent, and mortgage. Land transactions in terms of rental and sales had increased rapidly (Deininger and Jin 2003). Finally, the 2003 Land Law explicitly states that the names of both husband and wife should be included in the LUCs.

Study villages and sample households

Study villages

We had eight study villages that represent four distinct agroecosystems in Vietnam: (1) irrigated flood-prone areas in the MRD in the south, (2) rainfed lowland in the north and south, (3) irrigated lowland in the Red River Delta (RRD) in the north, and (4) upland in the northern mountainous regions. Our study villages are located in Hanoi and Thai Nguyen in the north[2] and Long An and Can Tho in the south. Hereafter, we will refer to "northern villages" as our study villages in Hanoi and Thai Nguyen and to "southern villages" as our study villages in Long An and Can Tho (Figure 5.1). One village in Hanoi represents the irrigated lowland, and one village represents the rainfed lowland ecosystem along the RRD. The two villages in Thai Nguyen represent the upland ecosystem. One village in Long An represents the irrigated lowland, and one village represents the rainfed lowland ecosystem in the outer region of the

Figure 5.1 Location of the study villages in Vietnam

MRD. The two villages in Can Tho represent the irrigated lowland along the MRD. These villages were selected and first surveyed in 1996 by Ut et al. (2000) with generous funding from the International Rice Research Institute (IRRI) in the Philippines. We did a resurvey of the same sets of households in these villages in 2009–10 with generous support from the Foundation for Advanced Studies on International Development (FASID) and the National Graduate Institute for Policy Studies (GRIPS) in Tokyo.

In 1996, we had a total of 376 households – 192 came from the north and 184 came from the south (Table 5.3). Average farm size declined from 3,967 m² in 1996 to 2,159 m² in 2009 in the north while, surprisingly, it rose from 10,276 m² to 14,220 m² in the south, which indicates consolidation of farms in the south. The irrigation ratio in the north rose from 54 to 88 percent and that in the south increased from 80 to 90 percent. Adoption of modern varieties (MVs) rose to 100 percent in 2009 in both the north and south.

In the north, 100 percent of households had access to electricity, 54 percent had tube water, and 50 percent had water-flushed toilets. In the south, the corresponding numbers were 100 percent for electricity, 46 percent for tube water, and 64 percent for water-flushed toilets. The living standard in our study villages was comparable with the average in Vietnam as a whole in 2010, when 97 percent of households had access to electricity, 91 percent had tube water, and 54 percent had water-flushed toilets (General Statistics Office of Vietnam 2010). Moreover, there was an improvement in housing standards: in the north, the proportion of households with concrete houses rose from 26 to 46 percent; in the south, the increase was from 26 to 37 percent from 1996 to 2009.

Sources of household income

There are seven major sources of household income: (1) agricultural wages, (2) rice farming, (3) production of nonrice crops and livestock, (4) nonfarm formal wage work, (5) nonfarm informal wage work, (6) nonfarm self-employment, and (7) remittances and other sources (Figure 5.2). Agricultural wage

Table 5.3 Characteristics of sample households in rural Vietnam, 1996 and 2009

Characteristics	1996	2009
	Northern villages	
Number of sample households	192	184
Hanoi	100	90
Thai Nguyen	92	94
Average farm size (m²)	3,967	2,159
Area irrigated (%)	54	88
Farmers using modern rice varieties (%)	66	100
	Southern villages	
Number of sample households	184	160
Long An	94	74
Can Tho	90	86
Average farm size (m²)	10,276	14,220
Area irrigated (%)	80	90
Farmers using modern rice varieties (%)	82	100

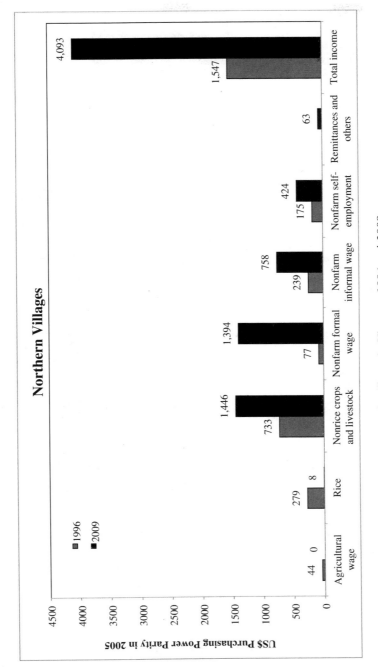

Figure 5.2 Sources of household income in sample villages in Vietnam, 1996 and 2009

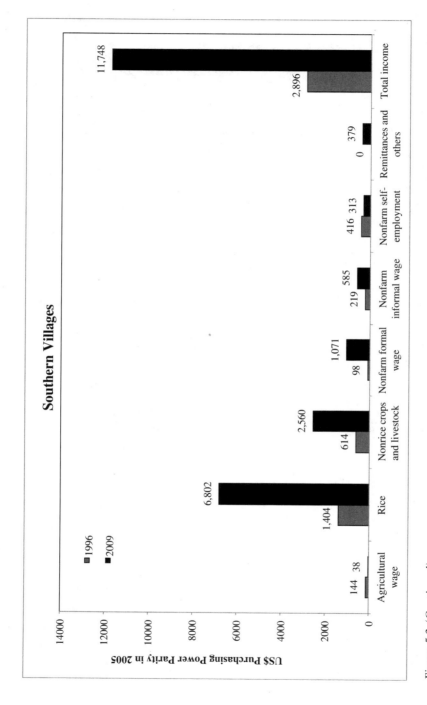

Figure 5.2 (Continued)

income is a minor source, as the number of landless agricultural worker households is very small. Nonrice crops refer to high-value crops such as fruits, vegetables, and cut flowers. Income from nonfarm formal wage work refers to income from regular jobs in the government sector in education, health, military, and other services and in the private sector in industries (e.g., factories) and services (e.g., hotels and restaurants). Nonfarm informal wage income comes from casual work from the informal sector such as construction and domestic work. Income from nonfarm self-employment comes from retail and trade, transport, rural restaurants, equipment and vehicle rentals, rural manufacturing, etc. Data on remittances and other sources were not collected in 1996, but we believe that income from this source was negligible at that time. In 2009, remittances remained a small portion of the total household income (1 percent in the north and 3 percent in the south).

Income data refer to international dollars in 2005. Household income in the northern villages rose 2.64 times from $1,547 in 1996 to $4,093 in 2009, whereas in the southern villages, income rose 4.05 times from $2,896 to $11,748 (Figure 5.2). The major sources of income growth in the northern villages are nonrice crop and livestock production, nonfarm formal wages, nonfarm informal wages, and nonfarm self-employment. In the southern villages, the major sources of income growth are rice production, nonrice crop and livestock production, and nonfarm formal wages. Rice farming is by far the most important source of income growth in the southern villages. In brief, household activities are increasingly concentrated on rice farming in the southern villages, while there has been a diversification of household activities away from rice farming to nonrice farming and nonfarm work in the northern villages. Considering that farm size expanded in the southern villages and contracted in the northern villages (Table 5.3), these observations suggest that large-scale rice farming has become profitable in the former, whereas the profitability of nonrice farming and the advantages of nonfarm jobs have increased in the latter.

Schooling, farmland, and job choice

We did a retrospective survey on schooling, farmland inheritance, and choice of occupation of three generations of household members. The first generation (G1) consists of the fathers (male G1) and the mothers (female G1) of respondents. We divided G2 into male G2 and female G2, which consist of the male and female respondents and their brothers and sisters. Our respondents are largely male heads of households. The third generation (G3) are the children of G2, consisting of the sons of respondents (male G3) and the daughters of respondents (female G3).

We had 181 female G1 and 183 male G1 in the northern villages and 160 pairs of female G1 and male G1 in the southern villages (Table 5.4). The data of completed years in school of G1 was very low and was higher in the south (less than 3 years) than in the north (less than 2 years). The male G1 in both the northern and southern villages completed significantly more years of

Table 5.4 Characteristics of three generations of household members in sample villages in rural Vietnam, 2009

Characteristics	Average	
	Male	Female
	Northern villages	
First generation (G1)		
Number of individuals[a]	183	181
Year of birth	N/A[c]	N/A
Completed years in school	1.9	1.4
Size of inherited farmland (m²)[b]	N/A	N/A
Second generation (G2)		
Number of individuals	545	473
Year of birth	1959	1957
Completed years in school	7.2	6.2
Size of inherited farmland (m²)	1,146	147
Third generation (G3)		
Number of individuals	238	221
Year of birth	1975	1976
Completed years in school	9.5	9.1
Size of inherited farmland (m²)	624	155
	Southern villages	
First generation (G1)		
Number of individuals[a]	160	160
Year of birth	N/A	N/A
Completed years in school	3.0	2.1
Size of inherited farmland (m²)[b]	N/A	N/A
Second generation (G2)		
Number of individuals	416	311
Year of birth	1954	1953
Completed years in school	6.1	4.8
Size of inherited farmland (m²)	7,114	1,374
Third generation (G3)		
Number of individuals	292	278
Year of birth	1974	1975
Completed years in school	7.4	6.4
Size of inherited farmland (m²)	2,710	778

a   Consists of those who are 19 to 60 years old at the time of the survey.
b   Refers to those whose bequests have been completed.
c   N/A = not available.

schooling than did the female G1, indicating the existence of a gender bias in schooling in favor of males among the G1.

We had 545 male G2 and 473 female G2 in the north and 416 male G2 and 311 female G2 in the south for a total of 1,745 individuals who were born between the mid- and late 1950s (Table 5.4). G2 received significantly more schooling than their parents – a difference of about 5 years in the north and about 3 years in the south. Like their mothers, the female G2 received significantly less schooling than did the male G2 and significantly less farmland, suggesting a strong pro-male bias in the bequest decisions of G1; this applies to both the north and south.

In the north, we had 238 male G3 and 221 female G3; in the south, we had 292 male G3 and 278 female G3 for a total of 1,029 individuals who were born in the mid-1970s (Table 5.4). Similar to G1 and G2, the female G3 received significantly less schooling and less farmland, a continuation of the traditional pro-male bias in the inheritance practice of the three generations. Yet, the gender gap in schooling narrowed from 1.0 to 1.5 years in G2 to less than 1 year in G3, indicating that parents have become more egalitarian in schooling investments in more recent years. This supports Hypothesis 5 on the improvement of women's welfare in terms of schooling attainment.

We classified jobs into three distinct categories: (1) farming, (2) nonfarm work, and (3) others (Figure 5.3). Farming refers to the self-cultivation of crops and livestock, fishing, forestry, and a negligible amount of casual agricultural wage work. Nonfarm work includes formal wage work, informal wage work, and self-employment. Formal wage work includes regular jobs in the government (e.g., teachers, military personnel, office workers, and rural health workers) and in manufacturing, mining, and construction. Nonfarm informal wage work largely refers to casual irregular construction and domestic work and irregular service work in hotels and restaurants. Nonfarm self-employment includes retail trade and commerce, operation of rural transport, and the traditional village manufacturing industry. Since overseas work is very thin in the context of Vietnam, we categorize it as nonfarm work. "Others" refers to housekeepers, the retired and unemployed, people with a disability, and those who are unreported.

Almost all the male G1 and female G1 were engaged in farming, implying that the nonfarm labor market is largely underdeveloped (Figure 5.3). A large majority of female G2 became farmers (helping their husbands, who are the principal farmers) or housewives, presumably because female G2 are less educated and receive smaller pieces of farmland. Yet, we notice an early evolution of the nonfarm labor market, as both the male G2 and the female G2 have started to diversify into nonfarm work.

Surprisingly, there was a higher proportion of farmers among the female G3 than the male G3 in the north – 69 percent versus 43 percent. Having more female farmers in the north is rather surprising, considering that the schooling gap between the female G3 and the male G3 was not too large and not statistically significant (9.5 for the male G3, 9.1 for the female G3) (Table 5.4). Indeed, Paris *et al.* (2009, Table 4b, p. 9) reported that the principal migrants

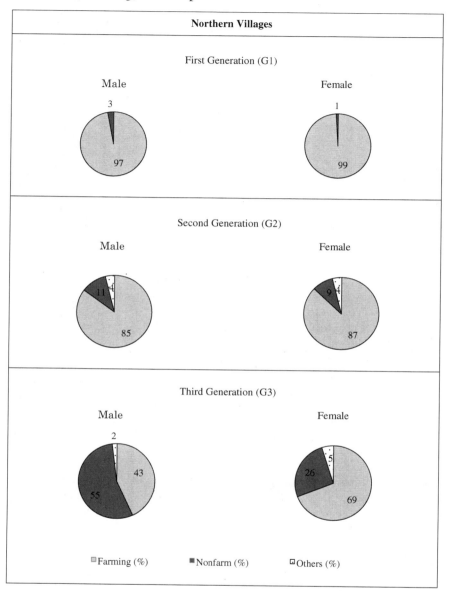

Figure 5.3 Choice of occupation of three generations in sample villages in Vietnam

in northern Vietnam are the male spouses, and hence farming in the north is dominated by female family labor, particularly among households with higher rates of male outmigration. In the south, the proportion of farmers was the same (55 percent) for both the female G3 and the male G3. Also, there was a higher proportion of housewives in the south, where women commonly work full time as housekeepers.

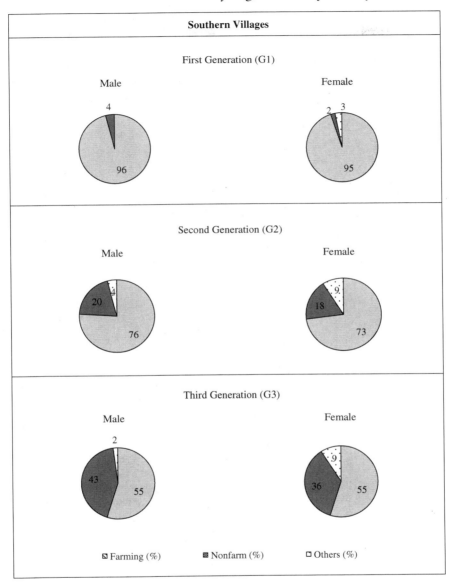

Figure 5.3 (Continued)

To sum up, our data show a secular increase in schooling attainment and a decline in inherited farmland from G1 to G3. Females are disfavored with respect to parental bequests, receiving significantly less schooling and smaller farmland, although such preference has declined over time. The female G3 in the north are more involved in farming, while the male G3 are more involved in nonfarm work outside the village. The female G3 in the north are not necessarily worse off being on the farm because they are involved in the production of high-value crops such as fruits, vegetables, and other horticultural crops and in raising poultry and livestock and thus are able to earn a decent income. A gender-specific pattern of job choice, however, is largely absent in the south, where both the female G3 and the male G3 are equally likely to participate in farming and other jobs. This supports Hypothesis 5 on the expansion of equal employment opportunities for women and men.

Regression model

Schooling and farmland inheritance

We explored the factors affecting schooling investments and farmland bequests from the older to the younger generations – (1) from G1 to G2 and (2) from G2 to G3. Completed years in school (E) and farmland inheritance (L) of an individual could be explained by the individual's and his or her parents' characteristics and village characteristics.

$$E = aX + bZ + cV + e_1 + e_2 \tag{1}$$
$$L = \alpha X + \beta Z + \delta V + e_3 + e_4 \tag{2}$$

where X is a vector of individual characteristics; Z are parental characteristics; V is provincial dummy; and e_1 and e_3 are the unobserved household-specific effects; a, b, c, α, β, and δ are regression parameters, and e_2 and e_4 are error terms that are assumed to be independently and identically distributed (i.d.d.) across individuals. X includes (1) year of birth, (2) birth order indicated by the youngest child dummy (1 = yes, 0 = no) and eldest child dummy (1 = yes, 0 = no), (3) female child dummy (1 = female, 0 = male), and (4) number of siblings. Z includes the father's and mother's completed years of schooling and size of inherited farmland of both spouses. The provincial dummy V is included to control for the supply of local schools and complementary infrastructure, among others.

We estimated Equations (1) and (2) separately, treating household-specific effects e_1 and e_3 as fixed effects (FEs) and random effects (REs). FEs address a possible estimation bias because children belonging to the same households share the same household-specific characteristics. Since some children did not receive any schooling or farmland, we estimated Equations (1) and (2) using tobit models with FEs (Honore 1992) (FE tobit model) and REs (RE tobit model). Equations (1) and (2) are estimated separately for the wealth transfers from G1 to G2 and from G2 to G3.

Job choice

Let us define Y as the probability of choosing farming as a job:

$$Y = \Phi G + \theta E + \psi L + e_5 + e_6. \tag{3}$$

Υ is affected by the individual's own characteristics such as year of birth, gender (G), schooling (E), and inherited farmland (L). The terms Φ, θ, and ψ are regression parameters; e_5 is the household-level random effect; and e_6 is the error term, which is i.d.d. We used the probit model in our estimation using other jobs as the base category (1 = farming, 0 = other jobs). We included housewives in the farming category because women commonly help their husbands with farm work. Our analysis applies for the northern and southern villages separately because of their distinct differences in farmland endowments, labor market characteristics, and gender relations.

Determinants of schooling, inherited farmland, and job choice

The major questions are: who among the daughters and sons inherits farmland, and who receives schooling? The FE and RE tobit model on education and farmland in G2 (Table 5.5) shows the following in the northern villages: (1) later-born children, the youngest child, and the eldest child received significantly more schooling; (2) the eldest child received significantly more farmland; and, importantly, (3) the female G2 were significantly disfavored, receiving 0.6 fewer years of schooling and receiving about 0.4 ha less farmland compared with the male G2. Although there seems to be no visible preferences on year of birth and birth order in the southern villages, the findings in the northern villages that female G2 were significantly disfavored in both schooling and farmland inheritance hold true in these villages as well. In general, the education of the parents affects the schooling of children, and the inherited farmland of the parents affects the amount of farmland passed on to their children. In brief, it is clear that, after controlling for parental schooling and farmland, the female G2 are significantly disfavored in schooling and farmland inheritance.

Table 5.5 Determinants of completed years in school and farmland inheritance of the second generation (G2) of household members in sample villages in rural Vietnam, 2009

Variable	Northern villages			
	Education RE tobit	Education FE tobit	Inherited farmland RE tobit	Inherited farmland FE tobit
Year of birth	0.05***	0.06**	52.19***	−3.00
	(3.028)	(2.457)	(2.823)	(−0.084)
Youngest dummy (1 = yes)	0.59***	0.59***	−167.33	8.26
	(2.700)	(2.598)	(−0.557)	(0.034)
Eldest dummy (1 = yes)	0.51**	0.58***	1,532.68***	1,016.48***
	(2.380)	(2.667)	(5.158)	(2.616)

(*Continued*)

Table 5.5 (Continued)

Variable	Northern villages			
	Education RE tobit	Education FE tobit	Inherited farmland RE tobit	Inherited farmland FE tobit
Daughter dummy (1 = yes)	–0.57***	–0.63***	–3,429.86***	–5,356.29***
	(–3.789)	(–3.621)	(–13.084)	(–2.821)
Number of siblings	0.01		53.96	
	(0.104)		(0.779)	
Education of mother	0.24*		–138.02	
	(1.882)		(–1.474)	
Education of father	0.05		191.20***	
	(0.530)		(2.594)	
Inherited farmland of parents	–0.00		0.25**	
	(–0.483)		(2.252)	
Constant	–90.06***		–102,875.84***	
	(–2.826)		(–2.843)	
Observations	787	787	786	786
	Southern villages			
Year of birth	0.03	0.02	–3.34	–38.22
	(0.973)	(0.535)	(–0.028)	(–0.178)
Youngest dummy (1 = yes)	0.22	0.29	2,076.34	4,160.65
	(0.668)	(0.885)	(1.245)	(1.197)
Eldest dummy (1 = yes)	–0.15	–0.22	1,971.96	3,275.36
	(–0.451)	(–0.558)	(1.198)	(0.976)
Daughter dummy (1 = yes)	–1.38***	–1.34***	–14,695.03***	–19,057.53**
	(–5.745)	(–4.757)	(–10.295)	(–2.401)
Number of siblings	0.13		–641.67	
	(0.987)		(–1.535)	
Education of mother	0.01		513.53	
	(0.089)		(1.176)	
Education of father	0.45***		–114.53	
	(3.195)		(–0.280)	
Inherited farmland of parents	–0.00		0.20	
	(–0.502)		(0.465)	
Constant	–46.39		11,551.45	
	(–0.886)		(0.050)	
Observations	497	497	497	497

*Significant at 10% level. **Significant at 5% level. ***Significant at 1% level.

Notes: RE = random effects and FE = fixed effects. Numbers in parentheses are *z*-statistics.

The following are the results for G3 in the northern villages (Table 5.6): (1) later-born children, the eldest child, and the youngest child received significantly more schooling, (2) year of birth and birth order did not significantly affect the amount of inherited farmland, and (3) daughters were no longer significantly disfavored in schooling but remained significantly discriminated in farmland inheritance after controlling for parental farmland holdings, which is consistent with Hypothesis 5 on the improvement of women's schooling attainment. In southern villages, the coefficient of the daughter dummy was negative and significant in both schooling and farmland, indicating that daughters remained significantly discriminated against in terms of both schooling and farmland inheritance. Yet, regression runs incorporating various interaction terms between the daughter dummy and variables

Table 5.6 Determinants of completed years in school and farmland inheritance of the third generation (G3) of household members in sample villages in rural Vietnam, 2009

Variable	Northern villages			
	Education	Education	Inherited farmland	Inherited farmland
Year of birth	0.05**	0.14***	6.22	−40.03
	(2.024)	(2.932)	(0.368)	(−1.249)
Youngest dummy (1 = yes)	1.00***	0.59*	87.86	341.43*
	(2.950)	(1.754)	(0.446)	(1.679)
Eldest dummy (1 = yes)	0.61*	1.00**	246.18	39.98
	(1.824)	(2.462)	(1.261)	(0.174)
Daughter dummy (1 = yes)	−0.41	−0.34	−1,483.15***	−1,792.51***
	(−1.535)	(−1.024)	(−8.592)	(−2.860)
Number of siblings	0.10		−47.99	
	(0.835)		(−0.565)	
Education of mother	0.15**		61.30	
	(2.229)		(1.230)	
Education of father	0.15*		−80.76	
	(1.942)		(−1.380)	
Inherited farmland of parents	0.00		0.31***	
	(0.110)		(5.162)	
Hanoi dummy (1 = yes)	−0.32		−385.17	
	(−0.774)		(−1.271)	
Constant	−92.08*		−12,525.36	
	(−1.873)		(−0.375)	
Observations	444	458	439	453

(*Continued*)

Table 5.6 (Continued)

Variable	Southern villages			
	Education	Education	Inherited farmland	Inherited farmland
Year of birth	0.09***	0.15***	−22.83	131.68
	(3.250)	(3.851)	(−0.351)	(0.882)
Youngest dummy (1 = yes)	0.69**	0.44	1,740.23**	1,158.87
	(2.155)	(1.475)	(2.280)	(0.596)
Eldest dummy (1 = yes)	−0.01	0.32	−40.99	565.22
	(−0.041)	(0.899)	(−0.055)	(0.565)
Daughter dummy (1 = yes)	−0.68***	−0.70**	−6,752.94***	−10,182.67***
	(−2.866)	(−2.542)	(−10.756)	(−3.799)
Number of siblings	−0.13		−589.23	
	(−0.774)		(−1.622)	
Education of mother	0.31**		160.16	
	(2.541)		(0.591)	
Education of father	0.13		−213.92	
	(1.254)		(−0.913)	
Inherited farmland of parents	−0.00		0.08**	
	(−0.910)		(2.000)	
Can Tho dummy (1 = yes)	1.25*		1,204.33	
	(1.781)		(0.779)	
Constant	−174.81***		46,154.80	
	(−3.148)		(0.360)	
Observations	567	567	567	567

*Significant at 10% level. **Significant at 5% level. ***Significant at 1% level.

Note: Numbers in parentheses are z-statistics.

such as number of siblings, education of mother and father, and inherited farmland of parents show that the coefficient of the daughter dummy was not significant. Thus, the regression results on significant daughter discrimination in G3 were not robust.

The results of the probit function of choosing farm work (Table 5.7) are the following: (1) education had a negative effect on choosing farm work in both G2 and G3; (2) inherited farmland increased the odds of choosing farming; and (3) daughters and sons had equal odds of choosing farming in G2 during the commune system, whereas, on the contrary, the female G3 was significantly more likely to choose farming in the northern villages, where male outmigration is more commonly observed. In brief, education enables a child to explore opportunities outside the farming community, which is consistent with Hypothesis 2 on the impact of education on job choice.

Table 5.7 Determinants of choice of farm jobs in two generations of household members in sample villages in Vietnam, 2009 (probit function)

Variable	Second generation (G2)	
	Northern villages	Southern villages
Year of birth	0.008	−0.013
	(1.090)	(−1.511)
Daughter dummy (1 = yes)	0.121	0.122
	(0.884)	(0.832)
Education	−0.212***	−0.180***
	(−8.028)	(−8.778)
Inherited farmland	0.0001*	0.0001***
	(1.802)	(5.032)
Constant	−13.401	27.702
	(−0.905)	(1.609)
Observations	785	497
	Third generation (G3)	
Year of birth	0.007	−0.007
	(0.991)	(−1.005)
Daughter dummy (1 = yes)	0.890***	0.075
	(6.235)	(0.613)
Education	−0.226***	−0.197***
	(−8.913)	(−10.779)
Inherited farmland	0.000	0.000**
	(0.709)	(2.276)
Hanoi dummy (1 = yes)	−0.397***	
	(−2.932)	
Can Tho dummy (1 = yes)		0.670***
		(5.232)
Constant	−12.480	14.970
	(−0.850)	(1.103)
Observations	453	567

*Significant at 10% level. **Significant at 5% level. ***Significant at 1% level.

Note: Numbers in parentheses are z-statistics.

Determinants of household income

To explain the divergent pattern of job choice between the northern and southern villages, we estimated the determinants of agricultural and nonfarm incomes separately for the two regions. Explanatory variables were (1) farm size; (2) the technology factor, represented by the availability of irrigation water; (3) number of working members; (4) proxies for the quality of labor of working members in terms of gender, age, and schooling; and (5) the Hanoi and Can Tho dummy variables. Income (in US$ PPP in 2005) functions were estimated using the ordinary least squares (OLS) method (Table 5.8).

Table 5.8 Determinants of household income in sample villages in Vietnam, 2009 (ordinary least squares)

Variable	Northern villages		Southern villages	
	Agricultural income	Nonfarm income	Agricultural income	Nonfarm income
Farm size	0.40***	−0.14	0.54***	−0.02
	(4.209)	(−1.257)	(3.389)	(−0.934)
Area irrigated (%)	1.25	4.54	−11.37	6.28
	(0.211)	(0.663)	(−0.126)	(0.563)
Number of working members[a]	151.8	1,011.47***	3,330.86**	246.35
	(0.847)	(4.906)	(2.243)	(1.342)
Composition of working members				
Female (%)	−48.32	−651.29	−14,808.42	−32.84
	(−0.054)	(−0.630)	(−1.214)	(−0.022)
Between 26 and 35 years old (%)	−1,279.99	3,606.72***	21,848.36**	1,016.43
	(−1.533)	(3.753)	(1.988)	(0.748)
Between 36 and 45 years old (%)	8.83	2,055.48	20,010.38	1,638.76
	(0.008)	(1.625)	(1.563)	(1.035)
Between 46 and 60 years old (%)	−802.89	1,811.55	20,598.04	809.89
	(−0.814)	(1.597)	(1.482)	(0.471)
With secondary education (%)	−55.45	2,176.62**	2,550.32	2,046.55**
	(−0.068)	(2.317)	(0.318)	(2.065)
With tertiary education (%)	2,475.16*	4,434.40**	−4,601.13	3,888.78**
	(1.662)	(2.587)	(−0.297)	(2.034)
Hanoi dummy (1 = yes)	−998.70**	275.68		
	(−2.559)	(0.614)		
Can Tho dummy (1 = yes)			4,309.27	−818.59
			(0.757)	(−1.163)
Constant	1,050.80	−4,184.45**	−21,830.86	−726.92
	(0.727)	(−2.516)	(−1.356)	(−0.365)
Observations	175	175	150	150
R^2	0.209	0.207	0.174	0.076

a   Between 15 and 60 years old.
*Significant at 10% level. **Significant at 5% level. ***Significant at 1% level.

Note: Numbers in parentheses are *t*-values.

The coefficients of the proportion of female working members were not significant in the agricultural income and nonfarm income functions. The agricultural income function suggests that women who are left on the farms are not necessarily worse off because they earn income from high-value products. The nonfarm income function indicates no significant gender barriers to entry in the nonfarm labor market, which is consistent with Hypothesis 5 on the expansion of equal employment opportunities for women and men. After controlling for gender, household members with secondary and tertiary schooling were significantly more likely to work in the nonfarm sector than those with zero and primary schooling (control). On the other hand, farm size was a significant factor affecting farm income in both the north and south. These findings are consistent with Hypothesis 1 on the importance of farmland in increasing farm income. This implies that females, particularly in the northern villages, are pushed to stay on the farm because they are less educated and returns to their labor are lower, although there is no significant gender bias in the nonfarm sector. Overall, it is clear that the low schooling attainment of females serves as the greater barrier in female labor force participation in the nonfarm sector, even though female labor is not discriminated against in nonfarm labor markets. This finding in Vietnam is different from that of Laos, where less educated women found low-paying jobs in the informal sector in Thailand. This difference may be partly explained by the fact that young female workers in Laos graduated only from primary school (Table 2.6), whereas their counterparts in Vietnam graduated from secondary schools (Table 5.3).

It is interesting to find that young workers tend to engage in nonfarm jobs in the north and in agriculture in the south, suggesting that small-scale farming in the north does not absorb additional young workers, whereas large-scale farming in the south provides employment opportunities for the young. Presumably, scale economies have emerged in rice farming in the south due to large mechanization, which attracts young workers.

Summary and conclusions

This chapter explored the determinants of schooling, farmland inheritance, and job choice of three generations of household members in Vietnam. The most important finding is that the oldest generation tends to discriminate against females by investing less in schooling and transferring less farmland. This discrimination has largely been eliminated in the younger generation. The older generations are more engaged in farming, while the younger generation has diversified into nonfarm work. We found that the female G3 in the northern villages (where male members tend to work outside the village in the nonfarm sector) are significantly more likely to choose farming. This does not necessarily make the female G3 worse off, as they are engaged in the production of high-value products such as fruits, vegetables, and cut flowers and in raising livestock. It is thus recommended to extend credit and give legal access to farmland to women. In addition, we suggest greater public investments in education and health and in infrastructure such as roads, electricity, and running water, as these are time-saving devices that can enable women to allocate more time to market-oriented activities. In contrast, large-scale rice farming provides lucrative employment opportunities for both men and women in the south. It is therefore recommended to support farm size expansion and further development of mechanized farming in the face of increasing labor costs in this rapidly growing economy.

Acknowledgment

The authors would like to thank Francis Mark. Quimba for excellent research assistance.

Notes

1 According to Kerkvliet (2005), by the late 1960s, 86 percent of agricultural households belonged to cooperatives in northern Vietnam.
2 Thai Nguyen officially belongs to the northeast region. In this study, we consider it part of the Red River Delta.

Part II

Infrastructure and the changing landscape of rural economies

6 Infrastructure and the transformation of the rural economy in the Philippines

Introduction

The Philippine government recognizes that household income growth and poverty reduction are important national agendas, as stipulated in the 2004–10 Medium-Term Philippine Development Plan (National Economic and Development Authority [NEDA] 2004). Considering that a large majority of the poor live in rural areas, it is important to investigate the evolutionary processes and locational dynamics of the rural nonfarm sector. To date, there are three strands of thought that trace the development of the rural nonfarm sector. The first strand – geography of economic development – states that rural nonfarm activities tend to proliferate in areas near urban centers and in areas where infrastructure is well developed (Haggblade *et al.* 2007; Renkow 2007). The second strand – the role of human capital – asserts the importance of schooling in facilitating labor mobility away from low-productivity farm activities to high-productivity nonfarm activities so as to stimulate the development of the nonfarm sector (Kijima and Lanjouw 2005; Takahashi and Otsuka 2009). The third strand – agricultural growth linkages – asserts that agricultural development resulting from techno-logical advancement could spur the development of the nonfarm sector through several forward and backward linkages (Haggblade *et al.* 2007).

This chapter aims to test the validity of the aforementioned three strands of thought in the rural Philippines with a particular focus on the role of infrastructure in facilitating structural transformation from the farm to the nonfarm sector. Such research and analysis is largely missing from the literature, although economists consider physical infrastructure to be an indispensable precondition of industrial-ization and economic development (Murphy *et al.* 1989). Many empirical studies demonstrate that the development of physical infrastructure improves an economy's long-term production and income levels (Lipton and Ravallion 1995; Esfahani and Ramirez 2003). Moreover, an increasing amount of micro-empirical literature has started to focus on the role of infrastructure in reducing poverty in a direct manner (Gibson and Rozelle 2003; Lokshin and Yemtsov 2005).

We explore the structural transformation at the provincial and township levels covering an 18-year period from 1988 to 2006. The towns are located in Central Luzon, CALABARZON (an acronym for the provinces of Cavite, Laguna,

Batangas, Rizal, and Quezon), Central Visayas, and Western Visayas, which are the most progressive regions in the country and where economic transformation away from the farm sector to the nonfarm sector has been more rapid and changes in the composition of the nonfarm sector have been more dramatic than elsewhere in the country. We divided our analysis into two periods of time: (1) 1988–97 (representing the period before the Asian currency crisis and a major drought) and (2) 2000–9 (representing the period thereafter).

This chapter has five remaining sections. The second section reviews the litera-ture on the development of the rural nonfarm sector and presents three testable hypotheses, whereas the third section describes the evolution of the rural nonfarm sector in the Philippines. The fourth section discusses the data and methodology, followed by the fifth section, which presents the regression results on the deter-minants of different income sources. The sixth section concludes this chapter by providing policy recommendations.

Testable hypotheses

The nonfarm sector consists of a wide diversity of activities in manufacturing, commerce, finance, construction, community, and personal services. Haggblade *et al.* (2007) show that the rural nonfarm sector is substantial in terms of its share in total employment and income. The share of the nonfarm sector in primary employment was 24 percent in Asia, 31 percent in Latin America, and 9 percent in Africa, and its share of household income was 51 percent in Asia, 47 percent in Latin America, and 37 percent in Africa. The magnitude of the rural nonfarm sector could be underestimated because a large number of rural nonfarm activities are undertaken as secondary employment during lulls in the agricultural season, and some are not remunerated, especially those undertaken by women in family-owned enterprises (Lanjouw and Lanjouw 2001).

In what follows, we provide testable hypotheses on the factors affecting the development of the rural nonfarm sector by extending and elaborating Hypoth-esis 6 on the role of infrastructure in promoting the development of the rural nonfarm sector postulated in Chapter 1.

Distance and infrastructure

Proximity to urban centers affects the sources of household income, specifically the composition of nonfarm income (Reardon *et al.* 2007) and household participation in nonfarm activities (Deichmann *et al.* 2008). Distance from major cities is also found to be an important determinant of the location of industries and composition of rural nonfarm activity (Sonobe and Otsuka 2006). In Nepal, for example, nonfarm employment is heavily concentrated in and around the cities, whereas agricultural wage employment dominates in villages located farther away (Fafchamps and Shilpi 2003).

The development of infrastructure could mitigate the negative impact of distance in the transformation of the rural economy, the "death of distance" coined by Weiss (2007, pp. 51–67). Improved roads have facilitated the emergence of subcontracting arrangements between urban traders and rural firms (Kikuchi 1998). The availability of electricity has induced an expansion of labor employment opportunities in export-oriented sectors in the Philippines (Fabella 1985) and in a wide variety of nonfarm activities in Indonesia (Gibson and Olivia 2010) and Nicaragua (Corral and Reardon 2001).

Given the aforementioned, we propose the following hypothesis:

Hypothesis 6.1 on the geography of economic development and the role of infrastructure: The rural nonfarm sector tends to develop in areas near the urban and rural town centers. The development of the infrastructure system, however, integrates distant villages with urban areas and rural towns, leading to the development of the nonfarm sector in distant rural areas.

Human capital

Only a few studies point out that education is important in enhancing farm productivity, as it facilitates the adoption of modern agricultural technology (Foster and Rosenzweig 1996). The majority of rural household studies find that education is important in raising nonfarm income. In the rural Philippines, for example, it is found that the more educated household members are those who are more actively involved in nonfarm activities and have a higher propensity to move out of the village to work in the cities and overseas (Kajisa 2007; Takahashi and Otsuka 2009). Jolliffe (2004) found that, in rural Ghana, returns to education are higher in nonfarm activities. Corral and Reardon (2001) found in Nicaragua that secondary and tertiary schooling increases income in formal wage employment and in other lucrative nonfarm jobs but does not have a significant impact on self-employment income. Interestingly, the impact of secondary and tertiary education on the probability of engaging in nonfarm work is found to be more pronounced among the females than among the males in the Philippines (Takahashi and Otsuka 2009) and China (Glauben *et al.* 2008). Indeed, the availability of an educated labor force could facilitate the transformation of the rural economy away from the farm sector to the nonfarm sector by inducing a movement of labor away from the former to the latter (de Janvry and Sadoulet 2001).

Given the aforementioned, we postulate:

Hypothesis 6.2 on the role of human capital: The availability of an educated labor force serves as an important factor in promoting the development of the rural nonfarm economy.

Modern agricultural technology

Studies on the determinants of different sources of rural household income show that adoption of modern technology (that is, modern varieties [MVs] of rice and irrigation) significantly increases farm income (Estudillo and Otsuka

1999; Estudillo *et al.* 2008; Hossain *et al.* 2009) through increases in yield and cropping intensity (Otsuka *et al.* 1994). Yet, Jayasuriya and Shand (1986) show evidence of acceleration in the use of labor-saving technologies because of increasing wages in Asia.

The agricultural growth linkage hypothesis postulates that modern agricultural technology propels the development of the nonfarm economy through several production and consumption linkages (Haggblade *et al.* 2007). On the production side, improved agricultural technologies may spur the birth and development of industries engaged in the provision of agricultural inputs (for example, fertilizer) and service-related support to the agricultural sector (for example, repair shops for agricultural machinery). Also, a dynamic agriculture sector breeds industries that have strong linkages with agriculture, such as food processing and agro-based manufacturing industries. On the consumption side, increase in farm income brought about by increased agricultural productivity stimulates consumer demand for locally produced nonfarm goods and services (Haggblade *et al.* 2007).

Given the aforementioned, we postulate:

> **Hypothesis 6.3 on agricultural growth linkage:** *The adoption of modern agricultural technology is critically important in stimulating the development of the rural nonfarm sector through various production and consumption linkages.*

Overall, our literature review emphasizes that infrastructure systems, human capital, and modern agricultural technology could propel the development of the rural nonfarm economy, which could lead to poverty reduction and equitable income distribution.

Evolution of the rural nonfarm economy in the Philippines

The economic importance of the rural nonfarm sector

Table 6.1 reports the changes in the sources of rural household income from 1988 to 2009 in the Philippines. Households in rural areas have been increasingly deriving their incomes from nonfarm sources – the share of nonfarm income as a whole, including nonfarm activities and remittances, rose appreciably during the 21-year period; correspondingly, the share of farm income decreased.

The increase in the share of remittance incomes in the Philippines could be explained by the increasing number of deployed overseas Filipino workers (OFWs), which more than doubled from 1988 to 2009. Almost 50 percent of the OFWs are women. The most popular destinations of OFWs are the United Arab Emirates, Saudi Arabia, and Hong Kong. Parallel to the increase in the number of OFWs is the huge increase in the amount of remittances from about US$1 billion to about US$13 billion in the same period, placing the Philippines in the top four recipients of foreign remittances next to India, China, and Mexico.

Table 6.1   Sources of household income of rural households in the Philippines and its progressive towns, 1988–2009

Income source	1988	2000	2009
Philippines			
Average household income (US$ purchasing power parity, 2005 constant)	2,371	3,849	5,130
Farm (%)	45	35	28
Nonfarm (%)	41	48	56
Remittances (%)	14	17	16
Domestic (%)	8	9	5
International (%)	6	8	11
Total (%)	100	100	100
Central Luzon, CALABARZON,[a] Western Visayas, and Central Visayas			
Average household income (US$ purchasing power parity, 2005 constant)	2,449	4,394	5,587
Farm (%)	38	26	21
Nonfarm (%)	45	54	61
Remittances (%)	17	20	18
Domestic (%)	9	10	5
International (%)	8	9	13
Total (%)	100	100	100

a   CALABARZON refers to the provinces of Cavite, Laguna, Batangas, Rizal, and Quezon.

Source: Authors' calculations from the Family Income and Expenditure Survey, selected years.

The bulk of the emigrants consists of the highly educated, although the percentage of emigrants with less than a high school education has increased over time.

The development of the infrastructure system has been an important stimulus behind the increasing economic importance of the rural nonfarm sector. Electrification coverage in the Philippines has expanded, starting with only 60 percent of households with access to electricity in 1988 and reaching as high as 86 percent in 2009 (Table 6.2). The progressive towns have displayed an even higher electrification coverage for the same period. Accomplishments in terms of increasing the quantity of roads and improving their quality, however, have been modest. The Philippine national government's spending on infrastructure is below the World Bank's 5 percent recommendation to enable the Philippines to meet its infrastructure needs in the coming decade (Llanto 2007).

The transformation of the economy toward the nonfarm sector is also facilitated by the increase in the proportion of the labor force with higher educational

Table 6.2 Infrastructure development indicators in the Philippines and its progressive towns, 1988–2009

Category	1988	2000	2009[a]
Philippines			
Electricity (% of households)	60	76	86
Total road density (km/km²)	0.61	0.75	0.75
National	0.11	0.12	0.12
Local	0.50	0.63	0.63
Paved roads (%)			
National	44	59	69
Local	7	14	14
Central Luzon, CALABARZON,[b] Western Visayas, and Central Visayas			
Electricity (% of households)	63	82	89
Total road density (km/km²)	0.69	0.83	0.83
National	0.12	0.14	0.13
Local	0.63	0.77	0.77
Paved roads (%)			
National	60	73	82
Local	12	19	19

a   Data refer to 2006, except for electricity data, which refer to 2009.
b   CALABARZON refers to the provinces of Cavite, Laguna, Batangas, Rizal, and Quezon.

Sources: Authors' calculations from the Family Income and Expenditure Survey, selected years, and the Department of Public Works and Highways.

attainment. Table 6.3 reports that the proportion of the labor force without schooling was very small (6 percent in 1988), and this has even declined in recent years. Furthermore, while the bulk of the rural labor force only attained the primary education level, the share of the rural labor force with secondary and tertiary education substantially increased from 1988 to 2009. The National Statistics Office (NSO) reports that the female labor force participation rate in the Philippines increased from 48 percent in 1990 to 50 percent in 2005. This is consistent with the egalitarian tradition in the rural Philippines of bequeathing farmland to males, who have the comparative advantage in farm work, while investing in the education of females, thereby providing them with opportunities to participate in the nonfarm sector (Quisumbing *et al.* 2004). As a result, the Filipino female labor force generally has a higher level of education compared with its female counterparts in Asia (Esguerra and Manning 2007). This gives Filipino women a clear edge in participating in the international labor market.

There has been a decline in the average farm size in the Philippines as a whole and in its progressive towns (Table 6.4). The average farm size in the

Table 6.3 Schooling characteristics of the rural labor force in the Philippines and its progressive towns, 1988–2009

Category	1988	2000	2009
Philippines			
No schooling	6	4	3
Primary (%)	56	47	42
Secondary (%)	26	34	38
Tertiary (%)	12	15	17
Total (%)	100	100	100
Central Luzon, CALABARZON,[a] Western Visayas, and Central Visayas			
No schooling	4	3	2
Primary (%)	58	47	41
Secondary (%)	27	34	39
Tertiary (%)	11	16	18
Total (%)	100	100	100

a CALABARZON refers to the provinces of Cavite, Laguna, Batangas, Rizal, and Quezon.

Source: Authors' calculations from the Labor Force Survey, selected years.

Table 6.4 Agriculture development indicators in the Philippines and its progressive towns, 1988–2009

Category	1988	2000	2009[a]
Philippines			
Average farm size (ha)	2.16[b]	2.00	2.00
Area irrigated (%)[c]	47	44	49
Area under MV (%)[d]	93	98	95
Central Luzon, CALABARZON,[f] Western Visayas, and Central Visayas			
Average farm size (ha)	1.75[b]	1.37	N/A[e]
Area irrigated (%)	56	49	50
Area under MV (%)	96	98	99

a Data refer to 2006, except for area irrigated data, which refer to 2009.
b Refers to 1991.
c National Irrigation Administration.
d Refers to modern varieties of rice.
e N/A = not available.
f CALABARZON refers to the provinces of Cavite, Laguna, Batangas, Rizal, and Quezon.

progressive towns is relatively smaller than the average for the Philippines, and the drop in the average farm size is greater in the former than in the latter. Interestingly, irrigation and MV adoption are higher in the progressive towns than in the country as a whole. In any case, MV adoption has been nearly 100 percent, and changes in the irrigation ratio were small during the period under consideration.

Overall, the changes in the composition of household income and labor force allocation away from the farm sector to the nonfarm sector clearly indicate the structural transformation of the rural economy in the Philippines.

Data and methodology

We explored the determinants of rural per capita income at the provincial and township levels. Income data were derived from the Family Income and Expenditure Survey (FIES), which is a nationwide survey of households undertaken by the NSO every 3 years.[1] In our analysis, we included eight rounds of FIES data from 1988 to 2009. For the town-level analysis, we included towns and large cities belonging to Central Luzon, CALABARZON, Western Visayas, and Central Visayas. We selected Central Luzon and CALABARZON because these regions are in close proximity to metropolitan Manila, and Western Visayas and Central Visayas because they are close to metropolitan Cebu, which are the two major cities and the main hub of economic growth in the country. Accordingly, we call the towns in these four regions the "progressive towns."[2]

We estimated the determinants of income consisting of (1) farm, (2) nonfarm, which is further subdivided into (3) formal salary work, (4) informal manufacturing, and (5) informal trade, transportation, and communication (TTC)[3] and remittance income, which is classified into (6) foreign and (7) domestic.[4] We represented the provincial (town) per capita rural income as the average of the real per capita income of all rural households belonging to each province (town). We deflated the per capita income using the purchasing power parity (PPP) based on the gross domestic product (GDP) with 2000 as the base year taken from the World Development Indicators (World Bank 2008a). Specifically, the functional form is

$$\log(y_{ijt}) = b + \Sigma_n \omega_n X_{nit} + u_{it}, \tag{1}$$

where $\log(y_{ijt})$ is the natural logarithm of real per capita income in province (town) i, sector j at time t; and X refers to the vector of explanatory variables. We used the logarithm of average real per capita income to reduce the heteroskedasticity of the error term, which is inherently large in nationwide survey data (Wooldridge 2000).

We divided our explanatory variables into five major categories: (1) infrastructure, (2) human capital, (3) agricultural technology, (4) geography, and (5) time. Following Duflo and Pande (2007), we exploited the unique spatial characteristic of the Philippines by using geographic characteristics as instrumental variables (IVs) to address the possible endogeneity of the infrastructure variables. A possibly good IV for electricity access and roads specific to the Philippines is the number of islands per province. Since the Philippines is an archipelago, expanding infrastructure coverage to the remote islands is an expensive endeavor. Being an archipelago, there could be habitable and uninhabitable islands within the same province.[5] We deleted the uninhabitable islands in each province because the infrastructure system will only be set up in islands where there are communities. One of the biggest constraints to expanding and improving the quality of infrastructure in the country is the scarcity of public funds. The local governments are largely dependent on the internal revenue allotment (IRA) from the national government for financing infrastructure investments. The amount received by the provinces from the IRA is stipulated under the Local Government Code (LGC) of 1991 and is primarily based on the size of the population and the land area regardless of provincial income. We, therefore, included population density, population, and land area as additional instruments for electricity and roads, considering that the local government's share of the IRA is exogenously determined as stipulated in the LGC.[6] To mitigate the endogeneity of population, we used data from the population survey prior to the rounds of the FIES (for example, the population census in 1990 was used for the 1994 FIES).[7]

To test the validity of our instruments, we performed various diagnostic tests for under- and weak identification. We verified the validity of the instruments, and IV regression was used in the estimation. The first-stage regressions show that electricity coverage was lower in provinces and progressive towns with a higher number of habitable islands, which substantiates the difficulty and high cost of connecting small islands to the main electricity grid in areas with a high number of widely dispersed islands. The number of inhabited islands was also negatively related with paved local roads in the progressive towns. While population and population density are generally positively related with electricity and paved local roads, the opposite sign was observed for land area, possibly reflecting the constraint to infrastructure expansion in large areas.

Determinants of income

Determinants of income at the provincial level

Table 6.5 shows the results of the second-stage IV regression runs on the determinants of the provincial real per capita rural income. Let us begin our discussion with the examination of the impact of infrastructure. Electricity did not significantly affect farm income, but it had a positive impact on increasing nonfarm income as a whole and, most importantly, incomes from formal salary work, TTC, and foreign and domestic remittances in 2000–6. The last finding suggests that good access to electricity facilitated the flow of money from overseas and major cities to the provinces. The more pronounced impact of electricity in 2000–6 is reflective of the efforts of the government to encourage players

Table 6.5 Determinants of real rural per capita income at the provincial level in the Philippines, 1988–2006 (second stage of the instrumental variable regression)

Variable	Farm		Nonfarm	
	1988–97	*2000–6*	*1988–97*	*2000–6*
	A	B	C	D
Access to electricity	−0.17	−1.70	0.58	1.45**
Proportion of paved national roads	0.37*	−0.04	−0.15	0.004
National road density	2.03	0.81	−1.25	−0.11
Proportion of paved local roads	−4.38***	−0.75	2.79**	0.76
Local road density	−0.12	0.07	−0.05	−0.13
Proportion of labor force				
Female	−0.50	0.30	1.84***	1.21**
Between 15 and 25 years old	2.54***	1.80**	1.18*	1.21*
Between 26 and 35 years old	3.17***	3.12***	0.85	0.79
Between 36 and 45 years old	1.75**	0.70	−0.46	0.77
Between 46 and 59 years old	2.91***	−1.86	−0.35	1.14
With primary schooling	−0.35	1.49	−0.01	−0.79
With secondary schooling	−0.05	1.32	−0.49	−1.17
With tertiary schooling	−0.76	3.16	3.99***	1.34
Proportion of irrigated area	0.04	0.05	0.15*	0.05
Land acquisition and distribution (LAD)	0.27	0.45	0.08	−0.20
Farmland–labor ratio	0.12***	0.04	0.11**	0.03
Distance	0.004***	0.000	−0.004***	0.000
Road × Distance	−0.003	0.003*	0.005***	−0.001
Number of observations	248	186	248	186
R^2	0.20	0.45	0.78	0.78

Variable	Formal salary work		Manufacturing		Trade, transportation, and communication	
	1988–97	2000–6	1988–97	2000–6	1988–97	2000–6
	E	F	G	H	I	J
Access to electricity	0.08	1.32*	2.85	–2.63	–1.33	2.73**
Proportion of paved national roads	–0.40	–0.10	0.71	1.34**	0.467	0.17
National road density	–3.53**	–0.52	4.38	–0.12	0.49	1.13
Proportion of paved local roads	5.39***	1.07	–4.55	2.03	0.63	–0.62
Local road density	0.19	–0.13	–0.96	0.10	0.28	–0.24*
Proportion of labor force						
Female	2.29***	1.09*	0.64	3.81*	1.26	0.76
Between 15 and 25 years old	0.68	1.28	–1.49	0.04	1.91	0.94
Between 26 and 35 years old	–0.05	0.73	–0.84	–0.87	0.97	0.72
Between 36 and 45 years old	–0.80	0.88	–1.90	–0.53	–0.42	–0.29
Between 46 and 59 years old	–1.08	1.27	–2.65	–0.29	–0.37	1.01
With primary schooling	–0.26	–0.03	2.11	5.60	2.25**	–3.15*
With secondary schooling	–0.17	–0.22	–1.73	4.27	2.20	–3.74*
With tertiary schooling	5.36***	2.66	2.92	10.11	7.66***	–2.94
Proportion of irrigated area	0.23**	0.08	–0.08	0.36	0.17	–0.14
Land acquisition and distribution (LAD)	0.13	–0.27	0.35	–0.04	–0.06	–0.31
Farmland–labor ratio	0.004	–0.004	0.72***	0.25	0.31***	0.06
Distance	–0.004**	0.000	0.004	0.008*	–0.005**	–0.001
Road × Distance	0.005**	–0.001	–0.009	–0.011*	0.009***	0.002
Number of observations	248	186	235	184	248	186
R^2	0.66	0.75	0.11	0.17	0.37	0.49

(*Continued*)

Table 6.5 (Continued)

Variable	Foreign remittance		Domestic remittance	
	1988–97	*2000–6*	*1988–97*	*2000–6*
	K	L	M	N
Access to electricity	1.02	6.02***	−0.13	2.49*
Proportion of paved national roads	0.55	−0.15	−0.14	−0.13
National road density	0.71	−1.08	0.50	1.64
Proportion of paved local roads	−2.24	−2.30	0.47	−1.50
Local road density	1.02	0.09	0.47	0.06
Proportion of labor force				
Female	0.24	2.30	2.05***	0.99
Between 15 and 25 years old	−2.83	1.80	−0.44	−2.04**
Between 26 and 35 years old	−3.01	0.57	−1.25	−2.04
Between 36 and 45 years old	−3.57	0.05	−0.62	−1.62
Between 46 and 59 years old	−1.24	3.23	0.51	−0.89
With primary schooling	−1.89	−3.52	2.21**	3.78**
With secondary schooling	2.68	−1.32	3.85***	2.78*
With tertiary schooling	0.27	−5.83	3.77**	2.71
Proportion of irrigated area	0.20	−0.22	0.12	−0.26
Land acquisition and distribution (LAD)	0.11	−0.52	0.05	−0.07
Farmland–labor ratio	−0.016	−0.30*	0.003	−0.14
Distance	0.005	−0.001	−0.001	0.000
Road × Distance	−0.003	0.002	0.002	0.000
Number of observations	244	186	248	186
R^2	0.56	0.57	0.59	0.62

*Significant at 10% level. **Significant at 5% level. ***Significant at 1% level.

Notes: The coefficients for the location and year dummies, the interaction term between distance and location dummies, and the constant term, which are not shown in the table, are available from the authors upon request. The full set of tables including both the coefficients and *t*-statistics is also available upon request.

in the provision of electricity through the deregulation of the electricity industry. It can be recalled that, during the 1990s, the Philippines experienced massive power shortages because of the abolition of the Department of Energy and the discontinuation of the Bataan Nuclear Power Plant during the regime of Corazon Aquino. Much of the demand for electricity was met in areas with high demand, mainly urban areas and wealthier towns. In 2001, the Philippine government enacted Republic Act 9136 (Electric Power Industry Reform Act), which aimed at encouraging entry of several power providers. The results were lower electricity rates and expansion in power coverage in the country. Thus, we found a significant impact of electricity on nonfarm income in 2000–6 both in the provinces and progressive towns but not in 1988–97 (Tables 6.5 and 6.6). The important lesson is that electricity can effectively increase nonfarm income only when there is extensive nationwide coverage.

Road densities do not affect any of the provincial income components, possibly because there has been a minimal threshold increase in road densities. Paved national roads have exerted a positive impact on increasing income from manufacturing, while paved local roads have a positive impact on nonfarm and on formal salary incomes, especially in 1988–97. Paved local roads exerted a positive impact on nonfarm income as a whole in 1988–97, but not in 2000–6, probably because the expansion of local paved roads was minimal during 2000–6, as evident in Table 6.2. Overall, these findings largely support Hypothesis 6.1 on the role of infrastructure in the development of the rural nonfarm sector.

Next, let us examine the impacts of gender, age, and schooling. The higher proportion of the female labor force was found to increase nonfarm income as a whole and, more importantly, income from formal salary work, manufacturing, and domestic remittances. Age compositions of the labor force had largely insignificant coefficients, indicating that the development of the rural nonfarm sector opens up labor employment opportunities to all workers alike, regardless of age. Tertiary schooling remained important in the nonfarm income as a whole, formal salary work, TTC, and domestic remittance income, especially in 1988–97 but not in 2000–6, implying that even the less educated and less skilled workers were employed in these sectors in later years. In particular, all schooling variables had negative coefficients in the TTC income regression in 2000–6, suggesting that less educated workers were engaged in informal jobs in trade, transportation, and communications, which is consistent with Hypothesis 4, which states that the less educated labor force is engaged in informal work. The positive relationship of tertiary education with domestic remittance income is consistent with the general observation that more educated workers have a higher tendency to migrate to cities or nearby provinces, presumably to engage in information and communications, technology-related industries, and the financial sector. The higher impact of education in the earlier period probably reflects the fact that a relatively smaller number of the labor force had attained higher levels of education, thereby creating a larger marginal impact of schooling on income. To sum up, there seems to be strong and consistent evidence that the availability of an educated labor force promotes the development of the rural nonfarm sector, as argued by Hypothesis 6.2.

Now, let us examine the impact of agricultural technology as represented by availability of irrigation as well as farm size. Unexpectedly, irrigation does not seem to have a positive impact on farm income because of two reasons: (1) irrigation data refer to coverage of the national irrigation systems, which are mainly gravity (or dam) irrigation (that is, covered by the National Irrigation Administration) with the exclusion of privately owned pump or groundwater irrigation systems, on which data are largely not available and (2) pump irrigation is used for high-value crops, while dams are used for rice, which is less profitable than high-value crops. In fact, our farm income consists of income not only from crop production but also from fishing, forestry, hunting, and growing high-value crops.

Irrigation is largely insignificant in the nonfarm income regression, indicating that production linkages are weak (Foster and Rosenzweig 2004; Haggblade *et al.* 2007). Yet, irrigation significantly increased nonfarm income in composite and formal salary work in 1988–97, presumably because irrigation increased the collateral value of farmland and pawning revenues that could be used to finance the fixed cost of moving from farm to formal salary employment. It has been a common practice in the Philippines to pawn out irrigated farmland to finance the education of children, which facilitates their participation in the nonfarm sector (Estudillo *et al.* 2006). Our results on the impact of irrigation on rural income could indicate that agricultural growth linkages on the production side have weakened, especially in recent years in the Philippines, contrary to Hypothesis 6.3 on agricultural growth linkages.

On the whole, the implementation of land reform (variable land acquisition and distribution [LAD]) does not show any significant impact on increasing provincial income, possibly because of insufficient support services in agrarian communities (e.g., extension services and credit). Provinces with larger per capita farmland endowment (farmland–labor ratio) tended to have larger income from nonfarm sources, which may imply that farmland largely represents household wealth and the web of contacts necessary for participation in the nonfarm sector. This is consistent with Hypothesis 7 on the relationship between farmland endowment and participation in nonfarm self-employment and overseas work. The impact of farmland endowment, however, has diminished, suggesting that different nonfarm activities have increasingly become accessible across rural households regardless of access to farmland.

Finally, we would like to examine the effect of access to cities, measured by the distance variable. As may be expected, the distance variable shows that farm income tended to be higher in areas far away from major cities. Nonfarm income in general and formal salary work and TTC services in particular tended to be concentrated in areas near the cities in 1988–97 (negative sign of the distance variable) but appeared to have spread out to remote rural areas in 2000–6. Indeed, infrastructure development could bring about the "death of distance" (Weiss 2007, pp. 51–67) by inducing the growth of nonfarm sectors, even in the peripheries. This is indicated by the positive sign of the interaction term between distance and the proportion of paved roads. Specifically, for every 10-km increase in the length of paved roads connecting the provincial capital to the major city, nonfarm (column C) and formal salary work (column E) incomes increase by 5 percent and income from TTC increases by 9 percent (column I). In contrast, manufacturing income is negatively affected by the interaction term between distance and paved road (column H), possibly supporting the argument of Renkow (2007) that infrastructure development can be a "double-edged sword," bringing the growth of some sectors while causing the demise of others. This may also imply that the manufacturing sector in the rural Philippines may be producing inferior products that cannot compete with urban-manufactured goods and imports, which are tradable. Aside from the IV regression, we also tried various model specifications for a robustness check. Results generally highlight the importance of infrastructure and human capital and weak agricultural growth linkages on the production side. Overall, our findings on the role of infrastructure, human capital, agricultural growth, and physical distance are robust regardless of model specification.

Determinants of income at the town level

The results of the IV regressions in the progressive towns are shown in Table 6.6. Our instruments in the IV regression include population density, land area and total population of the towns, and the number of habitable islands of the province to which the towns belong. There are a number of important findings. First, electricity has exerted a positive impact on the total nonfarm income, formal salary income, and domestic remittances, with its impact more pronounced in the progressive towns than in the provinces. Second, national road density positively and significantly affected nonfarm income in both 1988–97 and 2000–6 but, surprisingly, local road density negatively affected nonfarm income in the progressive towns in the two periods. This contradicting result is possibly because the national government devolved in 1992 a number of its functions to the local government units (LGUs), including service provision. Thus, in 2000–6, the LGUs took full responsibility for the expansion and maintenance of local roads, while the national government continued to make decisions on national roads. The expansion of local roads under the LGUs could have been done in a "piecemeal" fashion, concentrating only on a few favored localities where the local official could maximize her or his votes. This implies that, for a road project to be effective in increasing nonfarm income, it is necessary to have a massive and well-orchestrated effort on road projects, even in only a few adjacent localities where economies of scale in road projects can be attained.

Third, similar to the analysis at the provincial level, the coefficient of the female labor force was positive in the nonfarm income as a whole, as well as in formal salary work and informal manufacturing and TTC, giving support to Hypothesis 5 on the role of the nonfarm sector in improving women's status. Fourth, farm income was lower and nonfarm and formal salary work incomes

Table 6.6 Determinants of real rural per capita income in the progressive towns, 1988–2006 (second stage of the instrumental variable regression)

Variable	Farm		Nonfarm	
	1988–97	2000–6	1988–97	2000–6
	A	B	C	D
Access to electricity	-0.65	-2.10***	3.39***	2.74***
Proportion of paved national roads	0.01	-0.62	0.36	0.46
National road density	-2.70***	-2.30**	2.97*	1.99**
Proportion of paved local roads	1.05	0.82	-2.31	0.69
Local road density	0.18	0.58**	-0.57**	-0.90**
Proportion of the labor force				
Female	-0.35**	-0.40	1.11***	0.89***
Between 15 and 25 years old	-0.69***	-0.91**	1.37***	0.83*
Between 26 and 35 years old	-0.33	-0.67*	0.91*	0.74*
Between 36 and 45 years old	-0.47*	-0.50	0.94*	-0.06
Between 46 and 59 years old	0.03	-0.17	0.97*	0.44
With primary schooling	0.70*	1.39*	-1.08	-0.96
With secondary schooling	0.35	1.69	-1.50	-0.82
With tertiary schooling	0.49	1.94	0.29	0.28
Proportion of irrigated area	0.44***	0.34**	-0.66**	-0.07
Proportion of fully owned farmland	0.24	-0.73***	-0.79***	0.23
Farmland–labor ratio	-0.14***	-0.15***	0.04	0.04***
Distance	0.001	-0.006	-0.006**	0.003
Road × Distance	-0.004	0.008	0.013**	-0.006
Number of observations	933	763	923	760
R^2	0.32	0.02	0.32	0.54

Variable	Formal salary work		Manufacturing		Trade, transportation, and communication	
	1988–97	2000–6	1988–97	2000–6	1988–97	2000–6
	E	F	G	H	I	J
Access to electricity	3.21***	2.83***	-0.21	1.84	2.16**	1.13
Proportion of paved national roads	0.56	-0.04	-1.76*	1.90*	-0.75	0.85
National road density	3.79**	2.15**	-3.26	1.90	-0.07	1.34
Proportion of paved local roads	-2.49	1.01	9.93*	1.38	1.56	-0.31
Local road density	-0.51*	-0.92***	1.02*	-0.50	-0.53	-0.30
Proportion of the labor force						
Female	0.87***	0.80**	2.03***	2.82***	1.12***	1.07**
Between 15 and 25 years old	1.37**	1.03**	0.34	-1.26	0.90	-0.42
Between 26 and 35 years old	0.67	0.54	-1.06	-0.73	1.65**	0.55
Between 36 and 45 years old	0.52	0.12	0.91	-0.74	1.38*	0.16
Between 46 and 59 years old	0.67	0.63	0.97	-1.15	1.32**	0.02
With primary schooling	-1.62*	-1.97*	2.84	-4.03	-0.14	0.40
With secondary schooling	-2.01	-1.78	3.36	-3.96	-0.25	1.00
With tertiary schooling	0.30	-0.35	3.37	-4.16	0.34	1.10
Proportion of irrigated area	-0.66**	-0.15	0.08	-0.07	-0.10	-0.06
Proportion of fully owned farmland	-0.69***	0.24	-0.86*	-0.18	-0.53	0.14
Farmland:labor ratio	0.03	0.05***	0.17**	-0.09	0.10**	0.03
Distance	-0.007**	-0.004	0.012**	0.013	0.000	0.005
Road × Distance	0.014**	0.005	-0.016*	-0.018	0.003	-0.009
Number of observations	900	753	374	383	797	714
R²	0.34	0.49	0.26	0.14	0.20	0.28

(Continued)

Table 6.6 (Continued)

Variable	Foreign remittance		Domestic remittance	
	1988–97	2000–6	1988–97	2000–6
	K	L	M	N
Access to electricity	0.46	1.84	1.51*	1.35*
Proportion of paved national roads	0.38	1.61**	0.01	0.36
National road density	2.39	3.03*	1.08	-0.01
Proportion of paved local roads	1.81	-3.73**	2.06	-0.76
Local road density	0.74	0.74	-0.71***	-0.18
Proportion of the labor force				
Female	-0.12	0.14	0.71***	0.49
Between 15 and 25 years old	-3.53***	-1.72**	-2.80***	-2.32***
Between 26 and 35 years old	-3.36***	-1.23	-2.75***	-1.68***
Between 36 and 45 years old	-2.82***	-1.38	-2.56***	-0.95**
Between 46 and 59 years old	-1.56*	0.73	-2.22***	0.03
With primary schooling	4.33***	-0.89	-1.63**	-0.75
With secondary schooling	5.62***	0.32	-1.25	-0.26
With tertiary schooling	6.70***	1.53	-0.76	0.22

Proportion of irrigated area	0.05	0.06	-0.52**	-0.15
Proportion of fully owned farmland	-0.30	0.47	-0.40	0.30
Farmland–labor ratio	0.06	0.06**	0.01	0.06***
Distance	0.003	0.001	-0.001	0.004
Road × Distance	-0.003	-0.003	0.002	-0.007
Number of observations	**624**	**629**	**930**	**763**
R^2	**0.237**	**0.298**	**0.195**	**0.335**

*Significant at 10% level. **Significant at 5% level. ***Significant at 1% level.

Notes: The coefficients for the location and year dummies, the interaction term between distance and location dummies, and the constant term, which are not shown in the table, are available from the authors upon request. The full set of tables including both the coefficients and *t*-statistics is available online.

were higher in towns with a larger proportion of the labor force belonging to the younger age group.

Fifth, while a higher level of education is important in enhancing nonfarm income in the provinces, the education variables were generally not significant in the progressive towns. There could be three reasons for this. First, a relatively larger number of workers in the progressive towns have attained higher levels of education, creating a lower incremental impact of schooling on household income. Second, this might reflect the fact that a large proportion of migrants to the cities or urban areas and even abroad are those who obtained tertiary schooling. Third, the presence of a more vibrant nonfarm sector in progressive towns could have increased the demand for unskilled labor, thereby increasing the rates of returns to lower levels of schooling. In the provincial analysis, we have shown that the less educated are employed in the informal TTC sector, which could be even larger in magnitude in progressive towns where consumer demand for services is higher.

Sixth, irrigation has positively affected farm income in the progressive towns but not in the provinces, which probably reflects the greater access to irrigation by the progressive towns (Table 6.4). Irrigation did not significantly affect nonfarm income as a whole, even at a lower level of disaggregation, where goods and services could be easily traded. Seventh, the per capita farmland endowment and the proportion of land under full ownership were also less important in increasing farm income, especially in 2000–6. The proportion of land under full ownership, which is used as a proxy for LAD at the town level, did not seem to have a positive impact on the different nonfarm income components, a result similar to that at the provincial level. While this is rather surprising, we speculate that this is because farming has become an occupation less popular among the younger generation, while the older generation, who are the principal beneficiary of the land reform program, retrieve from farming because of their advancing age and the income effect brought about by the land reform. The beneficiary of the land reform oftentimes hires a landless worker to become a "permanent worker" ("porcientuhan") doing all the farm tasks and receiving 10 percent of the output at the end of the season. Since family labor is more efficient than hired labor, labor efficiency in farming has declined among the beneficiaries of the land reform program (Hayami and Otsuka 1993).

Eighth, and finally, the distance variable shows that nonfarm income as a whole and income from formal salary work tended to increase with the development of paved roads connecting the town capital to the major city. Similar to the provinces, manufacturing income tended to decrease with increased integration, as indicated by the negative sign of the road and distance interaction.

Overall, for both the provinces and the towns, the magnitude of the negative impact of distance has declined in recent years, implying that the dispersion of rural nonfarm activities to the remote rural areas has proceeded over time, along with improvements in infrastructure. This is consistent with Hypothesis 6.1 on the "death of distance" that is brought about by infrastructure development.

Additional robustness checks for the town-level regressions likewise provide the same conclusions on the critical role of infrastructure and human capital in the development of the nonfarm sector and weak effects of agricultural growth linkages.

Conclusions and policy implications

This chapter explored the evolutionary processes in the structural transformation of the rural economy with a focus on the changing importance of infrastructure, human capital, modern agricultural technology, farmland, and physical distance on various income sources in rural Philippines using household-level survey data spanning 21 years from 1988 to 2009. Structural transformation refers to the shift in the "center of gravity" of economic activity away from the farm sector to the industry and services sectors (Hayami and Godo 2005, p. 36). In the Philippines, the structural transformation is evident in the increasing share of the value added to the nonfarm sector as a percentage of GDP and the increasing share of the labor force employed in the nonfarm sector. In the rural Philippines, we found that informal TTC sectors are the most dominant and vibrant.

Our regression results show that the development of the rural nonfarm sector has been largely stimulated by the improvement in the "quality" (represented by electricity and paved roads) and "quantity" of infrastructure. Improvement in the quality of roads enhances income and addresses the constraints of distance in the development of the nonfarm sector as a whole, especially the TTC sector in the provinces. Overall, our results support Hypothesis 6.1 on the decisive role of infrastructure in the development of the rural nonfarm sector.

Our empirical findings show that a higher level of education (that is, the tertiary level) remains a binding constraint to attaining formal salary income, while its impact has become modest or not statistically significant in rural manufacturing and TTC, especially in recent years. The analysis of the effects of the age and gender composition of the labor force likewise indicates that the nonfarm sector opens up employment opportunities to all workers alike, regardless of age and gender. This is important in reducing poverty and attaining a more egalitarian income distribution insofar as the poor are characterized by a lower level of education.

The strength of agricultural growth linkages depends on income growth (which drives consumption linkages) and input use and mechanization (which drives production linkages). Our empirical findings point to weakened production linkages, given the large number of statistically insignificant coefficients of the irrigation variable in various nonfarm income sources. This implies that agricultural growth linkages on the production side have become weak in the Philippines at least during 1988–2006, which does not give full support to Hypothesis 6.3. It implies a shift of the drivers of rural nonfarm development away from agricultural- to urban-based motors driven by growing urban markets and high urban wages, which induce subcontracting, migration, and peri-urban production aiming to serve urban consumers.

This study suggests a twofold strategy to enhance the development of the rural nonfarm sector. The first is investment in electricity and paved roads. The benefits of these investments will likely trickle down to the poor because of their positive impact on the development of the TTC sector, which has a large informal sector employing a large number of poor people. The second is continuous investments in education. Although the labor market has been expanding and increasingly accommodating the less educated, it is important to improve the quality of education at all levels, but most especially in primary and secondary levels for poverty reduction. The focus should be on public schools since a large number of poor families send their children to public schools. Overall, with the strong commitment of President Benigno Aquino on the advancement of human capital, moving forward is the only way to go for the rural Philippines.

Acknowledgment

The authors would like to thank Francis Mark Quimba for his assistance in updating the descriptive tables. Some parts of this chapter are drawn from Ramos *et al.* (2012) with permission from Taylor & Francis under license number 3550530956762.

Notes

1 The NSO defines "household" as a group of individuals who are currently living together and sharing the same pot.
2 Progressive regions and towns are defined mainly on the basis of geography, and this has little to do with the structure and growth of agriculture.
3 We include in the TTC sector the income from hotels and restaurants, financial intermediation, business, and some income from mining and quarrying and construction.
4 Total income also includes income from community and personal services and other income not elsewhere classified, but no separate regression analysis was done for these income sources, as they comprise a small portion of total income.
5 The Census of the Philippine Islands summarizes the islands in the Philippine archipelago. We define as habitable those islands that have an area of more than 0.1 square mile, are named, and are not rocks or rock formations.
6 Data on population and land area are generated from the NSO Census of Population and Housing.
7 Population surveys were conducted in 1980, 1990, 1995, 2000, and 2007.

7 Infrastructure and sectoral income inequalities in Sri Lanka

Introduction

As we have seen in previous chapters, the nonfarm labor market could absorb excess agricultural labor force that is excluded from agriculture, offering job opportunities even for the unskilled and uneducated workers who belong to the poorer segment of the community. However, there seems to be a high concentration of nonfarm economic activities in urban or semi-urban areas because of the availability of infrastructure and agglomeration economies (Kanbur and Venables 2005; Renkow 2007; Sonobe and Otsuka 2006, 2011, 2014). Access to infrastructure – more importantly, paved roads and electricity – is a crucial determinant of nonfarm income (Chapter 6).This chapter aims to inquire about the long-term strategic processes that underlie income growth, the decline in poverty, and changes in sectoral inequality in Sri Lanka from 1990 to 2006, focusing on the role of infrastructure (electricity and pipe-borne water). We explore these processes in the urban, rural, and estate sectors separately, as the diverging endowments of infrastructure and distinct sectoral characteristics bring about differences in the underlying economic forces across sectors.

Sri Lanka has been experiencing a rapid relative decline in agriculture and expansion of the nonfarm sector. The contribution of agriculture to gross domestic product (GDP) declined markedly from 27 percent in 1980 to 12 percent in 2009, and agriculture's share in labor employment decreased from 49 percent in 1985 to 34 percent in 2009. This change in the composition of output and employment was accompanied by a remarkable growth of Sri Lanka's economy at more than 5 percent annually over the last two decades (World Bank 2007a). Income growth in Sri Lanka, however, is highly concentrated in the Western Province, which houses 89 percent of the total number of industrial establishments in the whole country (Central Bank of Sri Lanka 1998). The Western Province alone accounted for more than 45 percent of the country's GDP in 2009, and its GDP grew at an annual rate of 6.2 percent during 1997–2003; the growth rate was only at 2.3 percent in the remaining provinces. Clearly, income growth is concentrated in the Western Province, which is endowed with a better infrastructure system.

This chapter has five remaining sections. The second section reviews changes in the Sri Lankan economy in the last few decades, whereas the third section describes the data sets and examines the changing patterns of household income and poverty incidence over time. The fourth section statistically identifies the dynamically changing determinants of household income across the urban, rural, and estate sectors. The fifth section decomposes the causes of income gaps among the three sectors in 1990 and 2006. Finally, the sixth section concludes the chapter and draws policy implications from the present study.

Transformation of the Sri Lankan economy

The estate, rural, and urban sectors

A unique feature of the Sri Lankan economy is the large presence of the estate sector (or plantation sector), where poverty incidence is the most pronounced at present. About 0.9 million people who comprise 5.4 percent of the Sri Lankan population reside in the estate sector. Low and stagnant wage income that goes along with the incessant rise in the cost of living is the strongest direct factor that prevents the estate people from moving out of poverty (World Bank 2005). The limited growth in productivity in the tea and rubber sectors and the low and declining prices of plantation crops in the world market constrain the increase in estate wage rates. In addition, the nonfarm sector has failed to develop in areas where the estate sector is located because of remoteness and, importantly, lack of improvement in infrastructure.

Households in rural Sri Lanka traditionally depend on rice cultivation as a major source of livelihood (Central Bank of Sri Lanka 1998). Rice cultivation is characterized by high adoption of modern varieties (MVs) of rice, which cover 98 percent of the total rice area in 2009 (Central Bank of Sri Lanka 2010). Mechanization is also prevalent, as farmers substitute machines for labor because of the increasing scarcity of farm labor owing to the expanding nonfarm labor employment opportunities. The nonfarm sector in Sri Lanka is vibrant and highly heterogeneous where the low-productivity sector offers employment opportunities to uneducated people with a few assets and weak social capital. Thus, some segments of nonfarm employment are associated with low education. The high-productivity sector is also developing, which raises the returns to higher education. This may mean that the development of the nonfarm sector could increase income inequality across sectors.

In Sri Lanka, most of the industries are concentrated in urban areas, most notably in the Western Province. The introduction of export-oriented industrial policies adopted in 1977 further intensified the development of industries in the urban sector due to good access to urban markets and proximity to the ports. The increasing labor demand induced by such industrialization is likely to have resulted in high wage rates and a low incidence of poverty in urban areas. Intersectoral differences in wage rates stimulated rural–urban migration – internal migration doubled between 1996–7 and 2003–4 from 15 to 29 persons per 1,000 households. In 2003–4, 81 percent of migrants were job seekers with a better education coming from remote and lagging regions (World Bank 2007a).

Data description

The data source

The Department of Census and Statistics of Sri Lanka (DCS) conducts a large-scale nationally representative Household Income and Expenditure Survey (HIES) once in roughly every 5 years. The Northern and Eastern Provinces have been excluded from the surveys since 1990 due to civil conflict. This study used data from four HIES rounds – i.e., those held in 1990–1, 1995–6, 2002, and 2006–7. For simplicity, we henceforth use 1990, 1995, 2002, and 2006 to refer to 1990–1, 1995–6, 2002, and 2006–7, respectively.[1] The HIES data contained the demographic, income, and expenditure information of the sample households. The primary sampling unit (PSU) was the block containing 150 households, and the administrative districts were considered the strata. In each survey, a total of 2,200 PSUs were allocated among the strata and sectors, proportionate to the number of housing units and the standard deviation of the expenditure values reported in the respective domain in the previous HIES (Department of Census and Statistics 2008). Then, 10 housing units from each PSU were selected as secondary sampling units (SSUs). The total number of observations in each survey differed due to the varying response rates of the households.

Characteristics of sample households

Table 7.1 compares the changes and differences in household characteristics across the urban, rural, and estate sectors over time. From 1990 to 2006, average household size declined markedly and roughly equally in all sectors. Since the retirement age in Sri Lanka is 55 years, we considered family members between 15 and 55 years old as working-age members. Corresponding to the declining household size in the three sectors was the decrease in the number of working-age members in a household.

Household members who are actually engaged in work were categorized on the basis of their primary occupation in the agriculture, manufacturing, and service sectors. The urban labor force is basically engaged in nonfarm jobs (manufacturing and service), and its sectoral composition of employment has not changed significantly during the last two decades. The proportion of household members primarily engaged in agriculture in the rural sector declined from 33 percent in 1990 to 13 percent in 2006 and, correspondingly, those engaged in nonagriculture – industry and service combined – increased from 67 percent to 87 percent. It is clear that, in the rural sector, agriculture is no longer the dominant employer of labor. Interestingly, the estate sector has similarly experienced a decline in its share of the labor force in agriculture, from 92 percent

Table 7.1 Description of sample households in Sri Lanka, 1990–2006

	Urban			Rural			Estate		
	1990	1995	2006	1990	1995	2006	1990	1995	2006
Average household size	5.1	4.9	4.3	4.8	4.4	4.0	4.6	4.6	4.2
Average number of members in a household by age group									
Below 15 years old	1.4	1.3	1.0	1.5	1.2	1.0	1.7	1.5	1.2
Between 15 and 55 years old	3.1	3	2.6	2.7	2.6	2.3	2.5	2.6	2.3
Above 55 years old	0.6	0.6	0.7	0.6	0.6	0.7	0.4	0.5	0.7
Male working members (%)	48	48	47	49	49	48	49	48	47
Average number of employed members in a household	1.1	1.6	1.5	1.0	1.5	1.4	1.9	1.9	1.8
Agricultural sector (%)	3	3	2	33	27	13	92	87	68
Industry sector (%)	28	27	28	23	27	35	2	3	16
Service sector (%)	70	70	70	44	46	52	7	10	16
Total (%)	100	100	100	100	100	100	100	100	100
Schooling of members in a household at working age (%)									
No schooling	6	3	2	10	5	3	33	21	14
Primary (Grades 1–5)	16	12	10	27	19	14	42	40	38
Secondary 1 (Grades 6–10)	48	41	42	44	48	49	20	34	41
Secondary 2 (Grades 11–13)	29	40	41	18	26	32	5	4	7
University	2	3	4	1	2	2	0	0	0
Total	100	100	100	100	100	100	100	100	100
Access to infrastructure (%)									
Households with pipe-borne water	26	50	72	1	5	23	0	4	8
Households with electricity	64	79	94	22	38	78	3	10	55

Note: Total numbers may not reflect exact totals because of rounding.

Source: Authors' calculations using data from the Household Income and Expenditure Survey, Sri Lanka.

to 68 percent, indicating that estate households are increasingly diversifying their livelihoods away from traditional estate wage work to nonfarm work. Although slow, the estate is obviously following the structural transformation observed in the rural sector, where the nonfarm sector is becoming a dominant source of employment.

Table 7.1 also shows the percentage composition of the schooling levels of households' working-age members. Considering the Sri Lankan education system, we considered the following five schooling categories: (1) no schooling for those who did not have any formal schooling, (2) primary from Grades 1 to 5, (3) Secondary 1 from Grades 6 to 10, (4) Secondary 2 from Grades 11 to 13 and, finally, (5) university education at both the undergraduate and graduate levels. As shown in Table 7.1, almost all the working-age members in the urban and rural sectors have formal schooling, whereas one third of working-age members in the estate sector did not attend school in 1990, even though this ratio declined to 14 percent in 2006. It is also interesting to observe that the proportion of working-age members with Secondary 1 and Secondary 2 levels was comparatively high in the urban and rural sectors, whereas the proportion with primary and Secondary 1 levels was relatively high in the estate sector. The extent to which such sectoral inequality in schooling level is related to sectoral income gaps is a major issue to be explored in this study.

Infrastructure development in the urban sector is considerably high: in 2006, 72 percent of the households had access to pipe-borne water, and 94 percent had access to electricity. Electrification in the rural areas increased markedly – 56 percent more households obtained access to electricity during the last two decades. But only 23 percent of the rural households had access to pipe-borne water, even in 2006. Infrastructure was much less developed in the estate sector as a whole. In 2006, only 55 percent of households had access to electricity in the estate sector, even though such achievement is remarkable in view of the fact that only 3 percent of households had electricity in 1990. As late as 2006, only 8 percent of them had access to pipe-borne water beginning with none in 1990. Assuming that favorable access to infrastructure stimulates the development of the nonfarm sectors, we will explore to what extent such differences in infrastructure explain the sectoral income gaps in the following sections.

Changing sources of household income

Table 7.2 compares the average monthly per capita income (PCI) and its composition over time and across sectors. The estimated rental value of owner-occupied housing units is considered part of household income in the HIES. Since house rent tends to be incorrectly estimated due to the thinness or even absence of the house rental market, the rental value of owner-occupied housing units is excluded from the household income in this study. The value of in-kind income received from employers is considered as wage income. To compare income across the survey years, we employed the World Bank's 2005 purchasing power parity (PPP) conversion rates based on private consumption (Sri Lankan

Table 7.2 Changes in household income structure in Sri Lanka, 1990–2006

	Urban			Rural			Estate		
	1990[a]	1995	2006	1990	1995	2006	1990	1995	2006
Monthly per capita income (US$ purchasing power parity [PPP] in 2005)	69	110	159	44	64	120	39	47	77
Monthly household income (US$ PPP in 2005)	322	485	635	195	259	439	166	198	277
Household income share (%)									
Farm	5	3	3	34	29	18	80	67	49
Farming[b]	3	1	1	22	17	12	3	4	3
Agricultural wage[c]	2	2	2	12	12	6	77	63	46
Nonfarm	68	68	72	39	45	54	8	16	32
Nonfarm wage[d]	51	51	54	29	35	41	6	15	29
Self-employment[e]	17	17	18	10	10	13	2	1	3
Others[f]	27	29	25	27	26	28	12	17	19
Total[g]	100	100	100	100	100	100	100	100	100
Poverty									
Head count index	0.39	0.19	0.09	0.60	0.40	0.14	0.60	0.44	0.22
Poverty gap	0.13	0.05	0.03	0.24	0.13	0.05	0.20	0.12	0.06
Gini coefficient of income inequality	0.46	0.47	0.47	0.41	0.42	0.44	0.30	0.32	0.40

a 1990, 1995, and 2006 refer to Household Income and Expenditure Survey rounds in 1990–1, 1995–6, and 2006–7, respectively.
b Income from cultivating and managing farms and from fishery activities.
c Employment income from the agricultural sector.
d Employment income from the nonfarm sector.
e Income obtained by running one's own nonagricultural businesses and enterprises.
f Pensions, interests, current remittances, transfers, etc.
g Numbers may not reflect exact totals because of rounding.

Source: Authors' calculations using data from the Household Income and Expenditure Survey, Sri Lanka.

rupees to the US dollar) as a deflator. Concomitantly, we use $1.25 per capita per day as the poverty line.

As expected, the average urban household income has been much higher than others. It is also important to realize that the gap in PCI between the urban and rural sectors has become smaller over time; the ratio of rural to urban income changed from 0.64 in 1990 to 0.75 in 2006. Another important observation is that, while PCI was almost the same in the rural and estate sectors in 1990, an income gap between the two sectors has emerged and widened since then, resulting in an income ratio of 3:2 in 2006 in favor of the rural sector. Inasmuch as nonfarm activities have become the primary source of employment in the rural sector, it seems reasonable to hypothesize that the decline in the income gap between the rural and urban sectors and the rise in the income gap between the rural and estate sectors can be primarily attributed to the differential growth of nonfarm jobs across the three sectors. Household income in the estate sector is low because agricultural workers are engaged in simple tasks (Hayami 1996).

All the income received by the members of the household, whether in cash or in kind, was included in the household income. We grouped household income sources into three major categories (Department of Census and Statistics 2008): (1) farm, (2) nonfarm, and (3) others (Table 7.2). Farm income is made up of two components – farming income and agricultural wage income. Households generate farming income by cultivating and managing farms as either owner or tenant cultivators and by engaging in fishing and forestry activities.[2] Nonfarm income is also classified into two categories – nonfarm wage income and self-employment income. Self-employment income is income earned from running one's own businesses and enterprises. "Others" refers to nonlabor income, including pensions, interests, current remittances, transfers, etc.

In the urban sector, the composition of income sources has been quite stable, in which nonfarm wage income has accounted for more than 50 percent of household income. In contrast, income shares have changed remarkably in the rural sector: the nonfarm income share was already slightly higher than the farm income share in 1990, but the former increased and the latter decreased by 15–16 percentage points by 2006. It is also noticeable that the share of nonfarm wage income in the rural sector was much smaller than that in the urban sector in 1990, but it became somewhat comparable in 2006. It appears that urbanization of rural areas has been taking place, during which wage employment opportunities in the nonfarm sector have been increasing. The share of nonfarm income in the estate sector also increased rapidly. Yet, farm income, particularly agricultural wage income, has been the major source of estate household income, even though its share declined from 80 percent in 1990 to 49 percent in 2006. Therefore, it is likely that the increasing importance of nonfarm income in the rural sector resulted in faster income growth compared with those in the estate and urban sectors.

It is worth noting that, even though the difference in PCI between the rural and estate sectors was small in 1990, the schooling levels of the rural working-age household members were much higher than those of their counterparts in the estate households (Table 7.1). Thus, it is clear that returns to schooling or the income of educated workers was not much higher in rural areas than in plantation areas (i.e., the estate sector) in the early years. On the other hand, the income gap between the two sectors has become substantially larger over time, which suggests that returns to schooling have increased particularly in rural areas, where the nonfarm labor market has developed more rapidly.

The share of self-employment income was stable at 17–18 percent in the urban sector and 10–13 percent in the rural sector. The nonfarm wage income was the largest component in the nonfarm income in all three sectors, and its share has been increasing, indicating that nonfarm wage income is the major driver of household income growth. The share of nonfarm wage income, however, was also growing relatively fast in the estate sector – its share of income rose from 6 percent in 1990 to 29 percent in 2006 – yet, nonfarm wage income was hardly the strong driver of income growth in the estate sector. Presumably, the nonfarm labor market in the estate is thin and slow to grow, which could be a major cause of concern, as this could be the underlying cause of income disparity across sectors. Infrastructure differences across sectors could explain the extent of dynamism of the growth of the nonfarm labor market, which favors the urban and rural sectors where the supply of electricity and pipe-borne water is more extensive.

Changes in poverty and sectoral inequality

Using HIES data and the Foster *et al.* (1984) formula, poverty indices were calculated for all three sectors and are reported in Table 7.2. Poverty incidence has been declining considerably in all three sectors during the period under study. The HCI in the urban, rural, and estate sectors decreased by 30, 46, and 38 percentage points, respectively, from 1990 to 2006. Interestingly, 60 percent of households in both the rural and estate sectors were under the poverty line in 1990. But, 16 years later, only 14 percent were poor among the rural households; however, 22 percent have remained poor among the estate households. Thus, the persistence of poverty in the estate sector is a salient feature of Sri Lanka's economy. Household income, however, was much more equally distributed in the estate sector than in the others, even though the speed of deteriorating sectoral income distribution is conspicuous in this sector. Table 7.2 shows that the Gini coefficient of income inequality in the estate sector rose from 0.30 in 1990 to 0.40 in 2006, which indicates the formation of a richer income class based on nonfarm employment. It seems that the estate area has been increasingly characterized by a two-tier labor market consisting of lowly paid traditional estate workers and highly paid workers in the newly emerging nonfarm labor market.

The rise in sectoral income inequality is manifested in the Gini index for the whole of Sri Lanka. The Gini coefficient rose consistently from 0.324 in 1991 to 0.354 in 1996 to 0.410 in 2002 and to 0.402 in 2007. This corresponds to the declining income share of the lowest 10 percent of households, whose share of income declined from 3.75 percent in 1991 to 3.57 percent in 1996 to 2.97 percent in 2002 and to 3.05 percent in 2007 (World Bank 2011c).

In summary, the descriptive analysis of household income growth and reduction in poverty among the three sectors revealed considerable sectoral differences in economic performance during the period under study. The urban and rural sectors have achieved substantial improvements in income compared with the estate sector due to the high and stable nonfarm income share among urban households and the increasing nonfarm income share among rural households. Since the growth of nonfarm income is partly explained by infrastructure, we analyze how differences in infrastructure could have created differences in the magnitude of income growth and poverty reduction while creating income inequality across sectors.

Determinants of household income

We used the ordinary least squares (OLS) regression to identify the changes and differences in determinants of the PCI using separate regression runs for 1990 and 2006 data only, with the exclusion of 1995 and 2002. In 1995, there was a severe drought that affected the entire country; in 2001, there were terrorist attacks on key points of the Sri Lankan economy (the airport, central bank, and oil refinery stations), which led to a negative growth that year for the first time in the country's history (World Bank 2005). The specification of our income equation is as follows:

$$Y_{ijt} = \beta_{0jt} + \beta_{1jt}X_{ijt} + \varepsilon_{ijt}, \tag{1}$$

where Y_{ijt} is per capita income of household i in sector j in year t; X is a vector of covariates; β_0 is an intercept and β_1 is a vector of estimated coefficients; and ε_{ij} is the error term with the usual statistical properties. The set of covariates consisted of (1) human capital represented by the proportion of working-age members;[3] female head of household dummy variable (1 = yes); and age, gender, and schooling compositions; (2) infrastructure represented by dummy variables for access to electricity and pipe-borne water;[4] (3) asset ownership represented by the size of paddy land and upland ownership per household member; and (4) district dummies. The proportion of working-age members is supposed to capture the "quantity" of human capital of the household, and the age, gender, and schooling composition variables are expected to represent the "quality" of human capital. There are 17 districts in Sri Lanka – Moneragala (the poorest district) is used as the default (control).

We did regression runs for (1) monthly PCI, (2) monthly per capita farm income, and (3) monthly per capita nonfarm income separately for 1990 and 2006. We ran tobit models for farm and nonfarm incomes because some households do not receive income from the two income sources. Table 7.3 shows the estimation results of the monthly PCI function; Table 7.4 presents the results

Table 7.3 Determinants of household monthly per capita income in Sri Lanka, 1990–2006 (ordinary least squares)

	Urban		Rural		Estate	
	1990	2006	1990	2006	1990	2006
Constant	15.49**	−17.67	11.66**	−16.56**	16.21***	0.479
	(2.550)	(−0.752)	(5.145)	(−2.178)	(3.768)	(0.0389)
Proportion of working-age members	31.46***	111.1***	14.69***	74.34***	33.59***	80.93***
	(4.902)	(6.259)	(6.012)	(13.20)	(6.653)	(7.327)
Dummy for female head (1 = yes)	−8.885***	−11.40	1.830*	1.491	0.599	6.983
	(−4.469)	(−1.479)	(1.820)	(0.551)	(0.258)	(0.954)
Proportion of working-age members						
Female	−0.361	−2.169	−1.307	−0.639	−2.915	−22.77*
	(−0.0506)	(−0.121)	(−0.492)	(−0.0907)	(−0.351)	(−1.658)
Between 25 and 34 years old	6.929*	1.097	2.239*	7.637*	1.269	2.490
	(1.955)	(0.0858)	(1.672)	(1.856)	(0.500)	(0.301)
Between 35 and 44 years old	5.767	1.068	0.595	3.874	2.945	2.857
	(1.555)	(0.0960)	(0.370)	(1.032)	(0.877)	(0.435)
Between 45 and 55 years old	11.75**	16.10	3.372	9.234**	3.952	−0.0197
	(2.197)	(1.394)	(1.604)	(2.174)	(0.858)	(−0.00314)
With primary schooling (Grades 1 to 5)	−13.18***	24.62*	1.544	1.152	−2.446	−8.630*
	(−2.611)	(1.768)	(0.949)	(0.197)	(−1.107)	(−1.688)

With Secondary 1 schooling (Grades 6 to 10)	−8.957* (−1.831)	26.37** (2.437)	2.866* (1.707)	13.57** (2.480)	−5.891** (−2.249)	10.93 (1.451)
With Secondary 2 schooling (Grades 11 to 13)	37.42*** (7.039)	131.6*** (10.88)	34.83*** (14.56)	96.95*** (15.99)	32.11*** (3.764)	114.9*** (5.574)
With university schooling	178.2*** (8.023)	570.6*** (8.989)	165.6*** (9.844)	355.8*** (15.04)	81.35 (0.982)	850.4** (2.386)
Area of per capita owned land						
Paddy area per capita (ha)	94.22*** (2.969)	266.5** (2.298)	27.21*** (3.152)	155.4*** (3.369)	104.0 (0.660)	−506.3** (−2.308)
Upland area per capita (ha)	66.96*** (2.992)	176.9*** (4.055)	22.81*** (4.675)	84.30*** (4.469)	−6.385** (−2.470)	459.0** (1.985)
Dummy for electricity (1 = yes)	15.85*** (10.21)	27.62*** (4.404)	20.55*** (14.26)	17.34*** (8.508)	32.46*** (2.644)	7.497** (2.277)
Dummy for pipe-borne water (1 = yes)	20.34*** (6.471)	9.875 (1.189)	34.96*** (3.060)	19.09*** (6.074)		9.448 (0.876)
Number of observations	6,076	3,967	10,912	11,245	1,222	1,703
R^2	0.238	0.255	0.257	0.228	0.266	0.354

*Significant at 10% level. **Significant at 5% level. ***Significant at 1% level.

Notes: Robust *t*-statistics are in parentheses. Coefficients and *t*-statistics of district dummies are not reported in this table to save on space. The full set of regressions is available from the authors upon request.

Table 7.4 Determinants of household per capita farm income in Sri Lanka, 1990–2006 (tobit)

	Urban		Rural		Estate	
	1990	2006	1990	2006	1990	2006
Constant	8.551	1.999	2.617	22.20**	-10.75***	-46.93**
	(0.968)	(0.0394)	(1.462)	(2.381)	(-2.832)	(-2.544)
Proportion of working-age members	-13.93***	-32.59	8.131***	9.825**	44.38***	24.09**
	(-2.825)	(-1.312)	(6.944)	(2.122)	(15.49)	(2.145)
Dummy for female head (1 = yes)	-2.491	-42.80***	-2.265***	-12.53***	-1.662	-18.26***
	(-1.105)	(-3.535)	(-3.964)	(-5.572)	(-1.025)	(-3.080)
Proportion of working-age members						
Female	-2.101	-1.585	-6.097***	-16.53***	-4.809*	25.01***
	(-0.535)	(-0.0785)	(-6.451)	(-4.567)	(-1.790)	(2.705)
Between 25 and 34 years old	-5.310	-17.63	2.531***	-5.768	11.54***	-8.355
	(-1.489)	(-0.911)	(3.070)	(-1.621)	(5.045)	(-0.951)
Between 35 and 44 years old	-8.843**	-29.98	1.636*	-9.751***	12.87***	-7.010
	(-2.330)	(-1.465)	(1.829)	(-2.615)	(5.601)	(-0.710)
Between 45 and 55 years old	1.648	7.921	6.310***	12.93***	9.524***	12.86
	(0.339)	(0.358)	(5.338)	(3.088)	(3.299)	(1.244)
With primary schooling (1 to 5 years)	-8.619	81.59*	3.045**	5.202	-1.028	9.794
	(-1.080)	(1.771)	(2.166)	(0.629)	(-0.505)	(1.034)
With Secondary 1 schooling (6 to 10 years)	-13.13*	-49.94	0.419	-8.622	-4.433**	-11.65
	(-1.921)	(-1.254)	(0.341)	(-1.161)	(-2.321)	(-1.319)

With Secondary 2 schooling (11 to 13 years)	−3.348 (−0.478)	−44.99 (−1.132)	2.439* (1.853)	−11.28 (−1.488)	10.15*** (3.007)	−73.00*** (−5.195)
With university schooling (14 years and over)	−7.016 (−0.672)	−41.40 (−0.860)	−1.505 (−0.505)	−25.15** (−2.363)	7.844 (0.318)	446.0*** (12.22)
Area of per capita owned land (ha)					−158.0 (−0.965)	−380.5 (−1.513)
Paddy area per capita (ha)	87.79*** (10.81)	345.8*** (4.257)	28.51*** (16.06)	161.9*** (16.76)		
Upland area per capita (ha)	61.77*** (20.51)	175.6*** (7.283)	17.45*** (18.88)	125.6*** (17.49)	−5.029* (−1.715)	220.8** (2.080)
Dummy for electricity (1 = yes)	−3.055 (−1.420)	−40.95** (−2.165)	−2.488*** (−4.050)	−9.504*** (−4.016)	10.27*** (3.280)	−0.848 (−0.172)
Dummy for pipe-borne water (1 = yes)	−5.338** (−2.167)	−23.59** (−2.037)	−9.702*** (−3.672)	−22.38*** (−9.422)		31.93*** (−3.340)
Number of observations	5,889	3,715	10,416	10,490	1,185	1,582
Number of uncensored observations	1,397	427	8,457	4,706	1,144	1,140

*Significant at 10% level. **Significant at 5% level. ***Significant at 1% level.

Notes: z-statistics are in parentheses. Coefficients and z-statistics of district dummies are not reported in this table to save on space. The full set of regressions is available from the authors upon request.

of per capita farm income function; and Table 7.5, those of per capita nonfarm income function. To save on space, we decided not to include the coefficients and *t*-values (or *z*-values) of the district dummies.

Determinants of monthly PCI

A number of important observations can be made from Table 7.3. First, the coefficients of the proportion of working-age members were significant in 1990 and became significantly larger in 2006 in all sectors. The coefficient was largest in the estate sector in 1990, indicating that the estate sector provided relatively ample employment opportunities, particularly in the 1990s. In 2006, the proportion of working-age members had the largest coefficient in the urban sector, indicating that employment opportunities abounded in this sector. Second, the coefficients of the female head dummy and the proportion of female working-age members were generally insignificant. Yet, the negative and significant coefficients of the female head dummy in the urban sector in 1990 may indicate the presence of gender discrimination in the early years.[5] Third, the coefficients of the age composition variables were, in general, either insignificant or weakly significant, which indicates that age is not a major determinant of household income. Fourth, while the coefficients of working-age members who completed primary and Secondary 1 schooling were generally insignificant or sometimes even negative and significant, almost all the coefficients of Secondary 2 schooling and university were positive and significant. Furthermore, the coefficients were similar across the three sectors, except for university education in 2006. More important was the significant difference in the coefficients of university education between the urban and rural sectors in 2006. This indicates not only the increasing importance of higher education in the labor markets but also the increasing segmentation of the urban labor market for university graduates compared with that in the rural labor market. Fifth, the ownership of land, particularly paddy land, conferred significantly higher income in the urban and rural sectors. The coefficients of land variables in the urban sector were larger, presumably because there are absentee landowners residing in urban areas who own highly productive land in rural areas. Sixth, and finally, the coefficients of dummy variables showing access to electricity and pipe-borne water were found to be positive and significant across the three sectors, which indicates that access to electricity and water is almost equally conducive to increasing total income over time and across the sectors. Electricity and pipe-borne water are time-saving devices at home that enable women and young girls to save time on household chores and allocate this time to the labor market. They are also critically important infrastructure for many nonfarm businesses.

Determinants of per capita farm and nonfarm income

The coefficients of the proportion of working-age members were positive, significant, and increased over time in the farm income function in the rural sector

(Table 7.4), suggesting that additional household workers are engaged in farming in the rural sector. As may be expected, this was negative and significant in the farm income function in the urban sector in 1990. An interesting case is the estate sector: the coefficient of the proportion of working-age members was positive, large, and significant in 1990, but it declined significantly in 2006. These findings imply that the labor absorption capacity of the plantation sector was large but has declined over time, indicating the decreasing importance of the estate sector in providing jobs.

The effects of the proportion of working-age members on nonfarm income were markedly different (Table 7.5). First, the coefficients were far larger in the nonfarm income function than in the farm income function in the rural sector, showing greater employment opportunities in the nonfarm sector than in the farm sector. Second, the coefficients were significantly larger in the urban than in the rural sector (Table 7.5), which confirms the larger nonfarm employment opportunities in the former than in the latter. Third, the coefficients were not significant in the estate sector in 1990 but became positive and significant in 2006, which implies that the labor force in the estate sector is allocated increasingly to the nonfarm sector.

The effects of female head of household and the proportion of female working-age members were generally negative, but the sectoral differences tended to be small in both the farm and nonfarm income functions. As far as the rural sector is concerned, household members who are between 45 and 55 years old tend to be engaged in farming, judging from the significant coefficients of the proportion of this age class of members. The effects of working-age members between 25 and 34 years old on nonfarm income were contrasting among the three sectors: in both the rural and urban sectors, the effects were positive and increasing; in the estate sector, the effects were positive and significant only in 2006. It is also noticeable that workers between 45 and 55 years old worked actively in the nonfarm sector in urban areas. These results indicate that relatively young workers are more actively engaged in nonfarm jobs in the rural sector, both young and old workers are engaged in nonfarm jobs in the urban sector, and there is an emerging trend among young workers in the estate sector to move to the nonfarm sector. Perhaps, young workers in the estate sector tend to migrate to urban and rural areas and send remittances back home, as the proportion of other income, including remittances in the estate, rose from 12 percent in 1990 to 19 percent in 2006. These findings correspond to the recent development of the nonfarm sector in the rural area, its predominance in the urban area, and its slow development in the estate area.

In the farm income function in the rural sector (Table 7.4), primary schooling had a positive and significant effect in 1990, whereas the Secondary 1 and Secondary 2 schooling levels had no significant effects in both 1990 and 2006. Thus, schooling generally does not significantly contribute to farm management efficiency, as is found in many other Asian countries (Chapters 2–5; Otsuka *et al.* 2009), which is supportive of Hypothesis 1. Another interesting finding is the positive and highly significant effect of university education on farm

Table 7.5 Determinants of household per capita nonfarm income in Sri Lanka, 1990–2006 (tobit)

	Urban		Rural		Estate	
	1990	2006	1990	2006	1990	2006
Constant	-13.77*	-88.55***	-41.08***	-120.2***	-10.58	-60.22***
	(-1.859)	(-3.048)	(-11.07)	(-10.42)	(-0.717)	(-3.282)
Proportion of working-age members	67.26***	152.8***	41.83***	95.78***	17.56	67.62***
	(17.97)	(12.54)	(18.10)	(18.94)	(1.432)	(5.783)
Dummy for female head (1 = yes)	-17.12***	-30.02***	-3.347***	-22.29***	16.26**	-2.114
	(-9.916)	(-5.356)	(-2.970)	(-9.227)	(2.480)	(-0.339)
Proportion of working-age members						
Female	-31.52***	-72.82***	-19.01***	-46.69***	-36.64***	-50.97***
	(-10.21)	(-7.291)	(-9.964)	(-11.65)	(-3.293)	(-5.297)
Between 25 and 34 years old	27.17***	75.20***	16.73***	38.29***	-0.831	36.18***
	(9.926)	(7.787)	(10.12)	(9.889)	(-0.0857)	(3.978)
Between 35 and 44 years old	29.34***	64.58***	19.24***	42.97***	-16.03	23.06**
	(10.02)	(6.435)	(10.80)	(10.58)	(-1.567)	(2.245)
Between 45 and 55 years old	23.95***	80.98***	10.18***	29.02***	6.369	10.29
	(6.197)	(7.085)	(4.224)	(6.222)	(0.513)	(0.929)
With primary schooling (1 to 5 years)	-7.118	1.245	5.846*	11.95	-7.212	2.058
	(-1.101)	(0.0459)	(1.923)	(1.137)	(0.766)	(0.185)
With Secondary 1 schooling (6 to 10 years)	-3.339	37.86*	14.74***	51.65***	7.556	41.94***
	(-0.607)	(1.665)	(5.552)	(5.479)	(0.923)	(4.181)

	(1)	(2)	(3)	(4)	(5)	(6)
With Secondary 2 schooling (11 to 13 years)	22.18***	106.1***	40.73***	113.7***	32.30**	156.6***
	(3.955)	(4.671)	(14.62)	(11.92)	(2.526)	(11.95)
With university schooling (14 years and over)	116.7***	337.0***	130.1***	276.7***	99.29	391.3***
	(14.42)	(12.82)	(23.89)	(23.29)	(1.316)	(11.19)
Area of per capita owned land (ha)						
Paddy area per capita (ha)	-5.400	169.8***	-19.17***	-37.57***	522.6	16.90
	(-0.558)	(2.693)	(-5.104)	(2.980)	(1.114)	(0.0833)
Upland area per capita (ha)	-3.695	-0.824	-3.350*	-53.47***	8.045	386.0***
	(-1.086)	(0.0410)	(-1.762)	(-5.207)	(1.003)	(3.894)
Dummy for electricity (1 = yes)	9.121***	12.55	19.50***	22.74***	24.17**	7.659
	(5.523)	(1.161)	(17.15)	(8.192)	(2.132)	(1.466)
Dummy for pipe-borne water (1 = yes)	10.86***	5.504	30.03***	14.05***		29.40***
	(6.127)	(0.900)	(6.812)	(5.928)		(3.304)
Number of observations	5,889	3,715	10,416	10,490	1,185	1,582
Number of uncensored observations	5,148	3,276	6,110	7,865	169	786

*Significant at 10% level. **Significant at 5% level. ***Significant at 1% level.

Notes: z-statistics are in parentheses. Coefficients and z-statistics of district dummies are not reported in this table to save on space.

income in the estate sector in 2006, which indicates that a handful of university graduates are employed on plantations as administrative workers.

The effects of schooling on nonfarm income were dramatically different from those on farm income (Table 7.5). First, in the rural sector, the effect of Secondary 1 schooling was positive and significant in 1990; the effect of Secondary 2 schooling was positive, larger, and increasing; and the effect of university education was still larger and increasing, attesting to the increasing importance of higher education in securing appropriate nonfarm jobs. Second, in the urban sector, compared with the rural sector, schooling did not necessarily lead to higher nonfarm income. This may reflect the integration in the rural and urban markets of highly educated labor. Third, in the estate sector, the coefficients of schooling variables became positive and significant in 2006, suggesting that demand for educated labor tends to increase over time in the nonfarm sector of the plantation areas. Overall, these results are consistent with Hypothesis 1. As may be expected, ownership of both paddy land and upland had, in general, had positive effects on farm income in both the rural and urban sectors (Table 7.4). Rich people in the urban sector leased their land to poor rural farmers and received rent income.

More important for our purposes are the findings that, in the urban and rural sectors, access to electricity and pipe-borne water had negative and significant effects on farm income (Table 7.4) but positive and significant effects on nonfarm income (Table 7.5). These results confirm Hypothesis 6 on the effects of infrastructure on the development of nonfarm sectors. Yet, insignificant coefficients of electricity in the nonfarm income function in the estate sector in 2006 (Table 7.5) may reveal difficulties in developing the nonfarm sectors by simply investing in electrification.[6] Recall that these infrastructure variables were significant in the monthly PCI function in the estate sector reported in Table 7.3. Thus, it may well be that the development of infrastructure in the estate sector stimulates remittances and transfers from household members who work outside the estate sector. Overall, since the improvement of infrastructure significantly increases nonfarm income and since nonfarm income is the major source of income growth, we can reasonably presume that the expansion of infrastructure is one major underlying driver of household income growth.

Decomposition of sectoral income gaps

The decomposition technique introduced by Blinder (1973) and Oaxaca (1973) is widely used to examine factors that affect differences in the mean outcome between groups (e.g., wage gaps by gender and race). One form of the Blinder–Oaxaca decomposition formula to look at differences in income between two groups, as proposed by Reimers (1983), can be written as:

$$\hat{R} = (\bar{X}_A - \bar{X}_B)'[0.5(\bar{\beta}_A + \bar{\beta}_B)] + [0.5(\bar{X}_A + \bar{X}_B)]'(\bar{\beta}_A - \bar{\beta}_B), \qquad (2)$$

where $\hat{R}$ represents the difference in per capita income between Groups A and B; $\bar{X}_A$ and $\bar{X}_B$ are group means of determinants of income; and $\bar{\beta}_A$ and $\bar{\beta}_B$ are vectors of estimated coefficients, which can be derived from the estimated regression function reported in Table 7.3. The first term represents the difference in income due to the differences in endowment, whereas the second term captures the difference in income due to differences in returns to endowment. For ease of interpretation, we analyzed the positive difference in income, meaning that we compared urban income with rural income and rural income with estate income.[7] Tables 7.6 and 7.7 summarize the results of the decomposition analysis of differences in PCI between the pair of sectors in 1990 and 2006, respectively.

Table 7.6 Decomposition of differences in per capita income between sectors in Sri Lanka, 1990

	Urban versus rural		*Rural versus estate*	
	Difference in per capita income	*%*	*Difference in per capita income*	*%*
Due to differences in endowment	17.44	79	12.42	220
Working-age members	0.83	4	−0.14	−2
Female head of household	−0.09	0	0.03	0
Female members	−0.01	0	−0.05	−1
Age groups	0.08	0	−0.16	−3
School levels	6.88	31	4.85	86
Infrastructure	14.76	66	4.30	76
Paddy land	−2.03	−9	2.84	50
Upland	−2.98	−13	0.75	13
Due to differences in returns to endowment	4.77	21	−6.79	−120
Working-age members	9.71	44	−10.66	−189
Female head of household	−2.18	−10	0.22	4
Female members	0.35	2	0.57	10
Age groups	3.85	17	−0.44	−8
School levels	−7.74	−35	4.96	88
Infrastructure	−3.88	−17	−1.30	−23
Paddy land	1.79	8	−1.68	−30
Upland	2.87	13	1.54	27
Total difference in per capita income (US$ purchasing power parity in 2005)	22.21	100	5.64	100

Notes: Overall income differences in this table do not tally with actual differences in per capita income because differences in intercepts and district dummies are not taken into account. Numbers may not reflect exact totals because of rounding.

Table 7.7 Decomposition of differences in per capita income between sectors in Sri Lanka, 2006

	Urban versus rural		Rural versus estate	
	Difference in per capita income	%	Difference in per capita income	%
Due to differences in endowments	19.38	27	4.67	74
Working-age members	−1.23	−2	0.88	2
Female head of household	−0.16	0	0.04	0
Female members	−0.01	0	−0.33	−1
Age groups	0.02	0	0.09	0
School levels	16.31	23	34.33	62
Infrastructure	11.11	15	5.33	10
Paddy land	−5.34	−7	−5.09	−9
Upland	−1.33	−2	5.41	10
Due to differences in returns to endowment	52.93	73	14.46	26
Working-age members	22.66	31	−4.07	−7
Female head of household	−3.21	−4	−1.25	−2
Female members	−.064	−1	8.86	16
Age groups	−0.73	−1	3.52	6
School levels	27.00	37	−5.63	−10
Infrastructure	4.19	6	8.22	15
Paddy land	1.90	3	10.10	18
Upland	1.76	2	−5.30	−10
Total difference in per capita income (US$ purchasing power parity in 2005)	72.31	100	55.13	100

Notes: Overall income differences in this table do not tally with actual differences in per capita income because differences in intercepts and district dummies are not taken into account. Numbers may not reflect exact totals because of rounding.

According to Table 7.6, a major difference in PCI between the urban and rural sectors in 1990 was accounted for by the difference in the endowment of resources. Particularly important were the higher schooling levels of urban workers and the more developed infrastructure in the urban sector. Because of large employment opportunities in the urban sector, the higher returns that accrue to working-age household members in the urban sector also substantially contributed to the urban–rural income gap. The difference in PCI between the rural and estate sectors was small in 1990 (see the last line in Table 7.6). Yet, it is interesting to find that while higher schooling levels, more developed infrastructure, and larger paddy land ownership in the rural sector contributed to higher income in that sector, the higher returns to endowment of working-age household members – which could well be classified as unskilled labor – in the estate sector almost offset the aforementioned effects. In other words, the estate sector attracted unskilled workers in 1990, as it offered ample employment opportunities for them.

The results of decomposition analysis were substantially different for 2006 (Table 7.7). Unlike the results shown in Table 7.6, differences in endowment and differences in returns to endowment explain the income gap between the urban and rural sectors. In particular, the contributions of the differences in returns to the number of working-age members and educated workers to the income gap have become larger. Thus, although the nonfarm sectors have developed significantly in the rural sector, the returns to labor in general and the returns to educated labor in particular have become larger in the urban sector than in the rural sector. As to the comparison between the rural and estate sectors, it is remarkable that the differences in endowment levels and the differences in returns to endowment explained the income gap. While the contributions of the differences in infrastructure and land ownership declined, those of the differences in schooling remained important. Significantly changed was the effect of the number of working-age members: the advantage of the estate sector in the provision of employment opportunities had disappeared in 2006, when working-age members in the rural sector could find nonfarm jobs more easily than before. Also important to mention are the returns to infrastructure being higher in the rural sector than in the urban sector and higher in the estate sector than in the rural sector, attesting to the greater importance of infrastructure in increasing income in more remote areas.

Overall, the results of the decomposition analysis indicate that the importance of differences in the level of endowments in accounting for the income gap among sectors has declined. On the other hand, differences in returns to both "quantity" and "quality" of human capital have become critical contributors to sectoral income gaps. Such changes undoubtedly reflect the increasing development of nonfarm labor markets, particularly in the urban sector and, to a lesser extent, in the rural sector as well.

Concluding remarks

This study analyzed how changing sources of household income lead to income growth and a reduction in poverty. A unique feature of the Sri Lankan economy is the presence of the estate sector in addition to the urban and rural sectors. An important observation is that poverty is still more prevalent, particularly in the estate sector than in the other sectors, even though it has been declining steadily. In this study, we found that households in the rural sector were as poor as those in the estate sector in 1990 but, in subsequent periods, the income of rural households grew much faster than did that of estate households, thereby creating a significant income gap between the rural and estate sectors. A major proximate cause of this is the increasing importance of nonfarm income in the rural sector. According to our decomposition analysis of the income gap, higher schooling levels and more ample nonfarm employment opportunities in the rural sector are primarily responsible for the emerging income gap between the two sectors. Within the estate sector, only a limited number of educated workers can find lucrative jobs in the nonfarm sector, indicating the difficulty for poor households to enter the nonfarm sector. Thus, we may conclude that, in order to reduce poverty and income inequality between the rural and estate sectors, it is imperative to invest in schooling and develop the nonfarm sectors so as to increase the supply of educated labor and the demand for labor (even uneducated workers). Since the development of the nonfarm sector is affected by infrastructure, there is a need to invest in infrastructure, particularly in electricity, which induces the development of small industries and service sectors.

This conclusion is further reinforced by the comparison of income between the urban and rural sectors. Although the income of rural households increased faster than did that of urban households, owing to the rapidly increasing nonfarm income in the rural sector, the income of the former still lags behind that of the latter because of lower schooling levels, lower returns to an educated labor force, and less favorable employment opportunities in addition to less developed infrastructure. Thus, further investments in schooling and infrastructure, as well as the development of the nonfarm sectors, are required for the rural sector to catch up with the urban sector in terms of the standard of living.

It is important to recall that infrastructure is an important determinant of monthly PCI all three sectors in Sri Lanka. This suggests that, to improve the standard of living, it is critically important for the government to invest in infrastructure. It makes sense to invest in schooling, as it contributes to the development of nonfarm sectors by supplying a high-quality labor force to these growing segments. To reduce poverty and sectoral income inequality, investments in both schooling and infrastructure seem to be of utmost importance, as demonstrated in the case of Sri Lanka.

Acknowledgment

The authors would like to thank the Department of Census and Statistics of Sri Lanka for providing the data set. Some parts of this chapter are drawn from Kumanayake *et al.* (2014) with permission from John Wiley & Sons under license number 3550600823190.

Notes

1 Descriptive tables show data in 1990, 1995, and 2006 only for simplicity.
2 Note that land rent received by land-owning households is counted as farming income.
3 We assume that the number of working-age members is an important determinant of household income. Since the dependent variable is per capita income, we used the proportion of working-age members as an explanatory variable.

4 The use of an instrumental variable in correcting for the endogeneity of infrastructure is becoming the norm (Duflo and Pande 2007). Yet, in Sri Lanka, identification of appropriate instruments remains a formidable task, most importantly because of the inadequacy of regional geographical data.

5 It is also possible that female heads of relatively rich urban households preferred not to work.

6 Due to the absence of appropriate data, we cannot assess the impact of improving the road network in the estate sector, which may be a more important infrastructure in this sector.

7 Needless to say, if we make a comparison of two pairs, the comparison of another pair is redundant. Thus, we do not show the comparison between the urban and estate sectors.

8 Infrastructure, household income, and children's schooling in rural Bangladesh

Introduction

The international community has recognized the importance of education in the Millennium Development Goals (MDGs) set forth by the United Nations. Goal 2 of the MDGs (MDG2), "universal primary education," aims to "ensure that, by 2015, children everywhere, boys and girls alike, will be able to complete a full course of primary schooling." Goal 3 of the MDGs (MDG3), "promote gender equality and empower women," aims to "eliminate gender disparity in primary and secondary education, preferably by 2005, and in all levels of education no later than 2015."

The United Nations (2012) reported that many more children have been enrolled in primary school since 2000 and that girls have benefited the most. There is optimism that, if the current trend continues, the world will meet MDG2 (United Nations 2013). As to progress in achieving MDG3, the ratio between the enrollment rate of girls and that of boys in primary school in developing countries has reached 97, an acceptable measure for parity. The World Bank (2011d, p. 9) has reported that, in more than a third of developing countries, girls significantly outnumber boys in secondary education and, in more recent years, women's tertiary school enrollment has risen sevenfold (fourfold for men) since 1970. Contrary to historical patterns, more young women than men are now attending tertiary school in 60 developing countries (World Bank 2011d).

In this chapter, we examine the case of Bangladesh, a country in South Asia where, historically, girls have lower rates of school participation than boys, and where, surprisingly in more recent years, girls have become better off (World Bank 2011a). Using a rare nationally representative panel data set, our purpose is to investigate the individual-, household-, and community-level factors that affect the probability that a child will be enrolled in school in rural Bangladesh. We focus on the gender of the child at the individual level, parental education and household income at the household level, and infrastructure at the community level.

This paper has five remaining sections. The second section briefly presents the state of children's schooling in Bangladesh, whereas the third section examines the study villages, households, and child schooling. The fourth section describes the methodology, and the fifth section identifies the determinants of household income and child schooling. Finally, the sixth section provides the summary and conclusions.

Children's schooling in Bangladesh

The educational structure in Bangladesh is divided into the primary level (commonly between ages 6 and 10), the secondary level (commonly between ages 11 and 17), and the tertiary level (commonly between ages 18 and 21).[1] Table 8.1 shows the school enrollment rates of girls and boys in primary, secondary, and tertiary schools from 1985 to 2009. There is a consistent trend of girls' enrollment rates rising in all school levels. In the primary level, the girls' enrollment rate became even higher compared with that of boys in 2009 (103.9 percent versus 98.6 percent) and in the secondary level as well (50.1 percent versus 46.3 percent). The tertiary school enrollment rate has remained significantly below 20 percent for both girls and boys, and boys have consistently been better off since 1985.

The Bangladeshi pattern is quite different from that of the rest of South Asia, where boys' enrollment rates in all levels of schooling were consistently higher than girls' from 1985 to 2009. Yet, even in South Asia, girls are quickly catching up with boys: the ratio of girls' to boys' enrollment in primary school rose from 0.71 to 0.94 from 1985 to 2007; in secondary school, it was from 0.53 to 0.85; and in tertiary school, from 0.44 to 0.68. Briefly, evidence shows that parents in South Asia have started investing relatively equally in the schooling of their female and male children, whereas in Bangladesh, a clear pro-girl bias in primary and secondary schooling has emerged in more recent years.

Table 8.1 School enrollment rates in Bangladesh, 1985–2009

Gender	1985	1990	2000	2009
	Gross primary school enrollment (%)			
Male	79.5	87.2	N/A[a]	98.6
Female	55.1	73.7	N/A	103.9
	Gross secondary school enrollment (%)			
Male	28.3	26.6	N/A	46.3
Female	11.5	13.6	N/A	50.1
	Gross tertiary school enrollment (%)			
Male	7.8	6.7	7.2	13.1
Female	2.0	1.3	3.6	7.8

a N/A = not available.

Source: World Bank (2013a).

Study villages, households, and children's schooling

Villages and survey design

The Bangladesh data set contains information from 1,239 randomly selected households in 1988; 1,888 households in 2000; and 2,010 households in 2008 in 62 villages from 57 out of 64 districts in the country (Table 8.2).[2] Data in 1988 and 2000 were collected by the International Rice Research Institute (IRRI), while the 2008 data were collected by BRAC. All these surveys were undertaken under the leadership of Mahabub Hossain.

The data set consists of panel households that were chosen using a multistage random sampling method (Hossain and Bayes 2009). In the first stage, 64 unions were randomly selected from the list of all unions in the country. In the second stage, one village was selected from each union that best represented the union with regard to the landholding size and the literacy rate. A census of all households was undertaken in the selected villages in order to stratify the households based on landownership and land tenure. Finally, 20 households were chosen from each village representing households in each stratum on the basis of landownership and land tenure. The size of the sample rose from 20 households from each village in 1988 to 30 or 31 in 2000 and, over time, a few new households were included to replace people who migrated to other places.

Households and children

We had a total of 2,337 children in 1988; 3,378 in 2000; and 2,807 in 2008 (Table 8.2). These are children whose ages were between 6 and 22 years old at the time of the survey. There were a lower number of female children currently living in the households, possibly because of early marriage. Bangladeshi females, upon marriage, commonly move out of their original households to live with their husbands in their localities.

Table 8.3 gives a description of the sample households. Average household size declined from 6.14 members in 1988 to 4.94 members in 2008.

Table 8.2 Number of sample households and children in sample villages in Bangladesh, 1988–2008

Description	1988	2000	2008
Number of households	1,239	1,888	2,010
Number of children of school age[a]			
Male	1,338	2,016	1,591
Female	999	1,362	1,216
Total	2,337	3,378	2,807

a   Between 6 and 22 years old.

Table 8.3 Characteristics of sample households in Bangladesh, 1988–2008

Characteristic	1988	2000	2008
Household size	6.14	5.68	4.94
Number of household members of working age[a]	3.20	3.42	3.04
Proportion of working-age members			
Gender			
Female	49	48	54
Age			
Between 15 and 25 years old	39	33	31
Between 26 and 35 years old	31	30	27
Between 36 and 45 years old	17	22	21
Between 46 and 60 years old	13	15	21
Schooling			
With no schooling	59	40	35
With primary schooling	13	16	13
With junior high school	16	23	29
With secondary schooling	8	14	16
With tertiary schooling	4	7	7
Average farm size (ha)	0.74	0.67	0.60
Farmers using modern rice varieties (%)	44	48	47
Farmers with irrigation facilities (%)	30	45	46
Households with electricity (%)	29	40	39

a Between 15 and 60 years old.

Accordingly, the number of working-age members between 15 and 60 years old declined from 3.20 to 3.04 during the same period. Hossain and Bayes (2009, p. 28) attributed the decline in household size to the rise in education of heads of households; at the same time, the government has been implementing family planning programs in the past three decades that aim to lower the birth rate to 2.2. Indeed, there has been an improvement in the educational attainment of working-age members who are 16 years old and above. The proportion of working-age members who have never gone to a formal school declined from 59 percent in 1988 to 35 percent in 2008, whereas the proportion of those who attended tertiary school rose from 4 percent to 7 percent during the same period. Also, the average years in school completed by both male and female heads of households rose, and the increase was higher for female heads of households so that the gender gap in schooling in favor of male heads of households became smaller.

The average farm size declined from 0.74 ha in 1988 to 0.60 ha in 2008. This means that income from agriculture alone (from rice farming in particular) may have not been enough to support a household of about five members in 2008. Only about half of the farming households used modern rice varieties, and only about half had irrigation facilities, notwithstanding the clear expansion of irrigation (the proportion of rice farms with irrigation rose from 30 percent in 1988 to 46 percent in 2008). This is mainly because of the increasing popularity of shallow tube wells and power pumps that are made available cheaply from China. There was an expansion in electricity coverage, as shown by the increase in the proportion of households with access to electricity (from 29 percent in 1988 to 39 percent in 2008). Electricity is particularly important in the development of small-scale enterprises that create jobs for both women and men and reduce women's time spent on domestic duties.

Sources of household income

Households had two major sources of income (Table 8.4): (1) farm income consisting of crop cultivation (mainly rice), wage labor, and noncrop production and (2) nonfarm income consisting of income from wage employment and self-employment income from business and trade, services, industry, transport, and construction, as well as remittances. Household consumption of self-produced crops, livestock, forestry, and fishery products was imputed using prevailing market prices and then included in the respective income component.

Farm income (particularly crop production) was by far the most important source in 1988, while its importance declined over time as its share of total income declined from 58 percent in 1988 to 43 percent in 2008. Concomitantly, the share of nonfarm income rose from 42 percent to 57 percent. Quite visibly, the share of remittances rose from 5 percent in 1988 to 22 percent in 2008, making this income source as important as crop cultivation. Part of these

Table 8.4 Sources of household income in Bangladesh, 1988–2008

Source	1988	2000	2008
	In international dollars in 2000		
Farm income	962 (58)	1,307 (46)	1,448 (43)
Crop cultivation	544	684	869
Wage labor	253	142	216
Noncrop production	165	481	362
Nonfarm income	688 (42)[a]	1,543 (54)	1,885 (57)
Wages and self-employment[b]	597	1,212	1,128
Remittances and others	91	331	757
Total household income[b]	1,650 (100)	2,850 (100)	3,334 (100)

a Includes income from trade, business, services, and informal and formal wage employment.

Note: Numbers in parentheses are percentages.

remittances came from young girls working in garment factories in Dhaka. In brief, we can see a clear pattern of the shift in income-earning opportunities of rural Bangladeshi households away from crop cultivation to nonfarm activities.

Household income approximately doubled from US$ purchasing power parity (PPP) 1,650 in 1988 to US$ PPP 3,334 in 2008 (Table 8.4) with the shift of the household income structure away from farm to nonfarm sources. Since household income is a major source of funds for children's schooling (Estudillo *et al.* 2009), we can reasonably expect that investments in children's schooling have increased alongside the rise in household income. And with the rising importance of nonfarm income, schooling investments will become more profitable because returns to schooling are bound to be higher in the formal nonfarm sector, where skills obtained from formal schooling are valuable (Otsuka *et al.* 2009). We will examine in the next section to what extent income from farm and nonfarm sources has affected children's school attendance.

Schooling

Completed years in school of adult individuals, both females and males between 22 and 55 years old, have increased over time (Table 8.5). The difference in

Table 8.5 Schooling of adult population and enrollment in school of children in sample villages in Bangladesh, 1988–2008

Schooling and enrollment	1988	2000	2008
Average schooling of adult population[a]			
Male	4.1	5.0	5.2
Female	1.6	2.9	4.1
Difference (male–female)	2.5*	2.1*	1.1*
Primary school enrollment (%)[b]			
Male	60	89	91
Female	54	89	94
Secondary school enrollment (%)[c]			
Male	59	59	73
Female	50	51	83
Tertiary school enrollment (%)[d]			
Male	27	27	27
Female	19	19	38

a   Between 22 and 55 years old at the time of the survey.
b   Between 6 and 10 years old at the time of the survey.
c   Between 11 and 17 years old at the time of the survey.
d   Between 18 and 22 years old at the time of the survey.
*Significant at 10% level.

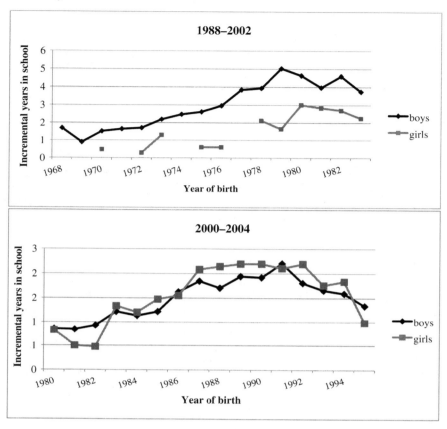

Figure 8.1 Incremental years in school of children of school age in sample villages in Bangladesh, 1988–2008

completed years in school in favor of adult males (which was statistically significant at conventional levels) declined from 2.5 in 1988 to 1.1 in 2008. According to Figure 8.1, girls' schooling progression (defined as the difference in completed years in school of the same child between two survey years) surpassed that of boys in 2000–4, and such a pattern became more evident in later years, indicating a stronger preference for parents to keep their girls in school longer than ever.

Table 8.5 shows that school enrollment rates were generally low and that the enrollment rates of girls were lower compared with boys in 1988 at all levels. Enrollment rates at all levels rose between 1988 and 2008, and enrollment rates of girls in secondary and tertiary school had become substantially higher relative to those of boys in 2008 (73 percent for boys, 83 percent for girls in secondary school; 27 percent for boys, 38 percent for girls in tertiary school). Hence, these data suggest that priority in education seems to have been recently conferred on daughters. The major question is: what factors drive the changes in schooling in favor of girls?

Methodology

We used regression models to identify the determinants of the probability that a child is in school.

Children who are the sons and daughters of household heads were between 6 and 22 years old at the time of the survey. We used a two-stage procedure: (1) ordinary least squares (OLS) regression of household farm and nonfarm income and (2) probit regression that a child is currently in school (1 = yes, 0 = no), in which their predicted values were used as explanatory variables of the probability that a child is in school.

The first-stage income function (ordinary least squares)

We would like to explore the determinants of farm and nonfarm incomes, as they are the main sources of school investment (Estudillo *et al.* 2009). The model specification for both farm and nonfarm income is as follows:

$$Y = \beta_0 + \Sigma \beta_i X_i + \varepsilon, \tag{1}$$

where Y = household income (farm or nonfarm), the βs are regression coefficients, and the X_i are explanatory variables such as (1) household demographic characteristics, including number of working-age household members and their characteristics in terms of (a) gender, (b) age, and (c) schooling; (2) farm characteristics in terms of farm size and proportion of area irrigated; and (3) infrastructure as represented by access to electricity.

In terms of age, we divided working-age members into four groups: (1) between 15 and 25 years old, (2) between 26 and 35 years old, (3) between 36 and 45 years old, and (4) between 46 and 60 years old. In terms of schooling, we grouped working-age members as follows: (1) with no schooling, (2) completed 1–4 years of schooling (primary school), (3) completed 5–8 years of schooling (junior schooling), (4) completed 9–10 years of schooling (secondary schooling), and (5) completed over 10 years of schooling (tertiary schooling).

The second stage: probability of being in school (probit)

The probability of being in school (P) has a value of unity if the child is currently a student and zero otherwise.

$$P = \alpha_0 + \Sigma \alpha_1 \text{ (child characteristics)} + \Sigma \alpha_2 \text{ (parents'}$$
$$\text{characteristics)} + \Sigma \alpha_3 \text{ (household income)} + \Sigma \alpha_4 \text{ (electricity)} + e_2. \tag{2}$$

Child characteristics include (1) the child's age at the time of the survey and (2) female dummy (1 = yes). Parents' characteristics include completed years in school of father and mother. Household income includes (1) farm income and (2) nonfarm income. Before examining the regression results, we discuss the hypothesized impacts of the explanatory variables, including age, gender, parents' education, household farm and nonfarm income, and availability of electricity.

The probability of being in school declines with age because free public primary school is extensive in rural Bangladesh, whereas secondary and tertiary schools are still limited and parents have to pay out-of-pocket costs for children's schooling, which remains unaffordable to a large majority of rural Bangladeshi households. Also, the opportunity cost of attending schools increases with age. We hypothesized that girls have a lower probability of being enrolled in school in earlier years, while this gender bias has been reversed in favor of girls in later years. As will be discussed later, this may be explained partly by the government schooling policies in favor of girls. Another factor, which may be more important, is increasing nonfarm work opportunities for women, headed by the development of the garment industry and created by the general development of the whole economy, which must have increased the rates of return to schooling, particularly for women. This means that the female dummy has a negative coefficient in earlier years and a positive coefficient in later years.

Fathers' and mothers' completed years in school represent the stock of human capital brought by parents to the households, and thus we expect these variables to exert a non-negative impact on children's schooling (Deolalikar 1993; Parish and Willis 1993).

Since household income could play a significant role in investment in children's schooling, we expect that the coefficient of household income will be positive. Indeed, a large number of studies have confirmed that income elasticity of schooling is positive in many developing countries (Behrman and Knowles 1999). According to Otsuka *et al.* (2009), many rural households in Asia were able to invest in children's schooling because of the rise in farm income through the adoption of modern rice technology and the gradual diversification of income sources away from farm to nonfarm activities. Increased participation in nonfarm employment has been more pronounced among the more educated children, whose education is facilitated by an increase in farm income brought about by modern rice technology. Thus, we expect that farm income will have a positive and significant impact on children's school enrollment in earlier years. Although nonfarm income is also expected to affect the investment in schooling of children positively, its effect may be less than that of farm income to the extent that nonfarm income is earned by children who want to support the livelihood of their parents but not necessarily that of their siblings.

Electricity is a time-saving infrastructure that enables young girls to abandon housekeeping activities in favor of school attendance. At the same time, electricity promotes nonfarm economic activities where schooling funds could come from. Thus, we expect a non-negative impact of electricity on school attendance directly or indirectly through increases in nonfarm income.

Determinants of household income and children's schooling

Determinants of household income

Before we discuss the determinants of children's schooling, we briefly discuss the determinants of household farm and nonfarm income, which is the first stage of the two-stage procedure (Table 8.6). As expected, farm size and proportion of irrigated area had positive and significant impacts on farm income.

Table 8.6 Determinants of farm and nonfarm income in sample villages in Bangladesh, 1988–2008 (household level)

Variable	1988		
	Total household income	Agricultural income	Nonfarm income
Farm size	870.193***	861.091***	9.102
	(17.963)	(36.562)	(0.203)
Proportion of area irrigated	0.736	3.062***	−2.326**
	(0.589)	(5.042)	(−2.010)
Number of working members[a]	305.599***	55.538***	250.061***
	(10.693)	(3.997)	(9.444)
Proportion of working members			
Female	−181.751	−435.541***	253.790
	(−0.671)	(−3.306)	(1.011)
Between 26 and 35 years old	561.547***	181.059**	380.488**
	(3.307)	(2.193)	(2.419)
Between 36 and 45 years old	187.893	95.302	92.591
	(0.939)	(0.979)	(0.499)
Between 46 and 60 years old	−165.935	−67.295	−98.640
	(−0.666)	(−0.556)	(−0.428)
With primary schooling (1–4 years)	1.838	−95.357	97.194
	(0.010)	(−1.063)	(0.569)
With junior schooling (5–8 years)	69.680	−228.929***	298.609*
	(0.409)	(−2.761)	(1.890)
With secondary schooling (9–10 years)	592.320**	−324.126***	916.445***
	(2.312)	(−2.603)	(3.862)
With tertiary schooling (more than 10 years)	1,605.735***	−441.226**	2,046.961***
	(4.191)	(−2.369)	(5.766)
Dummy for electricity (1 = yes)	348.522***	16.678	331.844***
	(3.901)	(0.384)	(4.009)
Constant	−296.543	328.699***	−625.241***
	(−1.460)	(3.329)	(−3.322)
Number of observations	1,237	1,237	1,237
R^2	0.468	0.629	0.184

(*Continued*)

Table 8.6 (Continued)

Variable	2000		
	Total household income	Agricultural income	Nonfarm income
Farm size	1,211.896***	1,520.844***	–308.947***
	(10.361)	(26.406)	(–3.290)
Proportion of area irrigated	1.473	5.900***	–4.427***
	(0.845)	(6.872)	(–3.163)
Number of working members[a]	753.193***	120.216***	632.978***
	(15.513)	(5.029)	(16.240)
Proportion of working members			
Female	–244.357	58.770	–303.127
	(–0.489)	(0.239)	(–0.756)
Between 26 and 35 years old	1,286.534***	119.053	1,167.481***
	(3.738)	(0.703)	(4.225)
Between 36 and 45 years old	1,291.134***	335.562*	955.572***
	(3.184)	(1.681)	(2.935)
Between 46 and 60 years old	830.230*	350.215	480.015
	(1.761)	(1.509)	(1.269)
With primary schooling (1–4 years)	–146.431	–285.511*	139.080
	(–0.436)	(–1.727)	(0.516)
With junior schooling (5–8 years)	777.303***	25.693	751.611***
	(2.601)	(0.175)	(3.133)
With secondary schooling (9–10 years)	2,072.306***	416.005**	1,656.301***
	(5.693)	(2.321)	(5.668)
With tertiary schooling (more than 10 years)	2,812.247***	1,462.266***	1,349.981***
	(6.014)	(6.350)	(3.596)
Dummy for electricity (1 = yes)	1,116.355***	229.091***	887.264***
	(7.030)	(2.930)	(6.960)
Constant	–2,025.057***	–337.462	–1,687.595***
	(–4.741)	(–1.605)	(–4.922)
Number of observations	1,870	1,870	1,870
R^2	0.324	0.419	0.219
	2008		
Farm size	1,761.956***	1,388.463***	373.492***
	(19.619)	(32.017)	(4.439)
Proportion of area irrigated	–3.854**	4.212***	–8.065***
	(–2.033)	(4.601)	(–4.542)
Number of working members[a]	928.439***	145.342***	783.097***
	(16.484)	(5.344)	(14.841)

Variable	2008		
	Total household income	Agricultural income	Nonfarm income
Proportion of working members			
Female	2,108.107***	−573.513***	2,681.620***
	(5.490)	(−3.093)	(7.455)
Between 26 and 35 years old	1,023.230***	314.808**	708.422**
	(3.209)	(2.045)	(2.371)
Between 36 and 45 years old	289.174	208.071	81.103
	(0.795)	(1.184)	(0.238)
Between 46 and 60 years old	260.033	249.132	10.901
	(0.668)	(1.326)	(0.030)
With primary schooling (1–4 years)	−19.411	−122.153	102.742
	(−0.057)	(−0.747)	(0.324)
With junior schooling (5–8 years)	558.373**	−154.669	713.041***
	(2.128)	(−1.221)	(2.901)
With secondary schooling (9–10 years)	1,502.548***	−276.454*	1,779.002***
	(4.632)	(−1.765)	(5.854)
With tertiary schooling (more than 10 years)	2,652.149***	526.644**	2,125.504***
	(6.072)	(2.497)	(5.194)
Dummy for electricity (1 = yes)	913.089***	155.703**	757.386***
	(5.895)	(2.082)	(5.219)
Constant	−2,763.842***	156.369	−2,920.211***
	(−6.300)	(0.738)	(−7.106)
Number of observations	1,957	1,957	1,957
R^2	0.389	0.457	0.208

a   Refers to household members between 16 and 60 years old.
*Significant at 10% level. **Significant at 5% level. ***Significant at 1% level.

Note: Numbers in parentheses are *t*-statistics.

Irrigation increased rice yield and the number of rice crops that could be grown in a year. The coefficient of additional working-age members increased from 1988 to 2008, particularly in terms of nonfarm income. Since the number of working-age members represents the quantity of labor resources in the household, the rise in the value of its coefficient could indicate the increased availability of employment opportunities, even to unskilled workers.

One striking difference between farm and nonfarm income was in the contribution of the educated members of the households. The contribution of an educated member of the household (those with secondary and tertiary schooling) to nonfarm income was considerably higher as compared with contribution to farm income. In fact, members with secondary and tertiary schooling tended to withdraw from farm work to engage in nonfarm work (as shown by the negative coefficient of secondary and tertiary schooling in agricultural income function). Indeed, the higher the educational attainment of a household member, the higher his or her contribution to nonfarm income, which may indicate greater returns to higher education in the nonfarm sector.

The consistently positive effects of farm size on agricultural income and the generally larger effects of education on nonfarm income (compared with agricultural income) are consistent with Hypothesis 1, which focuses on the declining importance of land and the increasing importance of human capital. Also, the availability of electricity is found to have significantly positive effects on income, particularly nonfarm income. The positive and larger effects of electricity and education on nonfarm income than on agricultural income are consistent with Hypothesis 6, which argues the importance of infrastructure and education in the promotion of nonfarm sectors.

Another difference was the impact of female members in the household, which was negative and significant on farm income (except in 2000) but positive and significant on nonfarm income in 2008. This suggests that girls in 2008 contributed significantly to increase nonfarm income. It may well be that the development of the formal nonfarm sector (most importantly the garment industry) in Bangladesh creates employment opportunities for female workers. Since the garment industry is located in urban areas, these girls contribute to nonfarm income by sending remittances. As we show in Table 8.4, the amount of remittances rose by 8.3 times, and its share of total household income rose from 5 to 22 percent between 1988 and 2008, making remittances an important source of household income growth in rural Bangladesh. These observations are consistent with Hypothesis 5, which asserts the significant contribution of nonfarm sector development to income-earning opportunities for women.

Determinants of children's schooling

Table 8.7 shows the determinants of a child being enrolled in school. We have the following results, which are largely in accordance with our expectations. First, younger children were more likely to be in school compared with older ones, perhaps partly because of the free public primary school and partly because of the low opportunity cost of time. Second, there was a recent increase in preference for the schooling of girls – the coefficient of the female dummy was negative and significant in the secondary and tertiary levels in 1988 and became positive in both levels in 2000 and 2008. Since the female dummy was largely not significant in primary school, the positive coefficient in secondary and tertiary school indicates that parents prefer to keep their girls in school longer than their boys. Why this has happened will be discussed further in the next subsection. Third, both fathers' and mothers' education increased children's schooling significantly with fairly equal impact. Fourth, the consistently positive and significant coefficient of farm income suggests its important role in schooling

Table 8.7 Determinants of probability of a child being enrolled in school in sample villages in Bangladesh, 1988–2008 (probit)

Variable	1988		
	Primary	Secondary	Tertiary
Age	0.276***	-0.190***	-0.205***
	(9.903)	(-6.436)	(-3.284)
Female dummy (1 = yes)	-0.127	-0.314***	-0.404*
	(-1.596)	(-3.197)	(-1.647)
Father's education	0.053***	0.077***	0.071**
	(3.662)	(4.374)	(2.198)
Mother's education	0.092***	0.062*	0.099*
	(3.591)	(1.939)	(1.763)
Agricultural income (US$ purchasing power parity [PPP] predicted)	0.098*	0.107*	0.131
	(1.777)	(1.801)	(1.590)
Nonfarm income (US$ PPP predicted)	0.169	0.393***	0.569***
	(1.609)	(3.458)	(3.293)
Electricity (1 = yes)	0.020	-0.195*	-0.733***
	(0.201)	(-1.679)	(-3.455)
Constant	-2.453***	2.141***	2.248*
	(-10.163)	(5.262)	(1.847)
Number of observations	1,159	793	318
	2000		
Age	0.007	-0.277***	-0.188***
	(0.189)	(-11.748)	(-4.586)
Female dummy (1 = yes)	0.019	0.426***	0.286**
	(0.177)	(5.207)	(1.967)
Father's education	0.044**	0.030**	0.017
	(2.112)	(2.163)	(0.889)
Mother's education	0.066**	0.141***	0.127***
	(2.331)	(6.932)	(4.678)
Agricultural income (US$ purchasing power parity [PPP] predicted)	0.056	0.283***	0.183***
	(1.033)	(7.244)	(4.853)
Nonfarm income (US$ PPP predicted)	0.078	0.158***	0.098**
	(1.142)	(3.428)	(2.056)
Electricity (1 = yes)	-0.163	-0.035	-0.059
	(-1.338)	(-0.382)	(-0.468)
Constant	0.889***	3.244***	2.199***
	(2.644)	(10.207)	(2.744)
Number of observations	1,103	1,455	626

(Continued)

Table 8.7 (Continued)

Variable	2008		
	Primary	Secondary	Tertiary
Age	0.162***	−0.299***	−0.175***
	(3.617)	(−10.366)	(−3.864)
Female dummy (1 = yes)	0.268**	0.395***	0.139
	(2.112)	(3.963)	(0.884)
Father's education	0.026	0.021	0.066***
	(1.058)	(1.203)	(3.256)
Mother's education	0.015	0.121***	0.093***
	(0.533)	(5.295)	(3.455)
Agricultural income (US$ purchasing power parity [PPP] predicted)	0.045	0.125**	0.158***
	(0.615)	(2.486)	(2.905)
Nonfarm income (US$ PPP predicted)	−0.014	0.049	0.007
	(−0.230)	(1.152)	(0.127)
Electricity (1 = yes)	−0.081	0.062	0.013
	(−0.592)	(0.588)	(0.086)
Constant	−0.142	4.190***	1.982**
	(−0.371)	(10.361)	(2.229)
Number of observations	902	1,075	497

*Significant at 10% level. **Significant at 5% level. ***Significant at 1% level.

Note: Numbers in parentheses are *z*-statistics.

investments. However, nonfarm income seems to be emerging as another important source of schooling funds for secondary and tertiary schooling – the coefficient of nonfarm income was positive and significant in 1988 and 2000, even though it was not significant in 2008. One possible interpretation is that parents who are primarily engaged in agriculture use agricultural income to invest in schooling of their younger children but do not use nonfarm income earned primarily by their elder children in schooling investment as much as agricultural income. Fifth, and finally, electricity did not seem to have a direct impact on children's schooling, indicating that the impact of electricity is largely indirect through increasing farm and nonfarm income, which are important sources of schooling funds. This suggests that village electrification programs support livelihoods directly and induce investments in children's schooling indirectly. Overall, our results give strong statistical evidence that Bangladeshi girls have been favored in schooling investments in more recent years.

Why are girls favored?

The World Bank (2011d) argues that (1) increasing household income, (2) removing institutional constraints, or (3) increasing employment opportunities for women is sufficient to increase female participation in education. Our regression results show that, indeed, increases in household income are tied to greater children's schooling, particularly schooling of girls. Now let us examine the possible role of institutions, policies, and the labor market.

Since independence in 1971, the government of Bangladesh has made serious efforts to put more children in school and lessen the gender gap in school participation. In 1990, the government established a policy of free and compulsory primary education for all. Education reforms such as the building of new schools, the rehabilitation of old ones, and the development of new curricula and new textbooks were implemented (Schuler 2007). The country's largest and most prominent nongovernment organization, BRAC, was able to establish more than 31,000 primary schools and 16,000 pre-primary schools by 2004. Creative strategies such as flexible class hours, establishment of schools near rural homes, and involvement of parents were used by BRAC to enable more girls to go to school (Schuler 2007).

In 1993, the government started the Food for Education (FFE) Program, which was later replaced by the Cash for Education Program. Under this program, households that have primary school-age children are eligible to receive a free monthly ration of wheat (or cash) if their children are able to attend 85 percent of classes each month. By 2000, the FFE program covered about 27 percent of all primary schools in Bangladesh, and out of the 5.2 million students enrolled in schools with the FFE program, about 40 percent received their entitlements (Ahmed and del Ninno 2003). Under the FFE program, all children, regardless of gender, are treated equally, and this might have contributed to the relatively equal enrollment rates of boys and girls in primary school.

In 1994, the government introduced a policy of free education of girls in secondary schools. In 2001, the Female Stipend Program (FSP), which provides small monetary stipends and tuition subsidies for each girl attending secondary school in the rural areas, was started. The program aimed to increase (1) the enrollment rate of girls, (2) the completion rate of girls, and (3) female age at marriage (Khandker *et al.* 2003). Yet, early marriage of girls within the 13- to 16-year-old age bracket remains widely prevalent in rural Bangladesh despite a law that mandates that the minimum marrying age is 18 for girls and 21 for boys. Nonetheless, Khandker *et al.* (2003) found a significantly positive impact of the program on the enrollment of girls and a negative impact on the enrollment of boys. Parents from poor economic backgrounds tend to withdraw male children early from secondary school to engage them in farm work.

Efforts were also made to promote female teachers in rural schools. Schools in Bangladesh were dominated by male teachers, with the female teaching staff comprising only 7 percent in 1980 and 10 percent in 1990 (United Nations Education, Scientific, and Cultural Organization [UNESCO] 2009). The Program to Train, Motivate and Employ Female Teachers in Rural Secondary Schools (PROMOTE), which started in August 1996, aimed to promote girl-friendly secondary schools and high-quality, gender-sensitive teaching in rural areas. Also, various community mobilization and communication initiatives were undertaken to address gender-based differentials in access to education. The World Bank–supported Female Education Awareness Program used various communication channels such as radio, television, printed materials, and personal communication to encourage women to participate in school. In brief, there has been strong institutional support for girls' schooling in rural Bangladesh since 1994.

Bangladesh ranks among the largest garment exporters in the world, thanks to the initial technology transfer from the Republic of Korea, the continuous investment in human capital, and the importation and assimilation of technological and managerial knowledge from advanced countries (Mottaleb and Sonobe 2011). The garment industry employs 3.6 million workers (80 percent of them are women) and generates US$12.5 billion worth of exports every year (World Bank 2012). A new generation of work opportunities for women in the garment industry enhances the returns to women's education. According to Heath and Mobarak (2011), school enrollment increased among girls after the garment factories were set up within commuting distance of their villages, while older girls dropped out of school to work in the factories. In anticipation of work opportunities for their daughters, Bangladeshi parents realize the gains from sending their girls to school. Employment opportunities in the garment sector stimulate investments in schooling, as workers in garment factories need considerably higher educational attainment than workers in agriculture.

Also being stimulated by the development of the garment industry, other industries, including the service sectors, have been developing quite fast in Bangladesh, which must have stimulated investment in children's schooling, particularly for females. These discussions suggest that because of the multiplicity of potential factors that may simultaneously affect schooling decisions for females, it is difficult to identify econometrically major factors affecting their schooling.

Summary and conclusions

This chapter aimed to identify the factors affecting completed years in school of school-age children in rural Bangladesh. This country has seen an unprecedented increase in school participation of children and has successfully eliminated the gender gap in school participation; these gaps are now reversing, with boys at a relative disadvantage in primary and secondary schools (Asian Development Bank 2010a). This research has three major findings: (1) girls of school age are able to increase their participation in school more than boys; (2) household income, particularly agricultural income, exerts a positive impact on children's schooling; and (3) electricity supports children's schooling indirectly through its positive impact on farm and nonfarm income. The question is why have girls been favored in school investment under the assumption that parents are basically egalitarian in schooling investment in their daughters and sons.

The policy environment and the labor market are likely to be strong outside forces that have tilted the balance in favor of girls. Importantly, the affirmative policy of providing free secondary education and a stipend for girls in secondary schools beginning in 1994 served as a magnet for young girls to attend schools. The expansion of the garment industry has increased the availability of labor employment opportunities for women, leading to the rise in returns to female schooling. Expansion of electricity coverage in rural areas enables nonfarm enterprises to grow and locate in rural areas, bringing jobs closer to rural households. Electricity also saves women's time on domestic chores, releasing time for girls to attend schools. Clearly, it is the synergy between household, institutional, and market factors that makes Bangladesh a successful case in increasing children's schooling.

What are the remaining issues? A large number of girls and boys in disadvantaged groups such as the poor, those living in remote areas, and those belonging to minority ethnic groups remain out of school and attendance is poor, particularly among girls (Asian Development Bank 2010a; World Bank 2011d). For these groups, we need to develop context-specific strategies that address specific issues. For poor households, the cash for schooling program should continue; for households in remote areas, community and satellite schools may work effectively; and for ethnic minorities, changing the school curricula to make schools friendly to all may encourage ethnic group participation. Another important issue is to enable the education sector to let students prepare for the job market by incorporating technical and vocational training that produces relevant market skills to strengthen the position of Bangladeshi workers in the job market. To sum up, increasing girls' schooling attainment and female participation in the labor market are important strategies to achieve MDG3, "gender equality and empowerment of women." At the same time, it must be clearly recognized that the development of female labor-intensive industrialization is a prerequisite for increased female participation in the labor market. Bangladesh is obviously moving in the right direction.

Notes

1 Secondary school is made up of the junior secondary level (commonly between ages 11 and 15) and the senior secondary level (commonly between ages 16 and 17).
2 There was a survey of 1,939 households in 2004, but we did not include 2004 in the analysis because 2004 is too close to the 2000 and 2008 surveys.

Part III
Summary and conclusions

9 Strategies for inclusive growth in Asia

Introduction

It is widely acknowledged that the pattern of rapidly growing Asian economies is broad based and inclusive of the large part of the county's entire labor force, including youth, women, and the uneducated. The nature of inclusive growth, however, is not well understood. The major purpose of the present volume is to inquire into the processes of inclusive economic growth through which Asian countries have achieved both economic growth and poverty reduction. Rapid growth of the nonfarm sector, including industry and services, that generates jobs for the poor is the main propeller of income growth and poverty reduction. The role of agricultural sector in decreasing poverty is modest in its limited ability to absorb labor in the rural areas. This study has found that the potential of agriculture in poverty reduction could be realized in the so-called high-value revolution in horticulture, livestock, and other high-value products.

We conducted a comparative case study of six countries in Asia – Laos, Myanmar, the Philippines, Vietnam, Sri Lanka, and Bangladesh. We paid special attention to the role of creating productive jobs, improving education, and providing access to good infrastructure, as it is productive jobs and improved education that can significantly improve the labor income of the poor, and it is infrastructure that connects jobs with workers by improving access to labor markets. We focused on rural households, as rural poverty is more persistent and widespread than urban poverty; about 70 percent of the poor live in rural areas.

This volume has demonstrated that individuals and rural households in Asia have been reallocating their labor away from agriculture and into nonfarm activities. The decision to take nonfarm jobs in rural areas or migrate outside the home villages is a common proximate cause for the reduction in poverty in rural areas of Asia. This is partly because of the rapid development of nonfarm sectors in Asia and partly because of the increasing scarcity of farmland, which limits employment opportunities in Asian agriculture. Agriculture may not be able to create a sufficient number of jobs for the burgeoning rural population because of the low elasticity of demand for food and because of the largely fixed supply of farmland, although there are prospects of increased employment in the high-value crop and livestock sectors.

In contrast, farm size has been expanding, and rice farming enjoys the scale economies in southern Vietnam, which is a major source of household income growth in this region. In northern Vietnam, women choose to farm high-value crops and raise livestock, while men choose nonfarm jobs outside the villages. However, we found that, in general, the development of the nonfarm sector confers particularly high benefits to women, as there is no difference in the ability to work in nonfarm jobs between men and women. Thus, in Asia, measures must be taken to increase nonfarm employment opportunities and facilitate intersectoral reallocation of both female and male labor from farming to nonfarm jobs, including those in foreign countries, through labor market adjustments in order to achieve gender equity and reduce rural poverty.

This study identified that investments in schooling and infrastructure are keys to increasing nonfarm income and eradicating rural poverty. Surprisingly, ownership of land is found to have lost importance as a determinant of income and poverty over time in rural areas. Instead, schooling has become a crucial determinant of income with the increasing share of income from nonfarm jobs where returns to schooling are high.

We postulated the two major hypotheses in Chapter 1: (1) income growth and poverty reduction take place when the rural poor find jobs in labor-intensive and profitable farming activities and labor-intensive informal nonfarm sectors and (2) women's status is enhanced primarily when women obtain higher levels of schooling, are able to migrate, and become employed in productive jobs not only in agriculture but also more importantly in nonfarm sectors. To substantiate these major hypotheses, we postulated seven more directly testable hypotheses. In this concluding chapter, we summarize the results of the case studies examining the empirical validity of these hypotheses and draw policy implications.

Test of hypotheses

Let us begin with the testing of Hypothesis 1, which states:

> *Hypothesis 1: Since access to farmland is a major determinant of farm income, whereas education is a major determinant of nonfarm income, as the nonfarm sector develops, the importance of farmland declines and that of human capital rises as a determinant of the total income of rural households.*

Table 9.1 summarizes the results of regression analyses on the effects of farm size and schooling on agricultural and nonfarm income.[1] It is overwhelmingly clear that farm size is the major determinant of agricultural income in a large number of cases. Exceptions are found in the Philippines in which respondents reside in Manila or overseas and in the estate area in Sri Lanka where the majority of people are employed by estates as hired workers. In stark contrast, schooling is the decisive factor affecting nonfarm income, with only one exception in Laos, where uneducated workers migrate to Thailand to engage in

Table 9.1 Effects of farm size, schooling, and gender on agricultural and nonfarm income

	Agricultural income			Nonfarm income		
				In Laos	In Thailand	Remittance
Laos in 2010[a]						
Farm size	+++					+++
Schooling					+++	
Female ratio						+
Myanmar in 1996 and 2012[b]	1996	2012		1996		2012
Farm size	+++	+++		+++		
Schooling		+		+++		+++
Female ratio						
Philippines in 2008[c]	Manila and overseas	Local towns	Villages	Manila and overseas	Local towns	Villages
Farm size		+	+++	+++	+++	+++
Schooling				+++	+++	
Female ratio						
Vietnam in 2009[d]	North	South		North		South
Farm size	+++	+++				
Schooling						
Female ratio				++		++
Sri Lanka in 1990 and 2006[e]	Urban area	Rural area	Estate	Urban area	Rural area	Estate
Farm size						
Schooling	+++	+++		++	- - -	
Female ratio			+++	+++	+++	+++
Bangladesh in 1988, 2000, and 2008[f]	1988	2000	2008	1988	2000	2008
Farm size	+++	+++	+++		- - -	+++
Schooling	- - -	++		+++	+++	+++
Female ratio	- - -		- - -		+++	+++

a From Table 2.10.
b From Table 3.7. Farm size refers to farm households only, whereas the effects of schooling and female ratio refer to both farmer and landless agricultural households.
c From Table 4.8. Data refer to married members residing in Manila and overseas, local towns, and study villages.
d From Table 5.8.
e From Table 7.4 for agricultural income and from Table 7.5 for nonfarm income. Significance levels are "averages" in 1990 and 2006, as the results are similar in the 2 years.
f From Table 8.6.
+++Positive and significant at 1% level. ++Positive and significant at 5% level. +Positive and significant at 10% level. ---Negative and significant at 1% level. --Negative and significant at 5% level. -Negative and significant at 10% level.

unskilled jobs. These workers are predominantly women who migrated to Bangkok and are engaged in the informal wage sector. These results clearly support Hypothesis 1.

Note that farm size has some positive effects on nonfarm income, presumably because income accrued from land is used to initiate self-employed businesses and finance migration abroad. This issue will be further discussed when we examine the validity of Hypothesis 7. It may also be worth pointing out that the coefficients of the number of working-age household members in the non-farm income regression are far larger than those in agricultural income regressions, suggesting that the nonfarm sector absorbs a greater number of workers in rural households. There are a few exceptions to this argument, as seen in Myanmar, where the nonfarm sector has not developed compared with those in the other countries under study, and in southern Vietnam, where a large-scale farming system has started to emerge.

As a corollary to Hypothesis 1, we postulated the following hypothesis:

Hypothesis 2: Inheritance of farmland positively affects the probability that children choose farming as a major occupation, whereas schooling investment increases the probability that children choose nonfarm jobs.

Taking advantage of the availability of job information for the second generation of farm households (G2), including the respondents and their spouses and siblings, and the third generation (G3) – i.e., the children of respondents – we estimated the job choice regressions in Laos, the Philippines, and Vietnam and summarized the results in Table 9.2. As is postulated in Hypothesis 2, schooling has significantly positive effects on the choice of nonfarm jobs, except for those in Thailand, where migrants from Laos are engaged in low-paying, unskilled jobs. Land inheritance or inherited farm area has generally negative effects on the choice of nonfarm jobs, except in Laos, where income from land appears to be used for start-up investment in self-employed nonfarm jobs or for covering migration costs. Although the intergenerational data are not available, the analysis of job choice using cross-sectional data in Myanmar is consistent with Hypothesis 2 (Table 3.6). Therefore, Hypothesis 2 seems to be generally supported empirically.

The question arises as to what determines investment in schooling. Summary results on the determinants of schooling using the intergenerational data are shown in Table 9.3. It is interesting to find that the female dummy has consistently negative effects on schooling for G2, but such effects largely disappeared for G3, except in southern Vietnam. Although the causes of such changes are not clear, it is evident that gender bias in schooling investment in favor of boys was no longer observed in rural areas in Laos and Vietnam. Year of birth has consistently and increasingly positive effects on schooling, indicating that expansion of free primary and secondary schooling, as well as increasing expected returns to schooling due to the rise in nonfarm job opportunities, favor larger investment in schooling.

Table 9.2 Effects of land inheritance, schooling, and gender on choice of jobs

Laos[a]	Nonfarm among G2	Nonfarm in Laos among G3	Nonfarm in Thailand among G3
Land inheritance	+	+	+
Schooling	+	+++	
Female dummy		+++	+++
Philippines, G2[b]	Nonfarm in local towns	Nonfarm in big cities	Overseas
Land inheritance	– – –	– – –	
Schooling	+++	+++	+++
Female dummy			
Philippines, G3[b]			
Land inheritance	– – –	– – –	– – –
Schooling	+++	+++	+++
Female dummy	+++	+++	+++

Vietnam, G2[c]	Farming in the north	Farming in the south
Land inheritance	+	+++
Schooling	– – –	– – –
Female dummy		
Vietnam, G3[c]		
Land inheritance		++
Schooling	– – –	– – –
Female dummy	+++	

a   From Table 2.9.
b   From Table 4.6 for the second generation (G2) and from Table 4.7 for the third generation (G3). The default is agricultural work in the study villages.
c   From Table 5.7.
+++Positive and significant at 1% level. ++Positive and significant at 5% level. +Positive and significant at 10% level. – – –Negative and significant at 1% level. – –Negative and significant at 5% level. –Negative and significant at 10% level.

The poorest of the poor in rural areas in Asia are landless agricultural workers (David and Otsuka 1994). They are poor as they are engaged in simple, manual, and seasonal tasks such as weeding and harvesting and, hence, they do not possess much farming- or farm-specific knowledge (Hayami and Otsuka 1993). As a result, the opportunity cost of the landless workers to leave agriculture is low, and they are more mobile occupationally and geographically than members of farm households. To the extent that the nonfarm sector develops faster and that earnings in nonfarm jobs grow faster than expected, the disadvantage of

Table 9.3 Determinants of schooling among second generations (G2) and third generations (G3) in Laos and Vietnam

	G2		G3	
	RE tobit	FE tobit	RE tobit	FE tobit
Laos[a]				
Year of birth	+++	+	+++	+++
Female dummy (FD)	− − −	− − −		
Education of father	++	N/A[c]	+++	N/A
Education of mother		N/A		N/A
Parents' inherited farmland (FL)	N/A	N/A	+++	
FD × FL	N/A	N/A	− − −	
Vietnam, North[b]				
Year of birth	+++	++	++	+++
Female dummy (FD)	− − −	− − −		
Education of father		N/A	+	N/A
Education of mother	+	N/A	++	N/A
Vietnam, South[b]				
Year of birth			+++	+++
Female dummy (FD)	− − −	− − −	− − −	− − −
Education of father	+++	N/A		N/A
Education of mother		N/A	++	N/A
Parents' inherited farmland (FL)		N/A		N/A

a From Table 2.8.

b From Tables 5.5 and 5.6.

c Not applicable, except for parents' inherited farmland for G2 in the Laos case, where data are not available.

+++Positive and significant at 1% level. ++Positive and significant at 5% level. +Positive and significant at 10% level. − − −Negative and significant at 1% level. − −Negative and significant at 5% level. −Negative and significant at 10% level.

Notes: RE = random effects; FE = fixed effects.

the landless labor class in income earnings compared with that of the landed class will decline over time. Such arguments led to the following hypothesis:

> *Hypothesis 3: Because of the increasing importance of nonfarm income and higher geographical and occupational mobility of landless households, the income gap between landed and landless households declines over time.*

The best data set we can use to examine this hypothesis is the income data of farmer and landless agricultural households in 1985 and their children in 2008 in the Philippines (Table 9.4). Although the landless households earned

Table 9.4 Comparison of income of farmer and landless households in 1985 and their descendant households in 2008 in the Philippines (US$ purchasing power parity in 2005)

	1985	
	Farmer households	*Landless households*
Household income	1,895	908
Proportion of farm income (%)	91	32
Proportion of sample households (%)	60	40
	2008	
	Married children of farmer households	*Married children of landless households*
Household income	8,142	6,629
Proportion of farm income (%)	76	9
Proportion of sample households (%)	78	22
	2008	
	Single children of farmer households	*Single children of landless households*
Household income	6,656	6,970
Proportion of farm income (%)	20	8
Proportion of sample households (%)	80	20

Note: Data are from Table 4.4.

nearly 70 percent of their income from nonfarm sources in 1985, their income was only half that of farmer households. Most children of landless households engaged in nonfarm jobs in nearby towns, major cities, and even abroad, resulting in income almost comparable with the income of children of farmer households in 2008. Expectation seems to have mattered, as the children of farmer households could have performed better, as they initially were wealthier and more educated. But there seems to be an underestimation of increases in nonfarm income over time.

Data similar to those shown in Table 9.4 are available for farmer and landless households in Myanmar in 1996 and 2012 (Table 3.4). The income gap between the two groups of households did not narrow considerably because the share of farm income of the landless (or labor income from farm tasks) remained relatively high at 38 percent as of 2012, reflecting the underdevelopment of the nonfarm sectors in this country.

Since the poor are less educated, we expect that the informal sector, which employs a larger number of uneducated workers than the formal sector, provides employment opportunities for a large number of the poor, which is conducive to poverty reduction. Thus, we postulated the following hypothesis:

Hypothesis 4: The formal nonfarm sector provides lucrative employment opportunities for the educated labor force, whereas the informal nonfarm sector provides employment opportunities for the uneducated labor force, thereby assisting them to move out of poverty.

Among our case studies, a clear distinction among formal (or regular), informal (or casual), and self-employed jobs is made in Myanmar. Consistent with Hypothesis 4, schooling has positive and significant effects on the choice of formal jobs but not on informal jobs (Table 3.6). The estimated coefficient of education in the formal job choice function is larger than that in the informal job choice function, indicating that schooling is much more important in formal than in informal sectors. Similarly, although the coefficients of schooling are generally positive and significant in the choice of self-employment regression, coefficients are much smaller than in the formal sector job regression. In contrast, parents' landholdings have generally negative effects on nonfarm jobs, which suggests that those who inherited large land areas choose farming.

Consistent with the results reported in Myanmar, schooling has a significantly larger impact on income in formal sectors than in other nonfarm sectors in Myanmar (Table 3.8). Although the distinction is not made between formal and informal jobs, schooling has larger effects on nonfarm income earned in Laos than in Thailand, where jobs are less skill intensive (Table 2.10), and outside the study villages than inside in the Philippines (Table 4.8).

We postulated that women do not have a comparative advantage in farming vis-à-vis men, particularly because crop farming requires muscle work. However, women may have a comparative advantage in the production of labor-intensive, high-value crops, such as flowers and vegetables, and in raising livestock, which requires careful management. Since labor markets in the nonfarm sector are likely to be generally competitive, as Becker (1957) argued several decades ago, discrimination by gender and race tends to be much lower in this sector. Thus, women generally have stronger incentives to work in the nonfarm sector, unless they are engaged in the production of high-value crops and livestock. Since the return to education in the nonfarm sector is high, there will be a strong incentive for parents to invest in the schooling of their daughters, who seek nonfarm jobs. Such arguments were summarized by the following hypothesis:

Hypothesis 5: The development of the nonfarm sector contributes to the improvement of women's educational and income status by providing equal employment opportunities for women and men.

Although direct testing of this hypothesis is difficult to do, there is some indirect evidence to support it. First, as shown in Table 9.1, the female ratio of working-age members of households has no impact on the nonfarm income of rural households in Laos, Myanmar, and Vietnam, whereas it has positive and significant impacts on nonfarm income in the Philippines and Bangladesh. In Sri Lanka, however, the female ratio has negative effects on nonfarm income due to the fact that women are engaged primarily in household activities. By and large, it seems clear that women find jobs in nonfarm sectors without handicaps vis-à-vis men. Second, as seen in Table 9.2, women tend to choose nonfarm jobs, and this tendency is strengthened over time. The exception is northern Vietnam, where women are increasingly engaged in the production of high-value crops and livestock, particularly in areas where there is a high rate of male outmigration. Third, as our results in Laos and Vietnam reveal, while the schooling of the female members of rural households was less than that of male members among the second generation, such a tendency largely disappeared among the third generation. Fourth, in the Philippines where females are more educated than males, the female ratio has positive and significant effects on income from various sources in the nonfarm sector (Table 9.5). Although more rigorous and direct testing of this hypothesis may be called for, it seems that the available evidence is at least consistent with this hypothesis.

Irrigation affects agricultural income by improving the efficiency of farming, whereas transportation and communication infrastructure affects both farm and nonfarm incomes by reducing transport as well as transaction costs.

Table 9.5 Effects of female ratio on per capita income, by source, in the Philippines

	1988–7	2000–6
Provincial level[a]		
Formal salary work	+++	+
Informal manufacturing		+
Trade, transportation, and communication (TTC)		
Foreign remittances	+++	
Domestic remittances		
Township level in progressive areas[b]	+++	++
Formal salary work	+++	+++
Informal manufacturing	+++	++
TTC		
Foreign remittances	+++	
Domestic remittances		

a   From Table 6.5.
b   From Table 6.6.
+Positive and significant at 10% level. ++Positive and significant at 5% level. +++Positive and significant at 1% level.

In the longer run, infrastructure development may affect the development of nonfarm sectors and access to nonfarm labor markets, including overseas markets. The development of nonfarm sectors may also be stimulated by the adoption of new agricultural technology through growth linkages and by an increased supply of the labor force from farm sectors in general and the educated labor force in particular. In this study, we analyzed the impact of infrastructure and education on household income generated from farm and rural nonfarm activities. More specifically, we postulated the following hypothesis:

> *Hypothesis 6: Development of the rural nonfarm sector is promoted by (1) invest-ment in infrastructure, (2) the availability of an educated labor force, and (3) the adoption of modern agricultural technology.*

We tested this hypothesis by using provincial and township data in the Philippines in Chapter 6, nationally representative secondary household data in Sri Lanka in Chapter 7, and nationally representative household survey data in Bangladesh in Chapter 8. As reported in Table 9.6, remarkably consistent results were obtained.[2] First, the availability of electricity has positive effects on nonfarm income without exception and largely negative effects on farm income, suggesting that electricity plays a more important role in the nonfarm sector than in the farm sector. In Bangladesh in 2008, the availability of electricity had a positive effect on farm income, but its effect was only one fifth of its impact on nonfarm income. Similar to the effect of electricity, the availability of pipe-borne water affects nonfarm income positively and farm income negatively in Sri Lanka; the higher density of national roads has similar effects in the Philippines.[3] Thus, Part (1) of Hypothesis 6 is supported by our analyses. Infrastructure is important to women because it reduces the burden of domestic duties, thereby allowing them to allocate more time to market activities.

Second, the ratio of irrigated area has positive effects on farm income, as may be expected, but negative effects on nonfarm income. Irrigation is a decisive factor affecting the efficiency of farming in Asia, and the availability of irrigation can be regarded as a good proxy for the adoption of modern agricultural technology (David and Otsuka 1994). Thus, its negative effect on nonfarm income contradicts Part (3) of Hypothesis 6. In other words, our analysis does not support the significant effect of growth linkages.[4] Third, the availability of an educated labor force is either unrelated with the development of nonfarm sectors, as in the Philippines, or positively related, as in the case of rural areas in Sri Lanka and Bangladesh. Thus, the results of the regression analyses are not inconsistent with Part (2) of Hypothesis 6.

Since ownership of farmland generates income and farmland can be used as collateral, access to farmland may be an important factor affecting investments in nonfarm businesses, including overseas migration. If this is the case, income inequality tends to persist across generations, and rural poverty arising from the

Table 9.6   Effects of infrastructure and schooling on farm and nonfarm incomes in the Philippines, Sri Lanka, and Bangladesh

	Farm income		Nonfarm income	
Philippines, progressive towns[a]	*1988 and 1997*	*2000 and 2006*	*1988 and 1997*	*2000 and 2006*
National road density				
Local road density	---	--	+	++
Electricity		++	--	--
% irrigated area		---	+++	+++
% secondary schooling	+++	++	--	
% tertiary schooling				
Sri Lanka, rural areas[b]	*1990*	*2006*	*1990*	*2006*
Electricity	---	---	+++	+++
Pipe-borne water	---	---	+++	+++
% secondary schooling	+		+++	+++
% tertiary schooling		-	+++	+++
Bangladesh	*1988*	*2008*	*1988*	*2008*
Electricity		+++	+++	+++
% irrigated area	+++	+++	--	---
% secondary schooling	---	-	+++	+++
% tertiary schooling	--	++	+++	+++

a   From Table 6.6.
b   From Tables 7.4 and 7.5.
c   From Table 8.6.
+++Positive and significant at 1% level. ++Positive and significant at 5% level. +Positive and significant at 10% level. ---Negative and significant at 1% level. --Negative and significant at 5% level. -Negative and significant at 10% level

lack of access to land may continue to prevail over time. Thus, we believe that it is worth testing the following hypothesis:

> *Hypothesis 7: Larger endowment of farmland relative to labor promotes nonfarm self-employment activities and overseas migration because land represents wealth that can be used to finance start-up costs in these activities.*

This study did not find strong evidence to support this hypothesis. As seen in Table 9.1, we did not find consistently positive effects of farm size on nonfarm income. Thus, the effect of farm size on nonfarm income is not as strong as what is suggested by Hypothesis 7. While farm size has positive and significant effects on total household income in the relatively low-income economies of Laos and Bangladesh (Tables 2.10 and 8.6, respectively), inherited farm land has largely insignificant impacts on total income in the comparatively higher income economy of the Philippines (Table 4.8). This may suggest that as an economy develops over time, the importance of access to land as a determinant of household income declines, which is also consistent with Hypothesis 1. In other words, the economic mobility of rural households in the process of inclusive growth in Asia seems to be considerably high, even though overall income inequality did not decline significantly, as was pointed out in Chapter 1. Clearly, inclusive growth in Asia means income growth and shared prosperity for all (World Bank 1989, 2000, 2014).

Policy implications

Consistent with the analytical framework shown in Figure 1.6, we found that investments in infrastructure and improvement of education are critical factors affecting the development of nonfarm sectors and access to nonfarm labor markets, which in turn affect the nonfarm income of rural households. Moreover, we found that it is the increase in nonfarm income that significantly contributed to the overall income growth in rural households in Asia. Furthermore, it was revealed that the increased employment opportunities in the nonfarm sector brought about significant increases in income earned by uneducated members of poor households and also by female workers, the marginalized groups in the community who are susceptible to spells of poverty and who have been traditionally handicapped in terms of access to land and schooling.

There are several policy implications of our study. First of all, the government should invest in such infrastructure as electricity, pipe-borne water, and high-quality roads in order to stimulate the development of nonfarm sectors and to improve the connectivity between the rural and urban labor markets. Second, the government should invest in agricultural research and irrigation, as modern agricultural technology is particularly important in the early stage of development because income from farming could be used as funds for children's schooling (Otsuka *et al.* 2009). Furthermore, new technology development may be needed for the efficient production of high-value crops and the promotion of scale economies in rice farming. Nevertheless, it is important to point out that, contrary to what is traditionally believed, the growth linkage effect of agricultural development on the development of the rural nonfarm sector is not as strong as generally perceived. Third, the government should recognize that schooling is the decisive factor affecting household income, which implies that schooling investment has significant impacts on the pace of economic growth as well as income distribution. Thus, in order to achieve truly inclusive growth, the government should make every effort to improve the education levels and the quality of education. Fourth, it must be clearly recognized that the development of nonfarm sectors contributes not only to the income of households but also to the improvement of women's educational and income status. In all likelihood, our basic hypothesis that women's status is enhanced primarily when women obtain higher levels of schooling, are able to migrate, and become employed in productive nonfarm jobs (Hypothesis 5) is empirically valid. It is true, however, that lucrative jobs can be created in farming by introducing high-value crops, as in the case of northern Vietnam. Nonetheless, it seems generally true that it is primarily the development of labor-intensive nonfarm sectors that provides lucrative job opportunities for women. That is, we can hardly expect to achieve gender equality without the development of nonfarm sectors.

While it is clear that the development of nonfarm sectors is indispensable for inclusive growth and that investments in infrastructure and education promote such growth, our knowledge of the strategy to develop nonfarm sectors and to provide employment opportunities to the poor and to women is far from adequate. Since there is low demand for the traditional products of rural enterprises, it is preferable to encourage the development of modern industrial clusters that are connected to international markets. Regarding the promotion of labor-intensive industrial clusters in Asia and sub-Saharan Africa, Sonobe and Otsuka (2006, 2011, 2014) argue based on numerous case studies that managerial and technological training for entrepreneurs, followed by support for promising entrepreneurs by means of providing credit and infrastructure, is the most effective development strategy. Creating dynamic and innovative enterprises, or "the gazelles" (a term coined by the World Bank [2012b]), is the central issue because they are the ones who remain in business for a long time and create jobs, even for the poor. We have, however, a sheer lack of knowledge on appropriate policies to stimulate the development of nonfarm sectors in general and the service sectors in particular. The question of how to link the analysis of household income and job choice, like our present study, with the analysis of the development of the nonfarm sector is a major remaining issue that needs to be explored in the future for a deeper understanding of inclusive growth in Asia.

Notes

1 The effect of gender is also summarized in Table 9.1, but it will be examined later in this section.
2 For simplicity, we show only the results of our study at the township level in the Philippines and in rural areas in Sri Lanka in Table 9.6.
3 In the Philippines, the higher density of local roads has the opposite effect, presumably because local roads connect villages with local towns, thereby stimulating the development of the farm sector.
4 There is the possibility that the development of farm sectors leads to the development of nonfarm sectors outside the locality by increasing demand for goods and services provided elsewhere.

References

Asian Development Bank (2005) *Viet Nam Gender Situation Analysis*, Manila: Author.
Asian Development Bank (2006) *Lao PDR: An Evaluation Synthesis on Rice*, Manila: Author.
Asian Development Bank (2010a) *Country Gender Assessment: Bangladesh*, Manila: Author.
Asian Development Bank (2010b) *Key Indicators for Asia and the Pacific 2010*, Manila: Author.
Asian Development Bank (2013) *Myanmar in Transition: Opportunities and Challenges*, Manila: Author.
Ahmed, A.U. and del Ninno, C. (2003) "Food for education in Bangladesh," in A.R. Quisumbing (ed) *Household Decisions, Gender, and Development: A Synthesis of Recent Research*, Baltimore, MD: Johns Hopkins University Press.
Baulch, B. (2011) *Why Poverty Persists: Poverty Dynamics in Asia and Africa*, Cheltenham, UK: Edward Elgar Publishing.
Becker, G. (1957) *The Economics of Discrimination*, Chicago: University of Chicago Press.
Behrman, J.R. and Knowles, J.C. (1999) "Household income and child schooling in Vietnam," *World Bank Economic Review*, 13(2): 211–56.
Blinder, A.S. (1973) "Wage discrimination: reduced form and structural estimates," *Journal of Human Resources*, 8(4): 436–55.
Capistrano, L.O. and Santa Maria, M.L.C. (2007) "The impact of international labor migration and OFW remittances on poverty in the Philippines," *Discussion Paper No. 2007-06*, Quezon City: University of the Philippines, School of Economics.
Central Bank of Sri Lanka (1998) *Economic Progress of Independent Sri Lanka*, Colombo: Author.
Central Bank of Sri Lanka (2010) *Annual Report 2009*, Colombo: Author.
Chaudhuri, S. and Ravallion, M. (2006) "Partially awakened giants: uneven growth in China and India," *World Bank Policy Research Working Paper Series 4069*, Washington, DC: World Bank.
Corral, L. and Reardon, T. (2001) "Rural nonfarm incomes in Nicaragua," *World Development*, 29(3): 427–42.
David, C. and Otsuka, K. (eds) (1994) *Modern Rice Technology and Income Distribution in Asia*, Boulder, CO: Lynne Rienner.
Deichmann, U., Shilpi, F. and Vakis, R. (2008) "Urban proximity, agricultural potential and rural nonfarm employment: evidence from Bangladesh," *World Development*, 37(3): 645–60.

Deininger, K. and Jin, S. (2003) "Land sales and rental markets in transition: evidence from rural Vietnam," *World Bank Policy Research Working Paper 3013*, Washington, DC: World Bank.

de Janvry, A. and Sadoulet, E. (2001) "Income strategies among rural households in Mexico: the role of off-farm activities," *World Development*, 29(3): 467–80.

Deolalikar, A. (1993) "Gender differences in the returns to schooling and in school enrollment rates in Indonesia," *Journal of Human Resources*, 28(4): 899–932.

Department of Census and Statistics of Sri Lanka (2008) *Household Income and Expenditure Survey, 2006/2007 Final Report*, Colombo: Department of Census and Statistics of Sri Lanka, Ministry of Policy Planning and Implementation.

Dollar, D. and Kraay, A. (2002) "Growth is good for the poor," *Journal of Economic Growth*, 7(3): 195–225.

Duflo, E. and Pande, R. (2007) "Dams," *Quarterly Journal of Economics*, 122(2): 601–46.

Esfahani, H.S. and Ramirez, M.-T. (2003) "Institutions, infrastructure and economic growth," *Journal of Development Economics*, 70(2): 443–77.

Esguerra, E. and Manning, C. (2007) "Regional labour markets and economic development in the Philippines," in A. Balisacan and H. Hill (eds) *The Dynamics of Regional Development: The Philippines in East Asia*, Cheltenham, UK, and Tokyo, Japan: Asian Development Bank Institute and Edward Elgar Publishing.

Estudillo, J.P. and Ducanes, G. (2014) "Infrastructure and Filipino women," *Philippine Daily Inquirer*, March 23, 2014, page A16.

Estudillo, J.P., Fujimura, M. and Hossain, M. (1999) "New rice technology and comparative advantage in rice production in the Philippines," *Journal of Development Studies*, 35(5): 162–84.

Estudillo, J.P., Mano, Y., Sawada, Y. and Otsuka, K. (2014) "Poor parents, rich children: the role of schooling, nonfarm work, and migration in the rural Philippines," *Philippine Review of Economics*, 51(2): 21–46.

Estudillo, J.P., Mano, Y. and Seng-Arloun, S. (2013) "Job choice of three generations in rural Laos," *Journal of Development Studies*, 49(7): 991–1009.

Estudillo, J.P. and Otsuka, K. (1999) "Green revolution, human capital, and off-farm employment: changing sources of income among farm households in Central Luzon, 1966–94," *Economic Development and Cultural Change*, 47(3): 497–523.

Estudillo, J.P. and Otsuka, K. (2006) "Lessons from three decades of green revolution in the Philippines," *Developing Economies*, 44(2): 123–48.

Estudillo, J.P., Otsuka, K. and Yamano, T. (2010) "The role of labor markets and human capital in poverty reduction: evidence from Asia and Africa," *Asian Journal of Agriculture and Development*, 7(1): 23–40.

Estudillo, J.P., Quisumbing, A.R. and Otsuka, K. (2001) "Gender differences in land inheritance and schooling investments in the rural Philippines," *Land Economics*, 77(1): 130–43.

Estudillo, J.P., Sawada, Y. and Otsuka, K. (2006) "The green revolution, development of labor markets, and poverty reduction in rural Philippines, 1985–2004," *Agricultural Economics*, 35(S3): 399–407.

Estudillo, J.P., Sawada, Y. and Otsuka, K. (2008) "Poverty and income dynamics in Philippine villages, 1985–2004," *Review of Development Economics*, 12(4): 877–90.

Estudillo, J.P., Sawada, Y. and Otsuka, K. (2009) "The changing determinants of schooling investments: evidence from the villages in the Philippines, 1985–1989 and 2000–2004," *Journal of Development Studies*, 45(3): 391–411.

Fabella, R. (1985) "Rural industry and modernisation," in S. Mukhopadhyay and P.L. Chee (eds) *Development and Diversification of Rural Industries in Asia*, Kuala Lumpur, Malaysia: Asia and the Pacific Development Centre.

Fafchamps, M. and Shilpi, F. (2003) "The spatial division of labour in Nepal," *Journal of Development Studies*, 39(6): 23–66.

Fields, G.S. (2012) *Working Hard, Working Poor: A Global Journey*, Oxford: Oxford University Press.

Food and Agriculture Organization (FAO) (2012, 2014) *FAOStat*, Rome: Author.

Foster, A. and Rosenzweig, R. (1996) "Technical change and human-capital returns and investments: evidence from the green revolution," *American Economic Review*, 86(4): 931–53.

Foster, A.D. and Rosenzweig, M.R. (2004) "Agricultural productivity growth, rural economic diversity, and economic reforms: India, 1970–2000," *Economic Development and Cultural Change*, 52(3): 509–42.

Foster, J., Greer, J. and Thorbecke, E. (1984) "A class of decomposable poverty measures," *Econometrica*, 52(3): 761–65.

Garcia, Y.T., Garcia, A.G., Oo, M. and Hossain, M. (2000) "Income distribution and poverty in irrigated and rainfed ecosystems: the Myanmar case," *Economic and Political Weekly*, 35(52–53): 4670–6.

Gibson, J. and Olivia, S. (2010) "The effect of infrastructure access and quality on nonfarm enterprises in rural Indonesia," *World Development*, 38(5): 717–26.

Gibson, J., and Rozelle, S. (2003) "Poverty and access to roads in Papua New Guinea," *Economic Development and Cultural Change*, 52(1): 159–85.

Glauben, T., Herzfeld, T. and Wang, X. (2008) "Labor market participation of Chinese agricultural households: empirical evidence from Zhejiang Province," *Food Policy*, 33(4): 329–40.

Haggblade, S., Hazell, P. and Dorosh, P. (2007) "Sectoral growth linkages between agriculture and the rural nonfarm economy," in S. Haggblade, P. Hazell and T. Reardon (eds) *Transforming the Rural Nonfarm Economy: Opportunities and Threats in the Developing World*, Baltimore, MD: Johns Hopkins University Press.

Haggblade, S., Hazell, P. and Reardon, T. (eds) (2007) *Transforming the Rural Nonfarm Economy: Opportunities and Threats in the Developing World*, Baltimore, MD: Johns Hopkins University Press.

Hayami, Y. (1996) "The peasant in economic modernization," *American Journal of Agricultural Economics*, 78(5): 1157–67.

Hayami, Y. and Godo, Y. (2005) *Development Economics: From Poverty to the Wealth of Nations*, Oxford: Oxford University Press.

Hayami, Y. and Kikuchi, M. (2000) *A Rice Village Saga: Three Decades of Green Revolution in the Philippines*, London: Macmillan Press.

Hayami, Y. and Otsuka, K. (1993) *The Economics of Contract Choice: An Agrarian Perspective*, Oxford: Clarendon Press.

Heath, R. and Mobarak, M. (2011, November 12–13) "Supply and demand side constraints on educational investment: evidence from garment sector jobs and girls' schooling subsidy program in Bangladesh," paper presented at Northeast Universities Development Consortium Conference 2011, New Haven, CT: Yale University.

Honore, B. (1992) "Trimmed LAD and least squares estimation of truncated and censored regression models with fixed effects," *Econometrica*, 60(3): 533–65.

Hossain, M. and Bayes, A. (2009) *Rural Economy and Livelihoods: Insights from Bangladesh*, Dhaka, Bangladesh: A.H. Development Publishing House.

Hossain, M., Rahman, A.N.M. and Estudillo, J. (2009) "Income dynamics, schooling investments and poverty reduction in Bangladesh, 1988–2004," in K. Otsuka, J. Estudillo and Y. Sawada (eds) *Rural Poverty and Income Dynamics in Asia and Africa*, London: Routledge.

Ianchovichina, E. and Lundstrom, S. (2009) "Inclusive growth analytics: framework and application," *Policy Research Working Paper 4851*, Washington, DC: World Bank.

International Fund for Agricultural Development (IFAD) (2000) *Rural Poverty Report 2001 – The Challenge of Ending Rural Poverty*, Rome: Author.

International Fund for Agricultural Development (IFAD) (2010) *Rural Poverty Report 2011: New Realities, New Challenges: New Opportunities for Tomorrow's Generation*, Rome: Author.

Jayasuriya, S.K. and Shand, R.T. (1986) "Technical change and labor absorption in Asian agriculture: some emerging trends," *World Development*, 14(3): 415–28.

Jolliffe, D. (2004) "The impact of education in rural Ghana: examining household labour allocation and returns on and off farm," *Journal of Development Economics*, 73(1): 287–314.

Kajisa, K. (2007) "Personal networks and non-agricultural employment: the case of a farming village in the Philippines," *Economic Development and Cultural Change*, 55(4): 669–707.

Kanbur, R. and Venables, A.J. (2005) *Spatial Inequality and Development*, New York: Oxford University Press.

Kerkvliet, B. (2005). *The Power of Everyday Politics: How Vietnamese Peasants Transformed National Policy*, Ithaca, NY: Cornell University Press.

Khandker, S., Pitt, M. and Fuwa, N. (2003) "Subsidy to promote girl's education: the female stipend program in Bangladesh," *MPRA Paper No. 23688*, Washington, DC: World Bank.

Kijima, Y. and Lanjouw, P. (2005) "Economic diversification and poverty in rural India," *Indian Journal of Labor Economics*, 48(2): 349–74.

Kikuchi, M. (1998) "Export-oriented garment industries in the rural Philippines," in Y. Hayami (ed) *Toward the Rural-Based Development of Commerce and Industry: Selected Experiences from East Asia*, Washington, DC: World Bank.

Kraay, A. (2004) "When is growth pro-poor? Cross-country evidence," *IMF Working Paper 4–47*, Washington, DC: International Monetary Fund.

Kumanayake, N.S., Estudillo, J.P. and Otsuka, K. (2014) "Changing sources of household income, poverty, and sectoral inequality in Sri Lanka, 1990–2006," *Developing Economies*, 52(1): 26–51.

Lanjouw, J. and Lanjouw, P. (2001) "The rural non-farm sector: issues and evidence from developing countries," *Agricultural Economics*, 26(1): 1–23.

Laos Ministry of Planning and Investment (MPI) (2009a) *The Household of Lao PDR*, Vientiane: Author.

Laos Ministry of Planning and Investment (MPI) (2009b) *Lao PDR Statistical Yearbook*, Vientiane: Author.

Laos Steering Committee for Census of Population and Housing (2006) *Results from the Population and Housing Census 2005*, Vientiane: Lao Government.

Lastarria-Cornhiel, S. (2006) "Feminization of agriculture: trends and driving forces," Background paper for the World Development Report 2008, Washington, DC: World Bank.

Lipton, M. and Ravallion, M. (1995) "Poverty and policy," in J. Behrman and T.N. Srinivasan (eds) *Handbook of Development Economics*, Amsterdam, Netherlands: Elsevier.

Llanto, G. (2007) "Infrastructure and regional growth," in A. Balisacan and H. Hill (eds) *The Dynamics of Regional Development: The Philippines in East Asia*, Cheltenham, UK, and Tokyo, Japan: Asian Development Bank Institute and Edward Elgar Publishing.

Lokshin, M. and Yemtsov, R. (2005) "Has rural infrastructure rehabilitation in Georgia helped the poor?" *World Bank Economic Review*, 19(2): 311–33.

Lopez, H. and Servén, L. (2004) "The mechanics of growth-poverty-inequality relationship," mimeo, Washington, DC: World Bank.

Mottaleb, K.A. and Sonobe, T. (2011) "An inquiry into the rapid growth of the garment industry in Bangladesh," *Economic Development and Cultural Change*, 60(1): 67–89.

Murphy, K., Shleifer, A. and Vishny, R. (1989) "Industrialisation and big push," *Journal of Political Economy*, 97(5): 1003–26.

Myanmar Central Statistical Organization (CSO) (2011) *Myanmar Statistical Yearbook 2011*, Naypyitaw: Author.

Myanmar Ministry of National Planning and Economic Development (MNPED) (2011) *Integrated Household Living Conditions Survey, 2009–2010: MDG Data Report*, Naypyidaw: Author.

Oaxaca, R. (1973) "Male-female wage differentials in urban labor markets," *International Economic Review*, 14(3): 693–709.

Otsuka, K. (1991) "Determinants and consequences of land reform implementation in the Philippines," *Journal of Development Economics*, 35(2): 339–55.

Otsuka, K. (2007) "Efficiency and equity effects of land markets," in R.E. Evenson and P. Pingali (eds) *Handbook of Agricultural Economics, Volume IV*, Amsterdam, Netherlands: Elsevier.

Otsuka, K., Estudillo, J.P. and Sawada, Y. (2009) *Rural Poverty and Income Dynamics in Asia and Africa*, London: Routledge.

Otsuka, K., Estudillo, J.P. and Yamano, T. (2010) "The role of labor markets and human capital in poverty reduction: evidence from Asia and Africa," *Asian Journal of Agriculture and Development*, 7(1): 23–40.

Otsuka, K., Gascon, F. and Asano, S. (1994) "'Second generation' MVs and the evolution of the green revolution: the case of Central Luzon, 1966–1990," *Agricultural Economics*, 10(3): 283–95.

Paris, T.R., Luis, J., Villanueva, D., Rola-Rubzen, M.F., Chi, T.T.N. and Wongsanum, C. (2009) "Labour out migration on rice farming households and gender roles: synthesis of findings in Thailand, the Philippines and Vietnam," paper presented at the FAO-IFAD-ILO Workshop on Gaps, Trends and Current Research in Gender Dimensions of Agricultural and Rural Employment: Differentiated Pathways out of Poverty, Rome, 31 March–2 April 2009.

Parish, W. and Willis, R. (1993) "Daughters, education, and family budgets: Taiwan experiences," *Journal of Human Resources*, 28(4): 863–98.

Philippines National Economic and Development Authority (NEDA) (2004) *Medium-Term Philippine Development Plan 2004–2010*, Manila: Author.

Philippines National Statistical Coordination Board (NSCB) (1990) *Philippine Statistical Yearbook 1990*, Manila: Author.

Philippines National Statistical Coordination Board (NSCB) (2000) *Philippine Statistical Yearbook 2000*, Manila: Author.

Philippines National Statistical Coordination Board (NSCB) (2012) *Philippine Statistical Yearbook 2012*, Manila: Author.

Pingali, P. and Xuan, V.T. (1992) "Vietnam: decollectivization and rice productivity growth," *Economic Development and Cultural Change*, 40(4): 697–718.

Quisumbing, A.R. (1994) "Intergenerational transfers in Philippine rice villages: gender differences in traditional inheritance customs," *Journal of Development Economics*, 43(2): 167–95.

Quisumbing, A.R., Estudillo, J.P. and Otsuka, K. (2004) *Land and Schooling: Transferring Wealth across Generations*, Baltimore, MD: Johns Hopkins University Press.

Quisumbing, A.R., Meinzen-Dick, R., Raney, T.L., Croppenstedt, A., Behrman, J.A. and Peterman, A. (2014) (eds) *Gender in Agriculture: Closing the Knowledge Gap*, New York: Springer.

Ramos, C.G., Estudillo, J.P., Sawada, Y. and Otsuka, K. (2012) "Transformation of the rural economy in the Philippines, 1988–2006," *Journal of Development Studies*, 48(11): 1629–48.

Ravallion, M. and Chen, S. (2007) "China's (uneven) progress against poverty," *Journal of Development Economics*, 82(1): 1–42.

Ravallion, M. and van De Walle, D. (2008) *Land in Transition: Reform and Poverty in Rural Vietnam*, Washington, DC, and Basingstoke, UK: World Bank and Palgrave Macmillan.

Reardon, T., Berdegué, J., Barrett, C. and Stamoulis, K. (2007) "Household income diversification into rural nonfarm activities," in S. Haggblade, P. Hazell and T. Reardon (eds) *Transforming the Rural Nonfarm Economy: Opportunities and Threats in the Developing World*, Baltimore, MD: John Hopkins University Press.

Reimers, C.W. (1983) "Labor market discrimination against Hispanic and black men," *Review of Economics and Statistics*, 65(4): 570–79.

Renkow, M. (2007) "Cities, towns, and the rural nonfarm economy," in S. Haggblade, P. Hazell and T. Reardon (eds) *Transforming the Rural Nonfarm Economy: Opportunities and Threats in the Developing World*, Baltimore, MD: Johns Hopkins University Press.

Rivers, D. and Vuong, Q.H. (1988) "Limited information estimators and exogeneity tests for simultaneous probit models," *Journal of Econometrics*, 39(3): 347–66.

Rosenzweig, M.R. (1995) "Why are there returns to schooling?" *American Economic Review*, 85(2): 153–58.

Rosenzweig, M.R. (2003) "Payoffs from panels in low-income countries: economic development and economic mobility," *American Economic Review*, 93(2):112–7.

Schuler, S.R. (2007) "Rural Bangladesh: sound policies, evolving gender norms, and family strategies," in M. Lewis and M. Lockheed (eds) *Exclusion, Gender and Education: Case Studies from the Developing World*, Washington, DC: Center for Global Development.

Schultz, T.W. (1964) *Transforming Traditional Agriculture*, New Haven, CT: Yale University Press.

Schultz, T.W. (1975) "The value of ability to deal with disequilibria," *Journal of Economic Literature*, 13(3): 827–46.

Sonobe, T. and Otsuka, K. (2006) *Cluster-Based Industrial Development: an East Asian Model*, New York: Palgrave Macmillan.

Sonobe, T. and Otsuka, K. (2011) *Cluster-Based Industrial Development: A Comparative Study of Asia and Africa*, Basingstoke, UK: Palgrave Macmillan.

Sonobe, T. and Otsuka, K. (2014) *Cluster-Based Industrial Development: Kaizen Management for MSE Growth in Developing Countries*, Hampshire, UK: Palgrave Macmillan.

Takahashi, K. and Otsuka, K. (2009) "Human capital investment and poverty reduction over generations: a case from rural Philippines, 1979–2003," in K. Otsuka, J. Estudillo and Y. Sawada (eds) *Rural Poverty and Income Dynamics in Asia and Africa*, London: Routledge.

United Nations (2010a) *The Millennium Development Goals Report 2010*, New York: Author.

United Nations (2010b) *Population Facts, No. 2010/6*, New York: Author.

United Nations (2011) *World Statistics Pocketbook 2010: Least Developed Countries*, New York: Author.

United Nations (2012) *The Millennium Development Goals Report 2012*, New York: Author.

United Nations (2013) *The Millennium Development Goals Report 2013*, New York: Author.

United Nations (2014) *The Millennium Development Goals Report 2014*, New York: Author.

United Nations Development Programme (2009) *Employment and Livelihoods Lao PDR, 2009: The 4th National Human Development Report*, Vientiane: Author.

United Nations Education, Scientific, and Cultural Organization (UNESCO) (2009) *Education for All Global Monitoring Report*, Oxford: Oxford University Press in association with UNESCO.

Ut, T.T., Hossain, M. and Janaiah, A. (2000) "Modern farm technology and infrastructure in Vietnam: impact on income distribution and poverty," *Economic and Political Weekly*, 35(52–53): 4638–43.

Vietnam General Statistics Office of Vietnam (2010) *Results of the Vietnam Household Living Standard Surveys 2010*, Hanoi: Author.

Vietnam General Statistics Office of Vietnam (2011) *Report on the 2011 Vietnam Labor Force Survey*, Hanoi: Author.

Weiss, J. (2007) "Globalization, geography and regional policy," in A. Balisacan and H. Hill (eds) *The Dynamics of Regional Development: The Philippines in East Asia*, Cheltenham, UK: Asian Development Bank Institute and Edward Elgar Publishing.

Wooldridge, J. (2000) *Introductory Econometrics: A Modern Approach*, Cincinnati, OH: Southwestern College Publishing.

World Bank (1989) *World Development Report 1990: Poverty*, Oxford: Oxford University Press.

World Bank (2000) *World Development Report 2000/2001: Attacking Poverty*, Oxford: Oxford University Press.

World Bank (2001) *Engendering Development through Gender Equality in Rights, Resources, and Voice*, Policy Research Report, Washington, DC: World Bank.

World Bank (2005) *Moving Out of Poverty in the Estate Sector in Sri Lanka: Understanding Growth and Freedom from the Bottom Up*, Washington, DC: Centre for Poverty Analysis.

World Bank (2007a) *Sri Lanka Poverty Assessment, Report No-36568-LK*, Washington, DC: Poverty Reduction and Economic Management Sector Unit South Asia Region.

World Bank (2007b) *World Development Report 2008: Agriculture for Development*, Washington, DC: Author.

World Bank (2008a) *World Development Indicators CD-ROM. 2009*, Washington, DC: Author.

World Bank (2008b) *World Development Report 2009: Reshaping Economic Geography*, Washington, DC: Author.

World Bank (2011a) *More and Better Jobs in South Asia*, Washington, DC: Author.

World Bank (2011b) *Vietnam Country Gender Assessment*, Washington, DC: Author.

World Bank (2011c) *World Development Indicators 2011*, Washington, DC: Author.

World Bank (2011d) *World Development Report 2012: Gender Equality and Development*, Washington, DC: Author.

World Bank (2012) *World Development Report 2013: Jobs*, Washington, DC: Author.

World Bank (2013a) *World Development Indicators 2013*, Washington, DC: World Bank.

World Bank (2013b) *World Development Report 2014: Risk and Opportunity: Managing Risk for Development*, Washington, DC: Author.

World Bank (2014) *Global Monitoring Report 2014/2015: Ending Poverty and Sharing Prosperity*, Washington, DC: Author.

Zhuang, J. and Ali, I. (2010) Poverty, inequality, and inclusive growth in Asia, in J. Zhuang (ed) *Poverty, Inequality, and Inclusive Growth: Measurement, Policy Issues, and Country Studies*, London: Anthem Press.

Index